"A fascinating account of Ed Larson's passion for aircraft and its history, his remembrances from flying in World War II combined with snapshots of Seattle life from 1924–1943. A must read!"

~ Jeffrey J. Nemitz
Colonel, US Army, Retired

"This book is wonderful! Mr. Larson has written an engaging and educational autobiography, full of rich detail with clever and often delightful turns of phrase. He provides the reader with a riveting narrative and wonderful asides full of insight and wisdom, and I was drawn in to his story immediately. Each episode he shares, it feels as if he is sitting with you at the kitchen table or by the campfire. This is not a romantic telling of his life as a pilot, but a frank and fascinating memoir—a clear view into the life of this World War II hero of the skies."

~ Lynda MacFarland
Author of *Drowning in Lemonade,*
Reflections of an Army Wife

"I have the model airplane plans that my father, born in 1925, had as a boy. He served in the Army Air Corps near the end of WWII as a radio operator bombardier hoping to see action onboard his B24. It was not until Korea as a pilot of an F86 Saber that he was in the fight. Ed's book helps me remember the times my dad talked about when I was a boy."

~ Larry Hart
Pilot

SPEAR-CARRIER
IN A
BACKWATER WAR

SPEAR-CARRIER
IN A BACKWATER WAR

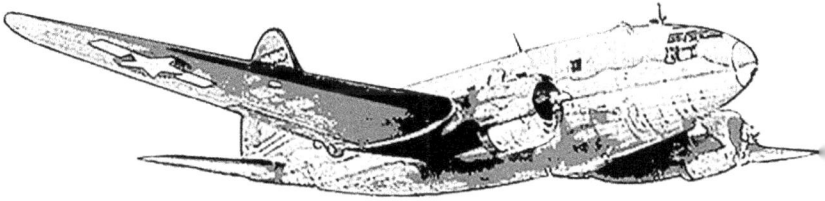

EDWARD C. LARSON

FLY·BY·NIGHT
GRAPHICS
SANTA CRUZ, CALIFORNIA

PUBLISHED IN THE UNITED STATES BY
FLY BY NIGHT GRAPHICS
222 2ND AVENUE
SANTA CRUZ, CALIFORNIA 95062

email: spear-carrier@journey2astar.net
www.journey2astar.net

Cover images:
US Army Air Forces Liberator departs on bombing mission, ca 1943.
National Archives Identifier: 535780. Public domain.
Ed Larson photographs from the author's collection.
Blood Chit photograph by Patricia D. Richards.

Cover and book design:
Sheila Setter

Photo Galleries:
Patricia D. Richards

Ed and Fiona photograph:
Patricia D. Richards

Printed in the United States
ISBN: 978-0965437646
18 17 16 15 14   1 2 3 4

I humbly dedicate this narrative to

Yeoman Marilyn K. Larson, USN

my fellow warrior and beloved wife.

IT IS NOT IN THE STARS TO HOLD OUR DESTINY,
BUT IN OURSELVES...

~ Shakespeare

Still at the threshold of youth, we met. In a time of peril and on winds of war, we journeyed to far-flung lands. At destiny's direction, for sixty-three years, we discovered together the wondrous adventure of two lives interwoven with love and respect.

She filled my days with joy and the anticipation of each new and thrilling tomorrow. She made me more than I imagined I could ever be.

In the end, with her passing, the music stopped.

One wonders if it will ever truly begin again.

CONTENTS

PART THREE

ILLUSTRATIONS

PROLOGUE

I n the parlance of legitimate theater, *spear-carrier* is that derogatory term applied to those who take no part in the drama played out before the audience. They are mute, living props inserted onstage to enhance the milieu in which thespians act out their roles. Destined to eternal unimportance, their sweet voices are silenced. Applause is the province of others; theirs is only to wear the dank cloak of the unheralded and unrecognized.

On the monstrous stage of World War II, there were no brighter stars than the fighter pilots who flashed across the skies like knights-errant, crushing the enemy and covering themselves in glory. We who flew the clumsy cargo planes were the spear-carriers, keeping our proper place, stage rear, in the shadows of our fighter plane brothers. Silent, save for the roar of our stone-dented airplanes—drab, dirty, tired, and worn—we creased the silence of the night skies and slogged through the mud of every battleground on earth dispensing the tools of war. As we traversed the trackless void, below us huddled souls without number: The dispossessed and dying cowering together before the ignoble coldness of terror, desperately seeking a faint breath of warmth, a promised surcease: salvation, peace. It would come only when our props ground to a final halt and our cooling engines ticked into silence. Only then would they know the curtain had descended on this worldwide tragedy.

On September 2, 1945, the show was over.

For the brotherhood of spear-carriers, living and dead, this would be quite enough.

Comedy and Tragedy. Drawing by Ed Larson, 2014.

Ed Larson 2014

PART ONE

ONE

I was born Edward Charles Garrett on the twentieth day of October 1924. Mine was a raucous entrance into an era of soft gentility characterized by white wicker bassinets, hand-hemmed diapers, pureed baby food, and the Thompson submachine gun (the latter item employed as the weapon of choice by the gangsters of my childhood years). I'm told I first appeared sometime in early evening in a local hospital; a couple of days later, I was delivered, via gray-blue Willys-Knight sedan, to a middle-class neighborhood in Seattle, Washington. In all probability, the trip occurred during a driving rainstorm so typical of my hometown-to-be.

As to my genealogical background, it pretty much resembles the end product of an overworked food blender. My birth father's lineage is dubious. Dad was an escapee from an abusive orphanage. Tennessee authorities never caught up with him, and from that time on, he was pretty well on his own. Painfully thin and with a mustache to match, he wasn't given a lot of breaks, but I'll give him this—he was tough.

His life was a series of self-indulgent exploits: itinerant tap dancer, saxophone player, airplane pilot; he was especially accomplished as an escape artist, particularly from that demon, *responsibility*. My dad didn't stick around too long after my arrival. He rotated in and out of my life with the frequency and excitement of Haley's comet. In the course of his orbits, he gave me rare moments of brilliant happiness—followed always by a sudden departure, the fading light of broken promises, and an ensuing silence that lasted years.

My mother, on the other hand, was the exquisite creation of my sainted grandparents who met on the frontier and married on New Year's Day 1900 in south-central Montana. My grandfather, a terrified midwife, delivered my mother on a storm-filled night in 1903 during a cattle drive near the venerable hamlet of Joliet. The size of the village was such that only one hitching post was required to serve the entire population. Although my mother grew up in Big Sky Country, she was more ballerina than cowgirl; and yet, her name—Violet—belies the fact that where I was concerned, she was as loving and protective as a female grizzly bear and remained so to the end.

I guess, like most kids, my mind was virtually a dial tone until about the age of three. For what it's worth, my first recallable memory was the sound of an Essex touring car and a Ford Model T violently converging outside my bedroom window at the corner of Sixty-Fifth Street and Palatine Avenue.

My bedroom was supplied through the generosity of my grandparents. My father had split after he and my mother divorced, and Mom and I had moved in with my grandparents and Mom's younger brother, who was just four years older than I. Out of financial necessity, we remained deadbeat boarders through most of my young formative years; but all together, we constituted a loving family, and they provided me with warmth and caring in a secure place, in a secure time.

I have enjoyed the pleasure of living during a time when the world has experienced vast and remarkable changes. This accounting is interwoven with many of those events. I hope, too, my story will serve to disclose what I regard as a wonderful and bizarre personal obsession. This malady invaded my mind at the first blush of reason and remains a compelling preoccupation well into the ninth decade of my existence. In truth, I have suffered a lifetime of manic devotion to airplanes and all things flying. I am deeply grateful for this malady and now feel compelled to knit together the story of my confessed fixation and its rather remarkable effect on a life I regard as having been truly well lived. Scarcely twenty-one years before my birth, the Wright Brothers accomplished the miracle of powered flight on the windy dunes of Kitty Hawk, North Carolina. In a miracle of progress, I have watched as another powered flight carried men to the moon. Between these two bookends of time, the pursuit of higher and faster has fired the imagination of entire generations, and mine in particular. This story will set forth the trivia of those wonderful days and years during which I spent more time looking up at the sky rather than down at my feet and where I was going.

My birth father learned to fly during the closing years of World War I, and though he was never truly in my life, my passion for flying must have been passed on through his genes. It was an endowment of gigantic proportion and just about the only gift he ever gave me that I got to keep. I imagine that I spent a great deal of 1925 and 1926 crashed out in a drop-side crib; but even then, spectacular aviation history was being forged. In August 1925, Commander John Rodgers and his crew set out from San Francisco on what was intended to be the first flight from North America to the Hawaiian Islands. They were forced down after covering about 1,800 miles. Since their craft was a PN-9 flying boat, they sailed it another 450 miles before being picked up by a submarine. All in all, it was a memorable trip.

The year 1926 was marked by the first flight over the North Pole, achieved by Richard Byrd and Floyd Bennett flying a Dutch Fokker F.VII A/3M. A few days later, Roald Amundsen made the first semirigid airship flight over the pole in the *Norse*. Again, I was probably asleep at the time.

According to my mother, however, the year 1927 was monumentally important. At the age of three, I built my first airplane model by nailing two random boards together to represent a fuselage and wings. I then teetered around the house drooling and making what my mother and others proudly perceived as the noise of an aircraft engine.

It was an auspicious beginning.

However, 1927 saw another, much more auspicious event. Perhaps the most legendary flight of all time, it captured the attention of the entire world: On May 20–21, an obscure airmail pilot named Charles A. Lindbergh flew the first solo, nonstop flight from New York to Paris. The world went crazy with adulation for the lanky young man. Everyone saw him as a hero, and as the media covered Lucky Lindy's accomplishment like a blanket, the history book of flight added a new page.

Marie and Al, two old friends of my grandparents, operated a large chicken farm outside Seattle, and we often visited them. I did not care too much for the chicken ranch; it smelled, and the house was festooned with flypaper strips hanging down from the ceiling with lots of dead flies attached. Someone gave them a collie that was born on the day of Lindbergh's famous flight. They named the beast Lucky Lindy, or just Lindy for short. Such was the extent of the adulation afforded the pilot of this historic flight.

Lindy grew from puppyhood into a serial chicken killer—*exactly* what one *needed* around a large chicken ranch. Because of his penchant for killing chickens, he was kept tethered to an unkempt doghouse by a chain large enough to moor a battleship. If anyone walked by, he would dash out of his shelter and run full speed at the terrified individual until the chain brought him up short and sent him sprawling in a cloud of dust. Lindy wasn't bright, and he wasn't just ill tempered; he was a savage sonofabitch—really, the antithesis of America's favorite flier—and we shared a mutual hatred for each other. That dog lived until 1940, his death approximately concurrent with Hitler's invasion of the Low Countries. One Sunday on a visit to the ranch, I noticed his chain and collar lying on the ground. I quite rightly deduced that the bastard had died. It was apparent the Rhode Island Reds were much more placid than before, and neither the flock nor I shed a single tear at his demise.

Nearly half a century after Lindbergh's historic 1927 flight, I was privileged to peer into the tiny, cramped cabin of the *Spirit of St. Louis* as it rested temporarily on the floor of the National Air and Space Museum. Ordinarily hung from the ceiling of the museum, the Ryan NYP single-engine monoplane was made accessible because of building remodeling. The situation offered me the opportunity of a lifetime to view the plane up close. The pilot's seat was a yellowed wicker. In sharp contrast, the fuel manifold's myriad of pipes and valves glowed in the rich colors of copper and brass.

Spirit of St. Louis. (US Air Force image.)

I imagined the cabin as being a place of overwhelming aloneness, particularly as Lindbergh crossed a rolling ocean in the darkness of night when the only other sounds in his universe were the drone of the Wright Whirlwind J-5C engine and the voice in his head quietly repeating, "I think I can make it! I think I can make it! I think I can. I think I can."

About the time of my visit to the *Spirit of St. Louis*, I was reminded of another footnote to the Lindbergh legend. As newlyweds, my wife Marilyn and I moved into a new house. Soon afterward, I discovered another airplane fanatic in the personage of our gregarious elderly neighbor, Dee Bristow. I never learned if it was "Dee" or just "D" because he didn't like his first name. At any rate, we spoke constantly about airplanes and flying.

Dee was an accomplished mechanic who had spent most of his life around planes. One of his most prized possessions was a pilot's license signed by Orville Wright when he served as administrator of the National Advisory Committee for Aeronautics.

One day in 1927, Dee got a call from his employer to go to the San Diego Airport (now Lindbergh Field). It was a special assignment. In a dramatic happenstance, he had been chosen to install the earth inductor compass in the *Spirit of St. Louis*. It would constitute the most treasured task in Dee's lifetime.

TWO

A few days after my fifth birthday, on the morning of October 29, 1929, the ticker tapes of American business began their doomsday dirge, and the nation collapsed with a terrible shudder into the Great Depression. Every family in America would be affected by the events on that fateful day, and the specter of poverty would soon paint itself across the land with a cruel brush.

That same month, another momentous event took place: I was enrolled in Mrs. Hall's Kindergarten. It was a humble little operation serving about ten kids from the neighborhood. The class was actually housed in Mrs. Hall's home, nestled beneath a huge horse chestnut tree, in a lovely room filled with small windowpanes. From the beginning, I believe I was looked upon as a pretty slow learner, and as primitive and nonselective as Mrs. Hall's class was, I was nearly expelled for repeatedly peeing on the toilet seat. Apparently, I didn't realize that it was hinged and should be raised. At any rate, it was a tempest in a teapot.

I enjoyed Mrs. Hall's Kindergarten, especially the constant availability of crayons and big sheets of paper and the fact that, quite often, I was left by myself to experiment with the various art tools she made available to her little charges. I wasn't reclusive, however, and I played my share of Kick the Can and other childhood games. I grew up in an age when doors were left unlocked and kids were safe to play in their neighborhoods. We built scooters cobbled from apple boxes and two-by-fours and used roller skates as running gear. It was a time when kids made their own toys and invented their own entertainment. That's always seemed to me to be a healthy way to grow up.

On Sundays, the family would usually take a drive as a means of entertainment; and quite often, we traveled through the downtown area past the old Georgetown Brewery to old Boeing Field, Seattle's air hub at the southern end of town. It was my very favorite place on earth. Airports of the day were pretty primitive; they were places of wooden hangers, oily tarmacs, mustachioed young men in leather jackets, and airplanes built of wood and fabric. I recall seeing salvaged remains of wrecked aircraft lying in scrap piles beside hangers and outbuildings in want of paint. The whole venue was wrapped in an air of excitement. Small, nondescript planes would accelerate their engines, race down the runway, and lift like birds into the sky. They would circle the field in a prescribed manner and then land, often bouncing down the runway like rubber balls. The engine sounds were, quite simply, spine tingling and unforgettable—even the grit-filled propeller wash was an experience to be pondered with awe. I was spellbound.

When I reached the age of six, I left the sanctuary of Mrs. Hall's Kindergarten and entered first grade at John B. Allen Elementary School. Classes were held in an ancient, two-story building with high-ceilinged rooms and wooden floors that were regularly oiled with some kind of petroleum-based product, making them very shiny and highly combustible. The whole structure was a pyrotechnic accident waiting to happen. Someone apparently noticed the inherent danger, and the school board reacted by constructing a wooden fire escape from the second floor to the ground. Every fire drill was an adventure. It was obvious to any thinking onlooker that the fire escape would be the first thing to burn, but at least its many stairs weren't soaked in flammable solution.

To describe me as an average student would be a bit of a stretch. My young uncle, Charlie, was a straight-A student. In comparison, my school performance was a source of constant concern for my mother and my grandparents. I was a dreamer—just getting by with my schoolwork. Life outside the classroom windows always seemed far more interesting than "2 x 2 = 4" or whatever. There was a magnificent world out there, infinitely more important than what was written on the blackboard, and my grades reflected this attitude.

As a preschooler, I had gravitated toward pencils and crayons, and it became apparent as I grew older that I possessed exceptional drawing ability. In elementary school, my favorite subject to draw was, of course, airplanes. I was intrigued by the romance of World War I aircraft and read voraciously about the technology of the early fighter planes. Even at a young age, I could render them with surprising detail, and my drawings were coveted by classmates and, to my ultimate astonishment, even a few teachers. In my advanced age, I now recognize that my drawing ability is a gift that only a few privileged enjoy. This skill, part genetically inherent and part commitment to a lifetime of observation and laborious practice, has brought me profound joy.

In the early 1930s, there was a staggering wealth of information available about aviation in general and particularly the famous pilots and planes of the 1914–1919 era.

G-8 and His Battle Aces was a pulp magazine filled with aviation intrigue. Set in World War I, it was fixed on the battle between good and evil. The plots revolved around G-8 and his daring pilots who fought not only the vile German Huns, but also an assortment of bizarre giant flying threats employed by the enemy to destroy Allied forces. Their gun platforms were the marvelous WWI aircraft: SPADs, Nieuports, Sopwith Camels, Albatross Scouts, and Fokker D.VIIs, and the action was breathtaking. I carefully read each beautifully drawn copy of *G-8 and His Battle Aces*. For a young kid who loved airplanes and art, this was literature at its finest.

Scorchy Smith, the story of a daredevil pilot and his adventures, appeared as a comic strip in the daily newspaper. I never missed it. The draftsmanship and graphics of these funny papers leapt to excellence in the mid-1930s, culminating with the magnificent drawings and design that constituted the action/adventure comic strip, *Terry and the Pirates*[1]. Created by Milton Caniff, *Terry and the Pirates* included parodies of real-life pilots and ground crews who were fighting a war set in the China-Burma-India Theater before and after the invasion of those countries by the Japanese. Before America's involvement in the war, Japanese forces were the thinly veiled "enemy" in the series, but young readers easily recognized their nationality and nefarious intent. Every kid I knew read *Terry and the Pirates* and identified with the characters and their mission. I loved Caniff's drawing style and avidly read and saved many of my favorite strips. In my case, this would prove to be monumentally prophetic in my life. Within the incredibly short span of ten years, I would actually be living the comic strip's adventures in the places where they occurred.

By the time I was nine years old, I had amassed a rather impressive volume of aviation knowledge. I had long before paired up with my next-door neighbor and pal, Art Nelsen. We were in the same grade and very close friends, and he also was interested in airplanes, although not to the extent in which I was. In or around 1934, we learned about the Jimmie Allen Flying Club. It started as a kids' radio adventure series and grew by leaps and bounds into a mini-institution. In my neighborhood, kids could join the club by merely signing up at the Richfield gasoline service station with an attendant named Erwin. Club members received a weekly newsletter featuring illustrated flying lessons, tips about airplanes, and general information about the club. In addition, we received Jimmie Allen Flying Cadet Wings and a nicely printed certificate of membership.

Jimmie Allen Flying Cadet Wings.

The Air Adventures of Jimmie Allen radio show was steeped in adventure and flavored with a moral touch. It featured all-American boy aviator Jimmie Allen and his buddy and mentor Speed Robertson, a WWI pilot and owner of a marvelous airplane named *The Monsoon*. With their mechanic Flash Lewis, they flew to exotic locations all over the world, solving mysteries and fighting for justice against the forces of evil. I never missed an episode.

Every Wednesday, the *Jimmie Allen Club News* was delivered to the gas station on Phinney Ridge. On those highly anticipated days, Art and I would ride our bikes to the tiny, worn-down, oil-soaked establishment about ten blocks from our homes. The gas station itself was a cottage-like structure guarded out front by two tall gasoline pumps. There was a sort of coziness about the little place. A blue enameled kerosene heater over which Erwin, the attendant, could huddle on cold, rainy Seattle nights kept the inside warm and comfortable. It was a long time between customers in those hard days when many drivers could pay for only a gallon of gas at a time and when a set of "new" used tires could break a family's budget. Erwin always saved copies of the flying club newsletters for us and regaled us with stories of his prowess as a part-time pilot.

As soon as I could be trusted with a single-edge razorblade, I began cutting balsa wood and building model airplanes. It quickly became a habit if not an obsession. There were two basic types of airplane kits available in those days: kits in which the fuselage and wings were carved or formed from solid blocks of wood, and flying models made with parts, much like real aircraft might be assembled. I much preferred the flying models because they were more intricate to build; and of course, they were light enough to fly! Depending on the size of the kit and its complexity, one might range in price from as little as fifty cents to as much as several dollars. Needless to say, I always bought the less expensive kits.

My aircraft-assembly "facility" consisted of an old pine table in the very small bedroom I occupied in my grandparents' home. The room itself was crammed with photos of airplanes and pilots—among them, Charles Lindbergh; air racing star Roscoe Turner; and Eddie Rickenbacker, racecar driver and leading American fighter ace of World War I. By the war's end, he had chalked up twenty-six victories and earned the Medal of Honor and Distinguished Service Cross among his many distinctions.

Outstanding in my pictorial pantheon of famous fliers was a photograph of Jimmy Doolittle. Doolittle was simply a giant in the annals of American aviation. Bright and tough, he was a boxer, military officer, aeronautical engineer, winner of all the major air trophy races, aircraft speed record holder, aerobatic champion, and unequaled herald of American air power. Doolittle would add to his impressive résumé by leading sixteen B-25s in a raid on the Japanese mainland in 1942. That raid would be just six short years from my childhood model-building days in the Dutch Colonial house on the corner of Sixty-Fifth Street and Palatine Avenue.

The men whose photos hung on my walls were not only my heroes, their exploits and the adventures of countless others made them constant topics in the media. Ensconced among these titans of the air, I spent countless hours hunched over my worktable drawing and building replicas of their famous World War I aircraft: The SPAD, Nieuport, Sopwith Camel, Albatros, and Fokker were beautifully

Lieutenant James H. "Jimmy" Doolittle made history as the first pilot to fly coast-to-coast in less than a day in a modified De Havilland DH-4, September 1922. (US Air Force photo.)

SPAD XIII, National Museum of the United States Air Force. (US Air Force photo.)

With the Fokker D.VII, this beautiful French fighter plane became famous as a lethal weapon of the sky during World War I. This plane bears the markings of Captain Eddie Rickenbacker of the 94th Aero Squadron.

decorated "steeds of the sky,"[2] and the drawings I made and models I built were exact replicas of the wood and fabric originals, replete with all their brilliant colors, shining engines, threatening machine guns, complex wire bracing, and intricate insignia. The fighter planes of World War I truly were, I believe, beautiful and romantic, exhibiting the elegance, imagination, and artistry of their talented creators.

This was the Golden Age of Flight!

THREE

Historically, wartime has provided fertile ground for accelerated technological advancement, and the period of World War I was no exception. Between July 1914 and November 1918, the world witnessed amazing advances in the conceptualization of warfare and the kinds of crafts required to wage it.

I was mainly interested in planes from the later part of the First World War—on both sides of the conflict. Studying the aircraft carefully, I believed then, as I do now, that the very configuration of these fighter planes mirrored the national characteristics of the countries that produced them. The French Nieuport really looked French. It was dainty, artful, seemingly more butterfly than warplane. On the other hand, German fighters such as the Fokker D.VII, Dr.I, and Albatros D.Va actually looked like Teutonic machines. They were burly and aggressive, colorful, and deadly when flown in capable hands. The Maltese cross was a standard insignia for German fighter planes, and the lettering and numerals appearing on the sides of their fuselages were unquestionably German.

National characteristics also appeared evident to me in the British fighters. The British S.E.5, built by the Royal Aircraft Factory, is a case in point. Stretching my imagination, I could liken its appearance to a parliament member in conservative dress. It was a squarish machine bearing a conservative Lewis machine gun that was mounted on the top wing and fired beyond the propeller arc. A Hispano-Suiza V-8 engine powered the S.E.5, and it proved to be somewhat troublesome: A problem in the gearing sometimes caused the propeller and the nose section to shear off and separate from the airframe—a very unfortunate occurrence indeed.

The Dutch plane builder Anthony Fokker used rotary engines in his famous Fokker Eindecker monoplane in the earlier part of the war and in his later design, the Fokker Dreidecker (three-winged) aircraft. The rotary engine offered advantages in weight and cooling over conventional, liquid-cooled engines but posed major disadvantages as well. In a conventional aircraft engine, the block and cylinder heads are stationary and the crankshaft, driven by the eccentric action of the pistons, drives the propeller. In the case of the rotary engine, the propeller is actually bolted to the front of the engine block, and the whole assembly—propeller and engine block—rotates about the crankshaft.

It is important to realize that although these wood-and-wire flying machines were beautiful examples of aviation artistry, they were powered by engines that were primitive and beset with troubles. The rotary engine was a German invention, taken over by the French and manufactured under license before World War I. These were the engines that powered the Nieuports, Sopwith Camels and Pups, and some of the Fokker planes; and often, they posed new and complex problems for mechanics and pilots because, like recalcitrant employees, they were subject to quit without notice.

In the physical world, torque and gravity are two irrefutable forces, and both exert constant pressure on a powered aircraft in flight. Essentially, torque tends to rotate the entire aircraft frame in a direction counter to the rotational direction of the propeller. The extent of torque is contingent on the weight and speed of the rotating propeller or engine block. The pilot must constantly compensate for varying magnitudes of torque either by using the control surfaces or by varying the rotational speed of the propeller or engine mass. In the case of the Sopwith Camel, turns to the right were whip-like; while turns to the left were so slow and difficult, they posed danger to the pilots who flew them. The effect of torque was so forceful in the Sopwith Camel that inexperienced pilots practicing full-power turns were warned to stay above 1,000 feet in altitude. The altitude cushion allowed them time to recover from violent dives or tailspins caused by the extreme pushing or pulling of the rotary engine.

With conventional engines, it is a simple matter to control engine speed by the use of an ordinary throttle, which regulates the flow of fuel to the cylinders. A throttle was incompatible for use in the rotary engine; thus, the only alternative to regulate its speed was to let the engine run full speed or turn it off entirely. This was accomplished by pushing a blip switch in the cockpit, which stopped the flow of electricity from the magneto to the firing chambers, momentarily killing the engine. As a result, the final approach to landing these little planes was an on-off, on-off, on-off proposition, making the engine sound as if it were suffering from stomach gas...a fascinating condition.

Fokker F.IV. (US Army photo.)

Fokker D.VII, National Museum of the United States Air Force.
(US Air Force photo.)

The top fighter of the German Air Force in World War I, this aircraft was so highly regarded that the Allies insisted on the confiscation of all D.VIIs as a part of the armistice agreement ending the war.

Nieuport Scout. (Haut-Rhin, France, 1917. Free of rights.)

First entering service in 1915, this aircraft was heavily used by Allied Forces during World War I.

Eberhart SE-5E, National Museum of the United States Air Force.
(US Air Force photo.)

This aircraft was assembled from S.E.5a spare parts by American company Eberhart Aeroplane.

Of interest also is the fact that rotary engines were lubricated with castor oil. Since the gasoline and lubricating oil were both drawn from the crankcase, it was mandatory to have non-petroleum-based oil for lubrication to prevent the gasoline and lubricating oil from mixing together. Castor oil, the bane of children from my generation, proved to be the answer to the problem since it would not mix with the aircraft's fuel. Nevertheless, it had its problems. Castor oil was messy, smelly, and leaked with rare abandon. The important thing was that it kept the little rotary engines ticking like clocks, and that was all that was needed.

The beautiful fighting planes of World War I had another problem. The very best location to place a machine gun on an airplane is directly in front of the pilot's eyes, with the breech within reach to permit the cleaning of jams. This axiom is straightforward and amounts to simple common sense; but with the machine gun so placed, another huge problem surfaced: The machine gun would have to be fired directly through the path of a spinning propeller!

Prior to the start of World War I, both the Germans and the French worked on devices to solve this problem. The British, on the other hand, were not too concerned in the search for a solution since they flew almost entirely pusher-type aircraft (which posed no problem for a forward-firing machine gun). German and French designers worked furiously on what they termed a "gun synchronizer," and each side came up with workable models. However, the devices were initially ignored by officials of their respective nations, perhaps with good reason. The French developed a system that must be recognized as verging on the ridiculous. Their method consisted of placing a belt of armor around that section of the propeller that was directly in the line of fire. Thus, if a bullet hit the propeller, it would be deflected by the armor plate without damaging or severing the propeller blade. This primitive approach reduced the efficiency of the propeller and provided the opportunity for dangerous ricochets back toward the pilot.

The concept of an armored propeller was not, however, entirely ridiculous. In the early months of 1915, French Ace Roland Garros shot down three German aircraft using this primitive system. On April 18, 1915, his airplane was in turn forced down; and before he could burn the machine, he was captured by German ground forces. German authorities found the armored propeller system on his aircraft archaic and ineffective; but in typical fashion, they quickly (with the aid of Anthony Fokker) designed a new and very practical gun synchronizer based on a crankshaft cam principle. It worked, and its advent introduced a new era of World War I aircraft combat on the western front that would be known as the Fokker Scourge. By mid-1916, Allied forces' synchronizing gear had caught up, and this would once again level the field of play in air combat.

These famous warplanes spurred my imagination, and dreams of flight carried me (and a myriad of other kids my age) out beyond the privation and sorrow of the Depression years into the sunshine and clouds of dawn patrols, dogfights, and blazing victories in far-away skies. It was heady stuff—a far cry from the doom and gloom of my adolescent years.

FOUR

The process of model building is painstakingly slow and involves cutting parts and fashioning details from small sheets of balsa wood. The WWI flying models were invariably built of one-sixteenth-inch square stringers of balsa wood, meticulously cut, joined, and glued to form the skeleton of the particular aircraft. Colored tissue was then glued to the frame and sprayed with water from a perfume atomizer. If properly applied, the tissue dried drum tight and rendered beautiful surfaces to the wings and fuselage of the aircraft. Rounded fuselages, such as those present in the German Albatros D.Va and the Pfalz D.XII fighters, were more difficult to assemble than the flat-sided Sopwiths, Nieuports, German Fokker series, and British S.E.5.

Whenever my friend Art or I ran out of construction materials, we rode our bikes around Green Lake to the mecca of model builders: Doug's Model Airplane Store. There, we would gaze longingly at the wonders inside the small place, most of which we couldn't begin to afford.

Hanging from the ceiling was a gorgeous black and white replica of a Waco UPF-7, a magnificent two-seater biplane that Doug had built for display.

I don't remember ever talking with Doug, the namesake of the enterprise. He was an older kid who saw us, I'm sure, as young punks; and by this time, Art and I had begun looking like Depression kids. Our uniforms of necessity were dirty cord pants, hand-me-down shirts, and sweaters with patches on the elbows; and our bikes were a dead giveaway, too, both of them dingy, rusty, and with tires needing air.

Doug's mother actually ran the model shop; and she was always kind to us kids, maybe seeing in our grubby hands the coins that would help feed her family and pay the rent. This was a survival business—actually a part of their humble living space. The most intriguing things in the shop were the new tiny gasoline engines for larger flying models. As I recall, they retailed for fifteen dollars or so and were as far beyond our reach as the stars.

All of our models were powered by rubber bands, which, when twisted, gave a few hundred revolutions to the props, and that was about all we could expect. A couple of times, to achieve longer powered flights, we wound the rubber bands so tightly they actually crushed the fuselages of our little planes like worn-out accordions. We gave up that idea and usually settled for just gliding our models from a high porch on the back of Art's house. These little planes glided pretty well after we adjusted the center of gravity to make them a bit nose heavy. When the models were beyond their prime, we tried putting small firecrackers in them and sending them off the porch on a death glide. As I remember, we never got the desired result. In every case, the firecracker either went out or blew up before the glide was accomplished. Our flaming crashes were simply failures.

I got pretty good at model building; and one day, a lady from the Seattle Public Library on Phinney Avenue called my grandmother to ask if they might display one of my models in their front window. Naturally, I was delighted and took one of my best models to the library for the world to view. They displayed it in the window for a month, and what I got back was a shambles. The heat from the sunny window had withered the structure and tissue paper into a rather pathetic configuration of stuff. They were very apologetic, and it was OK. I'd had my fifteen minutes of fame.

About the same time, spurred by the excitement of *G-8 and His Battle Aces*, I decided to write my own World War I aviation adventure story. It would be serialized and offer all the action that the professional publications could produce. My teacher asked me to read the first chapter to the class, and it went over very well. I followed up with a chapter every Friday for about ten weeks until I ran out of steam and had to annihilate most of the main characters. My teacher, classmates, and I were pretty well pleased at the end of the saga, but it was never chosen for a literary award and didn't help my math score a bit.

During the inauguration of my authorship phase, a truly unique event occurred. About eight o'clock one night, there was a knock on the front door (the doorbell was broken); and when Gram answered it, there stood my father. He had dropped out of one of his earthly orbits and landed on our front porch. This was a major event in my life. Even though years had rolled past without birthday cards, phone calls, or any other type of communication on his part, he was still my dad. The family always welcomed him with a great deal of grace; and to give them credit, no one, including my mother, ever spoke ill of him in my presence. This would be a wonderful thing for all divorced parents to remember.

After the first greetings were exchanged, Dad insisted that I accompany him out to the dilapidated coupe he was driving. He opened the trunk with a flourish; and although it was dark, I saw the treasures inside. He had liberated an empty fifty-pound aerial bomb and a belt of .30-caliber machine gun bullets from an airfield where he had been working at the time. To my astonishment, he presented them to me!

These gifts were a treasure for a kid that was into all things military, and I couldn't have been more excited. I didn't sleep that night; and the next morning, we were both up early. He loaded me into his car, and we headed for the most important location I could think of: Boeing Field! We traipsed all over the airfield until about noon, checking out the Stinsons, Eaglerocks, Wacos, and a Travel Air or two—a virtual gallery of pre-World War II aircraft. Then he left me standing by the corner of a hanger while he engaged in an animated conversation with a guy in a billed cap and leather jacket. They talked for perhaps ten minutes. When he strode back toward me, he announced, "C'mon, yah mug, we're goin' flying!"

Sometimes there are moments that authenticate an obsession. *I couldn't believe it! I was really going flying!*

We headed toward what was probably the smallest, most primitive aircraft I had ever seen. The little Aeronca C-3 looked like the hybrid offspring of a wind-shredded umbrella and a lacrosse racquet. There were wires all over; some were attached to a huge, two-legged pylon on top of the wings—obviously intended to keep it from folding up while the craft was in flight. A single bench, barely wide enough for two, provided seating. When my dad plunked me in the cockpit, the Aeronca was so low to the ground I could reach over the open side and nearly touch the gritty black asphalt of the tarmac.

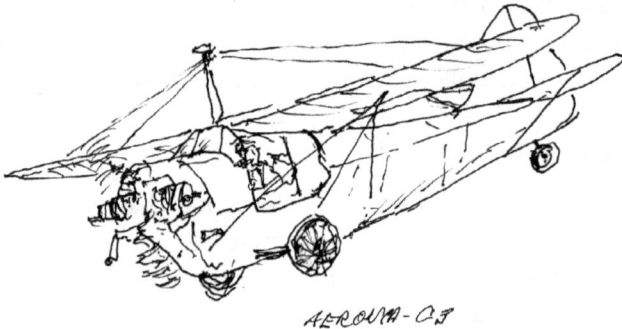

Aeronca C-3. Drawing by Ed Larson, 2014.

My first flight with my father was an indescribable thrill. The little Aeronca proved a gateway to my future.

My dad climbed in and fastened the single seat belt around both of us. Since a self-starter had never been considered for the waspish power plant on the Aeronca, Dad shouted to a promising onlooker in mechanic's overalls who gladly volunteered to prop the plane for us. It took several tries before the engine caught its breath and reluctantly consented to start. It ticked over with a small sound, rattling a bit like a chipmunk on a tiny treadmill. Dad checked the instrument panel and controls; then with a sudden increase in rpm, we taxied across a small, grassy area and headed into the wind. In a minute, I saw his hand push the throttle all the way forward, the prop blurred, and we accelerated down the runway. The ground rushed by ever faster, and suddenly, the noise from the rolling landing gear stopped...we were airborne! Looking out the open side of the little plane, I saw the ground drop away; it was simply one of the greatest thrills of my life!

In a matter of minutes, we were a hundred times higher than Art Nelsen's back porch, and things would never be quite the same for me. We circled over the old Georgetown Brewery and then headed for downtown and the waterfront. We were in a different dimension with the slipstream speeding by and my hometown unfolding beneath me like a glorious open book. To the west, the whole expanse of Puget Sound sparkled in the rare sunshine of a Seattle afternoon...my whole world was suddenly alive with the thrill of new adventure. I looked over at my dad. He was smiling at me.

As we returned to Boeing Field, he set the little C-3 down as gently as a feather and then thanked the guy who apparently owned the aircraft. I never saw any money change hands, and I suspect my dad actually conned him into loaning his airplane to a total stranger. We spent the rest of the day together; and when we got home, my grandmother had baked him a special lemon meringue pie. Dad stayed overnight in the spare bedroom, and I went to sleep dreaming about real airplanes and flying.

The next day was devoted to decorating the new aerial bomb and the machine gun bullets he had brought to me. We went to the store, and Dad bought a couple small cans of enamel paint and a brush. I remember we painted the bomb a battleship gray color and the nose cone shiny black. The bomb casing stood on its fins about three feet tall, and the belt of machine gun bullets, shining like gold, fit perfectly around it like a belt on a pair of dress pants. The bomb casing was dry by nightfall, and I lugged it upstairs where I'd rearranged my room so it could stand in the corner by the window. It was beautiful, and with all my airplane pictures and model bench, the room was now a pilot's paradise.

Bomb casing, machine gun bullets. Drawing by Ed Larson, 2014.

To a kid who loved aviation, the bomb casing and machine gun bullets were a supreme gift from my father.

Dad was looking for work and after a few days found a job repairing musical instruments in a music store in Bremerton, Washington. While he was staying with us, he ate quite a bit; and as young as I was, I still figured out that maybe he'd missed a few meals before he showed up at our place. Like everybody else, he wasn't doing all that well as far as money was concerned. The tires on his old car were so bald you could almost see through them, and that was sort of a dead giveaway.

Dad had been in Bremerton for maybe three days when he stopped back by the house late one rainy afternoon. He patted me on the back and asked if he could borrow the bomb and bullets for a couple of days to decorate the window in the music shop where he was working. When he put them in the trunk of the old coupe, like any kid, I was pretty disappointed. The last thing I saw was the taillights on the back of his old, beat-up car vanishing in the rain. I never saw the bomb or the bullets again.

I was down in the basement maybe a couple of weeks later and saw the two cans of paint that we'd used on the bomb casing. In our excitement, we'd both forgotten to clean the brush, and it was stuck to a piece of newspaper and as hard as a rock.

By 1934, the Great Depression had become a heartbreaking, long-lasting reality. I sometimes saw my grandparents in whispered conversation and overheard them say that we owed more than $200.00 at Mr. Riis's grocery store down the block. That was a king's ransom in those days, and that wasn't all we owed. Some mortgage payments on the house hadn't been made, and that was a lot worse.

We were all doing our best. My grandfather worked at small carpentry jobs when he could find them, and my mother worked at several office jobs and as a cashier in a fancy French restaurant in downtown Seattle. Both Charlie and I had paper and magazine routes, and he worked weekends for a butter and egg merchant down by the Pike Place Market.

*OUR CHILDREN HAVE SCHOOLLESS DAYS AND
SHOELESS DAYS....(W)HY ARE WE REDUCED TO
POVERTY AND STARVING AND ANXIETY AND
SORROW....WHY NOT END THE DEPRESSION
HAVE YOU NOT A HEART?*

~ Letter from a New Jersey Parent to President Herbert Hoover[3]

I got a big break when I auditioned for and won a part in a radio show called *Jimmy and Gyp, A Boy and His Dog.* It was on a local station and sponsored by Friskies Dog Food. Some of the shows were live, and some were transcriptions, which meant they were recorded on large vinyl disks for later presentations. I got three dollars for a live show and five dollars for a transcription.

We needed everything we could earn just to survive.

FIVE

In aviation history, 1935 was a year of triumph—characterized particularly by the success of one of my favorite airplanes in the Bendix Trophy Race—and tragedy—marked by the stunning crash on August 15, which took the lives of Wiley Post and Will Rogers.

The 1935 "Bendy" competitors flew from Burbank, California, to Cleveland, Ohio; and among the field of eight competitors, I had built models of four of the aircraft involved in that year's race: the winner, *Mr. Mulligan* (Howard DGA-6), the Wedell-Williams Model 44, the Gee Bee Racer, and a Lockheed Vega flown by Amelia Earhart. These planes were esthetically beautiful save for the Gee Bee, a short, barrel-shaped, blunt-object described by Jimmie Doolittle as simply a death trap.[4]

As a kid, I loved the Gee Bee; there was an air of outlaw about the plane—perhaps because of its startling red and white paint job with the rolled dice separated by the large numeral seven on the fuselage. This was a totally malicious airplane that killed or maimed nearly every pilot who crawled into its cockpit. Jimmie Doolittle, who won the

Mr. Mulligan (Howard DGA-6)—Winner of the 1935 "Bendy." (Photo courtesy of the San Diego Air & Space Museum SDASM Archives. No known copyright restrictions.)

Wedell-Willams Model 44, Racer NR61Y—1935 "Bendy" runner-up. (Photo courtesy of the San Diego Air & Space Museum SDASM Archives. No known copyright restrictions.)

The Gee Bee met a fateful end with Cecil Allen at the start of the 1935 "Bendy." (Photo by William S. Porter, released to public domain.)

Thompson Trophy closed-course race in a Gee Bee in Cleveland in 1932, was thoroughly relieved to climb out its cockpit alive. He later said of the aircraft, "This is the most delicate plane I have ever flown...flying it was like balancing a pencil or an ice cream cone on the tip of your finger."[5] As its last will and testament, this man killer met its end with Cecil Allen, a skilled pilot and racer, who perished during takeoff at the start of the 1935 Bendix Trophy Race.

Mr. Mulligan, on the other hand, was as lovely as the Gee Bee was malevolent. The Bendy Trophy winner was a beautiful, high-winged monoplane, painted white, with a graceful fuselage made distinctive by a necklace of teardrop projections encircling the engine cowling. *Mr. Mulligan* was flown by Benny Howard, a talented and experienced pilot, and the plane looked like it was racing even when it was sitting on the ground. Practically every kid I knew had built a model of this aircraft, and the model I built was one of my favorites for its sheer beauty alone.

Fate is fickle, and it's an aggressive hunter. After winning the 1935 race, *Mr. Mulligan* was entered in the 1936 Bendix with Benny Howard again as pilot and his wife Maxine, also a skilled pilot, registered as copilot. The starting location was Floyd Bennett Field in New York, and the finish line was at Mines Field in Los Angeles. While racing across New Mexico, *Mr. Mulligan* suffered the monstrous mechanical failure of shedding a prop blade. It crashed in the desert, pinning both pilots in the crushed cabin. After several hours, they were discovered by a passing local youth who ran for help. Both pilots were badly injured but recovered. Benny Howard lost a foot in the accident; *Mr. Mulligan* was totally destroyed.

Aviation enthusiasts everywhere were intensely interested in the anticipated expedition of Wiley Post. His plans included surveying Alaska in search of a mail-passenger air route between the US West Coast and Russia. Post had an illustrious past. He'd gained enormous fame as a flying figure following two record-setting flights in his famous Lockheed Vega, *Winnie Mae*; and the patch he wore (due to an industrial accident in which he lost his vision in one eye) lent him an added air of adventure. Will Rogers, at the time surely the nation's most dearly beloved cowboy humorist, writer, and philosopher, enjoyed a close friendship with Post and convinced him he should accompany him on the journey so he could record the exploits for his syndicated column.

Their aircraft—revamped in Seattle just prior to the trip—was a hybrid designed by Post consisting of a fuselage from a Lockheed Orion Model 9E Special joined to a longer wing that had been removed from a Lockheed-Explorer Model 7 Special. The resulting combo plane was to be fitted with pontoons for water landings, and the floats ordered by Post were originally set for installation in Burbank, California; but the shipment was delayed, so instead, just prior to the flight, Post mounted a larger pair of floats he had located in Seattle. At the time, there was a rather widespread contention that the floats were too large for the airplane, making it nose heavy, a potentially serious problem.

A monument to the two fliers now memorializes the starting point of the flight, which began August 7, 1935, on Lake Washington at a small seaplane harbor near the town of Renton. The Orion seemed to handle well with the new floats, and the trip to Juneau was uneventful, with Post and Rogers arriving to the greetings of a crowd of well-wishers.

There was, of course, a consuming interest in aviation in Alaska—in many cases, airplanes were about the only way to get from one place to another. The pair left Fairbanks on August 15, bound for Point Barrow on Alaska's far northwest corner. About fifteen miles from their destination, Post set the airplane down on a small river inlet to question a group of hunters and get his bearings. The hunters pointed out the direction to Point Barrow, and it was noted that Post tinkered with the engine for a few minutes while Rogers talked with the men. Finally, the pair boarded the aircraft; and Post started the engine, headed the Orion into the wind, and began their takeoff run. As the native hunters watched, the aircraft rose slowly off the water. At a height of about fifty feet with a nose-up attitude, the engine suddenly quit cold. In an instant, the nose dropped violently; and the plane plunged into the shallow water below, flipping over on its back. Both men were killed instantly, and another tragic page was entered in the annals of American aviation.

SIX

While 1935 was not a vintage year for fliers, neither was it a good year for the family in the house on the corner of Sixty-Fifth Street and Palatine Avenue. There was, in truth, genuine worry. Our family had managed to pay off the grocery bill at Mr. Riis's store, but I knew we were passing through very rough financial times. My grandparents had shielded my uncle and me from the certainty that foreclosure on our home was imminent. As I write this, eighty or so years after the fact, I consider the amount of money needed to save our home as chump change (at this moment I have twice that amount in my checking account), but now is now and then was then, and the heartbreak of losing our home and the effect it had on our family still lingers like a bad dream.

Families like ours that had failed after doing their best to meet their obligations were spread across the country like a blanket of sorrow. We were luckier than most. As a family, we turned away from that which had been ours and sought other means of survival. The Eddie Garrett aircraft factory that had been my bedroom was shuttered, and I said goodbye to the neighborhood where I had grown and to

Art Nelsen's back porch from which we'd hurled so many small airplanes that I smile now as I recall the memories.

My grandparents rented a small home in Ballard, an ethnic Scandinavian neighborhood of neat houses and nice people a couple of miles from the home we had lost. It wasn't a big deal for me to change schools. It was easy for me to make friends; and of course, I was beginning to notice girls. Airplanes continued to be my passion, and I resumed my model building on a smaller scale in the basement of the new place. Uncle Charlie was in high school now—a top student and achiever in every field; I was still spending a lot of time looking out of classroom windows and dreaming of airplanes and far off places.

I went to Boeing Field every chance I could get—usually, with my family, and each visit was like renewing an old friendship. When we'd arrive, I'd usually take off by myself, but not without an admonition to return to the car at a prescribed time. (I was always late.) In those days of innocence, the excursions to Boeing Field were ever more exciting because there were no restrictions on getting close to the airplanes—no fences, no yellow tape—only the beauty of the aircraft and the excitement of the entire milieu.

I recall one such visit, probably in late 1935, when I rounded the end of a hanger, and before me, standing in polished splendor, was a Boeing P-26 pursuit fighter. I had followed the development of this plane since it first flew in 1932 and had built models and drawn countless sketches of it, considering it to be arguably one of the most beautiful machines ever taken to the sky. For reasons I never completely understood, the pilots who flew this beloved aircraft had nicknamed it "Peashooter"—admittedly a moniker affectionately given.

Boeing P-26A, National Museum of the United States Air Force. (US Air Force photo.)

While retaining the old-style open cockpit and exterior wing braces common in fighter aircraft of an earlier era, the P-26 was the first all-metal plane built for the United States Army Air Corps (USAAC). It served in the Philippines until 1941 and as a frontline fighter for the Chinese during the war against Japan. One aircraft also served in the Spanish Civil War, and amazingly, the Boeing P-26 was flown by the Guatemalan Air Force until 1956 when the P-51 Mustang finally replaced it.

What the P-26 possessed in artistic beauty, it lacked in performance. The landing gear was nonretractable, which created a serious drag problem; and although it was reportedly easy to fly, it had a fast landing speed and a worrisome habit of flipping on its back due to its short nose. Accidents were so common that a huge neck rest was added behind the cockpit to protect those pilots who flipped on landing.

The P-26 aircraft served in 1935 as the first-line fighter of the USAAC. That same year, two other fighter aircraft were being test flown in Europe. In a few ensuing years, each of these airplanes would change the history of the world. The German Messerschmitt Bf 109 would prove deadly against British and American bombers in World War II, while the Hawker Hurricane and its prettier cousin, the Supermarine Spitfire, would win the Battle of Britain.

In many ways, 1936 and 1937 were jade steppingstones in my climb toward adulthood.

About this time, we moved into a house my grandfather had built on Queen Anne Hill, a neighborhood known for its historical homes just northwest of downtown Seattle. I really liked the place. There was room in the basement for a worktable and more sophisticated model building.

Of course, I changed schools again, but it was a minor adjustment. I still hated math, and I looked out the classroom window a lot, but my drawing skills were building into a capability of which I could be justly proud, and I was beginning to use a pencil to speak in the magical terms of linear perspective—a language that, once mastered, becomes a new and stunning way to communicate one's world. My airplane drawings were now flavored with the wonderful seasonings of depth, placement, and foreshortening that made them come to life. I was also becoming aware of the incredible changes in aircraft configurations, particularly in fighter planes, and I did hundreds of drawings of the many aircraft that fascinated me. These images are still engraved in my memory, and I hope they will be till the end.

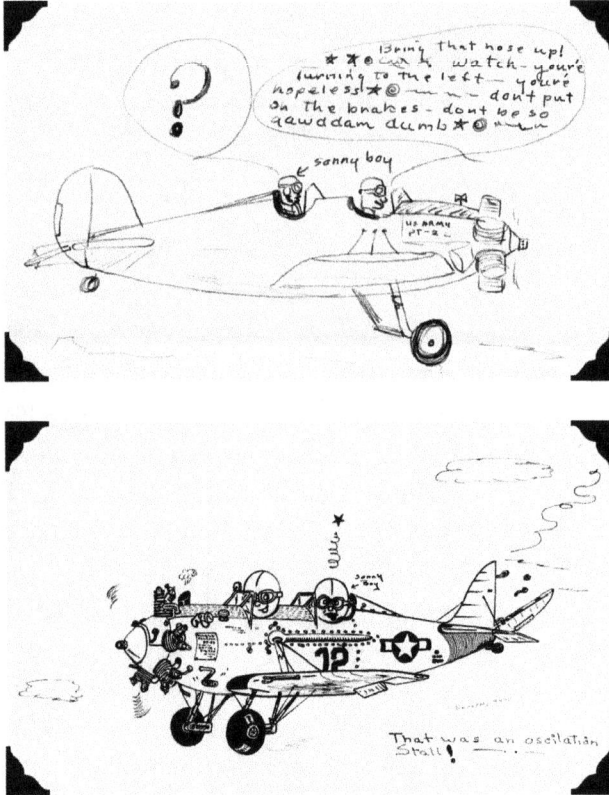

Cartoon drawings created by the author during primary training at Visalia, 1943.

A nice blacktopped boulevard with a really smooth surface wound through our Queen Anne neighborhood. It was great to skate on, and since there wasn't much traffic, we kids played a lot of hockey there. If your skate wheels were worn down, you could still get a pretty good skate on the soft blacktop.

As a kid, I could never keep my hands on the skate key needed to clamp the scats to my Depression-sole shoes. A few of the other kids had their skate keys hung with grubby white strings around their necks, sort of like rusty rosaries. They were the kids who had everything in order and would probably grow up to be lawyers and accountants.

I was different. I always had to borrow a key.

Things were picking up.

On Sunday evenings, my grandfather "Pop" and I would drive down to the drugstore on Greenwood Avenue and pick up a half gallon of their lemon custard ice cream. It was cheap, and to coin a flying phrase, the guy at the counter always "put the flaps up" on the carton and overfilled it by at least twenty percent. It was a great deal, and we never missed our weekend excursions.

Along with the new house and new school, I was enjoying a new feeling of independence that came with my growing height. Art Nelsen and I often took the streetcar downtown where we would walk into Don's Restaurant on Fifth Avenue and order the clam chowder that was served in big abalone shells. Don's was a businessmen's-class restaurant, really an upscale eatery, and the chowder cost thirty-five cents. The sight of two twelve-year-old Depression kids walking in the front door probably gave the management pause for concern; but after awhile, they quit asking to see our money before serving us.

On January 19, 1937, Howard Hughes set a new transcontinental air-speed record of 7 hours, 28 minutes, 25 seconds in a specially powered Northrop Gamma. His elapsed time equated to a speed of 332 mph.[6]

As I said before, things were picking up.

SEVEN

For me, 1937 was the "best of times and the worst of times." Early in the year, my mother met a widower named Oscar Larson, and she began seeing him on a regular basis. He would become everything to me that my biological father had never been: quite simply, one of the most significant, positive influences of goodness in my life. On the other side of the coin, 1937 should be remembered as the Earhart Year, when the attractive and vibrant aviatrix and her navigator, Fred Noonan, would fly into tragic immortality.

Oscar Larson had spent most of his life in the salmon business and had risen to the position of superintendent with the Alaska Pacific Salmon Company. His job entailed spending six to eight months each year at the Port Althorp Cannery in Alaska and returning to Seattle in the fall after the salmon season closed.

Port Althorp, located on the north end of Chichagof Island, is noted for its high concentration of native Alaska brown bears, an offshoot of the American Grizzly; and Oscar constantly regaled me with stories of bears, the beauty of Alaska, and the many flights he'd made in the area around the cannery. He was on a first-name basis with all of the bush pilots who pioneered flying in southeast Alaska; and he was also an avid sports fan, having played football and semipro baseball in his youth. I shared his interest in flying and sports, and we soon became fast friends, attending all kinds of sporting events at the University of Washington and other Seattle venues.

Waco-ZQC-6, ca 1937. (Photo courtesy of the San Diego Air & Space Museum SDASM Archives. No known copyright restrictions.)

My stepdad arranged for his friend to fly us over Seattle in an airplane similar to this one.

Oscar and my mother totally included me in the life they were building together, and sometime early in their relationship, he arranged with a friend to take me on a flight in a Waco YQC-6 cabin biplane. It was a beautiful machine with a plush interior and an impressive instrument panel. We circled over the Sound and the city a couple of times, and my fascination with flying magnified exponentially. I have to admit that my earlier open-air flight in the Aeronca C-3 was a bit more exciting; but the Waco's posh seating was a nice touch, and the instrument panel was a wonderland of intriguing gauges that until then I had only read about.

With the exception of Lindbergh's transatlantic flight, certainly Amelia Earhart's flying accomplishments must be considered some of the most dramatic in the history of American aviation. Her participation in any flying event engendered a sense of excitement that was hard to ignore; and all my life, I had followed her career with intense fervor. Earhart was an icon by the early '30s when America and the world desperately needed a heroic figure. In the Depression era, when poverty and futility choked the land, she stood as a tousle-headed champion in a field of adventure traditionally available only to men; and dressed in a leather jacket and standing in front of romantic aircraft that few could afford or even operate, she proved that women could fly as well as men.

Earhart was born in Atchison, Kansas, in July 1897. Her childhood was checkered by an alcoholic father, and her family bounced around a lot—experiences that obviously nurtured her wanderlust and spirit of adventure. In 1921, while working three jobs to pay for flight lessons, she purchased a secondhand yellow Kinner Airster nicknamed *The Canary*. It was a rather primitive-looking machine resembling an anemic World War I scout plane.

From that point forward, Amelia Earhart was destined for fame. In October 1922, she set a women's altitude record of 14,000 feet at Rogers Field in Chester, California. On June 17, 1928, she accompanied pilot Wilmer Stutz and copilot/mechanic Louis Gordon on a transatlantic flight. (The trio landed in Wales 20 hours, 40 minutes later, and a New York ticker-tape parade greeted them upon their return.) In May 1932, Earhart, in a Lockheed Vega 5B, became the first woman to fly solo across the Atlantic. That same year, she became the first woman to complete a solo transcontinental flight, crossing the United States and setting a new speed record. In 1933, as a contestant in the National Air Races, she broke her own coast-to-coast speed record; and in January 1935, she became the first person (man or woman) to fly solo from Hawaii to California. (This was also the first civilian flight utilizing two-way radio communication.) In April 1935, she became the first person (again, man or woman) to fly solo from Los Angeles to Mexico City; and in May of that year, she became the first person to fly solo nonstop from Mexico City to New York. For her accomplishments, she was twice awarded the Harmon Trophy as America's most outstanding aviatrix.

In July 1936, Purdue University provided funds to Earhart for the purchase of a twin-engine Lockheed Electra Model 10E to be used as a flying laboratory. The Electra prototype had been designed to serve as a light-airliner type and first flew in 1934. To serve Earhart's purposes, the 10E underwent significant modifications in instrumentation, tankage, and equipment. Powered by two 600-horsepower Pratt & Whitney R-1340 engines, this one-of-a-kind aircraft was smooth and lovely in the fashion of the modern transport planes being designed and produced by Boeing and Douglas, and it would be maintained, so to speak, as the newest thing around. In a portent of things to come, the

Electra would also be seen as a suitable airplane for Earhart's planned around-the-world flight.

Amelia Earhart requires study. Her open relationship with her husband, publisher George "G. P." Putnam, is an interesting story fraught with speculation. Extensive reading[7] suggests that G. P. was a bit pushy about Earhart's activities and an aggressive promoter as well as a devoted husband. My personal opinion of him is less favorable. In contrast, Amelia soared above the relationship, and her popularity and celebrity status continued to grow, not only in America, but also across the world.

Earhart's first attempted circumnavigation flight began on March 17, 1937. Accompanying her on the heralded journey was Fred Noonan, a highly experienced navigator who had previously been responsible for establishing flying routes for Pan American Airways. Also onboard were another skilled navigator, Harry Manning, and Paul Mantz, a famous and well-regarded Hollywood stunt pilot. The first leg of the flight was from Oakland, California, to Honolulu, Hawaii. Mantz served as Earhart's mentor in planning the flight and grew in fame in the following years until he was killed in a dramatic airplane crash while filming *The Flight of the Phoenix*.

Upon landing in Hawaii, an examination of the Electra disclosed some lubrication problems in the variable pitch propeller hubs. Repairs were made; then three days later, the Electra with Earhart, Manning, and Noonan aboard initiated takeoff on the second leg of the flight. During takeoff, the Electra ground looped and was severely damaged.

There was much conjecture about the cause of this crash. Earhart thought the right tire had blown out or that the right landing gear had collapsed. Paul Mantz, who had watched the attempted takeoff, stated that in his opinion, the ground loop was the result of pilot error.

Severely damaged Electra following Earhart's ground loop. (US Army photo.)

There should be a twelve-step program for those pilots who have ground looped a perfectly good airplane. Absent a blown tire or landing-gear collapse, there is no legitimate reason for this totally embarrassing situation to occur. Through the years, I have read some indictments regarding Amelia Earhart's skills as a pilot; however, I prefer to believe her accident was sheer happenstance—as was the time I myself ground looped an airplane.

The remainder of Earhart's trip was cancelled, and the Electra was transported by steamship back to the United States for repair. Although it was not an easy task, Amelia and G. P. raised the funds to rebuild the plane.

On May 21, 1937, Earhart departed the Burbank Lockheed facility for Miami, Florida, where it was announced that she and Noonan would again attempt the 'round-the-world flight. This time, because of prevailing weather, they would fly eastward. Just prior to departure on the first leg of the journey, she stated, "I have a feeling that there is just about one more good flight left in my system, and I hope this trip is it."[8]

Earhart's route took her and Noonan first to San Juan, Puerto Rico, and thence along the northeast coast of South America through Paramaribo, Fortaleza, and finally Natal, Brazil—Natal being the jumping-off point for the transatlantic flight to Dakar on Africa's western bulge. The Electra arrived in Dakar on June 10 and then headed almost due east through Gao, Fort-Lamy, and El Fasher, reaching Khartoum on June 13. From Khartoum, Earhart and Noonan flew northeast to Karachi, where they arrived on June 17. Then on they flew to Calcutta before moving southward through Rangoon, Burma, Singapore, and Bandoeng. From Java, their route led southeasterly to Port Darwin, Australia, then on to Lae, New Guinea, the departure point for the long, overwater leg to Howland Island. Upon reaching Lae, they had logged 22,000 miles; only 7,000 miles of the journey remained—all over vast and lonely reaches of the Pacific. In an act that was more than symbolic, Earhart and Noonan shipped their parachutes home from Port Darwin because they created additional weight and would be useless over the remainder of the overwater flight.

My retelling of the details of this critical segment of the Earhart-Noonan journey is based on review of analyses reported by the Waitt Institute Flight Reconstruction Team.[9]

In my opinion, this study presents the most plausible and defensible account of the last flight of Electra 10E NR16020.

Amelia Earhart and Fred Noonan took off from Lae, New Guinea, at exactly 0:00 Greenwich Mean Time (GMT) on July 2, 1937. They carried 1,080 gallons of fuel, sufficient for them to remain aloft for 22 hours. The estimated time en route to Howland Island was 18 hours at cruising speed. Their anticipated fuel reserve would thus provide them with four additional hours in which to search for and pinpoint the island and then land the plane. In view of the necessity of finding an island one and a half miles in length after an overwater night flight of 2,556 miles, the reserve seemed adequate but not excessive.

An aircraft fuel tank is ever so much like a checkbook. One starts out with a balance of so many dollars or gallons and draws on the account as needed; hoping that planning and judicious spending will make the dollars last till the end of the month or the fuel till the end of the journey. However, one must couple this metaphor with the lines often taken from Robert Burns's poem, *To a mouse*:

> *The best laid schemes o' Mice an' Men,*
>
> *Gang aft agley,*
>
> *An' leave us nought but grief an' pain,*
>
> *For promis'd joy!*

Their departure time—10:00 a.m. local time—gave Earhart and Noonan an abundance of daylight hours to progress toward their far-off destination. Earhart's first withdrawal from her fuel "account" was occasioned when she diverted twenty degrees to the right of her flight path to avoid thunderstorms visible directly ahead. Passing the line of thunderstorms, she later reverted to her original path, but inevitably, as darkness of night raced across the sky, the plane and the sea were enveloped in total blackness, and overcast skies with intermittent showers challenged Noonan's celestial navigation skills. The only light the pilot and her navigator would know would be the blue flames from the exhaust stacks and the phosphorescent glow of the gauges on the instrument panel.

Radio reception in the area of Howland Island was mediocre. To ensure the safety of the flight, the USCG *Itasca* had been ordered to Howland Island and was standing by to monitor Earhart's radio traffic. The Coast Guard Cutter was equipped with the latest in radio direction finders (RDF), a relatively new technology for the time. The RDF would indicate the direction from the Electra to the ship by picking up radio transmissions from the aircraft. By determining the plane's direction, the *Itasca* could then actually "steer" Earhart and Noonan toward the vessel and safe landing at Howland Island.

The night flight continued calm, but in the green glow of the instrument panel, there now lurked the insidious probability of disaster. Earhart's Electra was likewise equipped with state-of-the-art technology, including a supremely essential instrument: a Cambridge Fuel Analyzer (CFA). This complex monitor measures exhaust gases and improves engine performance by enabling a pilot to set the fuel-air mixture control to achieve optimum fuel economy and thus maximum aircraft range. This equipment is simply essential to long-distance flights.

From the beginning, the CFA on the Electra 10E had been problematic. On the Khartoum-to-Karachi leg of the journey, the CFA had failed; and Earhart expressed concern that repairs or replacement must take place, stating in a telegram to G. P., "Hesitant to attempt Pacific without (it)."[10] A second breakdown of the CFA required a return trip to Bandoeng, Java, from Surabaya, Indonesia, to effect repair of the troublesome analyzer.

Were the CFA readings to lead the pilot to run the engines on too lean a mixture, there would be an almost immediate warning by an acute rise in the cylinder head temperature gauge, indicating detonation in the engine from insufficient fuel. The pilot would then ignore the readings of the CFA and take immediate action to enrich the mixture and end the problem. On the other hand, if a malfunctioning CFA misled the pilot by allowing him or her to run the engines on too rich a mixture, there would be no warning at all. In other words, the "checking account" would run out of "funds," and the "check register" would be stamped in red ink: "ACCOUNT OVERDRAWN."

When a position is to be determined by RDF, it is essential for the target—in this case, the Electra—to operate the transmitter for sufficient time to allow the seeking party to obtain a fix, or position. All Earhart's messages were too short in length to allow the *Itasca* to determine her actual direction from the ship. At 19 hours, 30 minutes into the flight, the *Itasca* received the following message[11] from Earhart:

> KHAQQ calling ITASCA: We must be on you but cannot see you...gas is running low.

This message, received loud and clear by the *Itasca*, indicated that Earhart was close to the Coast Guard Cutter and to Howland Island. Had fuel consumption been as planned, she should have had ample fuel reserve to remain in the air for an additional two and a half hours.

Amelia Earhart and Lockheed L-10E Electra NR16020, ca 1937. (Public domain.)

Amelia Earhart's Lockheed Model 10 Electra, NR16020, Oakland, California, March 20, 1937. (US Air Force photo.)

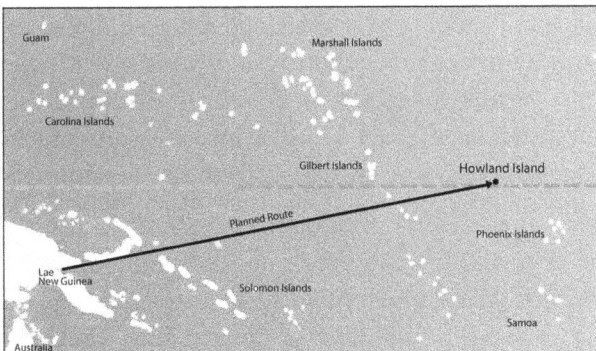

Planned route for last leg of Earhart's transworld flight.

The Electra was apparently not receiving any of the transmissions from the vessel.

Sixty-one minutes later, the *Itasca* received another transmission in a harried voice:

KHAQQ TO ITASCA: We are on the line 157 337. Will repeat the message. We will repeat this on 6210 kcs. Wait. We are running (on) line (north and south).

These were the last words ever heard from NR16020.

The last minutes of the flight can be easily imagined. The sunny morning sky was dotted with cumulus clouds casting dark shadows on the incredibly broad expanse of the western Pacific. Each shadow might contain the reality of the tiny island, the haven so desperately sought. Eyes would be constantly scanning the horizon for some sign of land, and the needles on the gasoline gauges would be hovering ever closer to their zero markings. An attempt would surely be made to lean out the fuel-air mixture even more, but the slightest additional reduction would bring about a rise in cylinder head temperature, followed by detonation in the engines from insufficient fuel. The mixture simply could not be leaned out anymore and still keep the engines running.

Since the Electra was not fitted with fully feathering[12] propellers, there was no possibility of turning the blades to feathered position, thus eliminating the terrific drag created by the powerless windmilling of dead engines. Undoubtedly, one engine would run out of fuel first, and the drag of the propeller on that side would create a severe yaw in the aircraft's direction of flight. This yaw would require excessive rudder application and probably the reduction of power to the remaining good engine if any directional stability were to be maintained. In a dreadful sequence, that power reduction would, in turn, mandate that the nose of the aircraft be dropped to sustain sufficient air speed to preclude a disastrous stall and tailspin.

When the second engine ran out of fuel, the powerless aircraft would have to assume an extremely steep rate of descent to overcome the drag of two dead engines. Such an excessive nose-down attitude would probably prevent a successful ditching procedure, and entrance of the aircraft into the water would most likely be catastrophic.

The Electra 10E NR16020 disappeared on the morning of July 2, 1937. Massive search efforts by the US Navy, Coast Guard, and others to find Earhart, Noonan, and the plane officially ended on July 19. Privately funded expeditions to solve the mystery continue to the present.

The disappearance of NR16020 has developed a life of its own—filled with all the drama and suspense of a well-written novel. At the time of this writing, the tragic flight has intrigued the world for more than seventy-five years. It is a story whose conclusion may well remain forever unwritten.

EIGHT

The maiden flight of the first military aircraft produced by Bell Aviation Corporation occurred in 1937. Called the Airacuda, the twin-engine design concept was unique in that the wing-mounted engines were reversed, and the engine pods housed pusher-type engines. Although this concept was not entirely new (there were several pusher-type aircraft used in World War I), the front of each of the engine pods was fitted with a glass nose to provide a gun platform for a gunner who would operate a forward-firing 37mm cannon. The Airacuda was essentially a twin-engine interceptor of stunning beauty and atrocious practical design; and at the time, I considered it one of the most beautiful airplanes I had ever seen. I ascribe my original admiration for this beast to my immature age of thirteen and commensurate lack of common sense. The same might be said of the airplane's designer.

In a miscarriage of good sense, thirteen Airacudas were built for the US Army Air Corps between 1937 and 1940. None ever saw action; and by 1942, all were accounted for. Two had crashed with one fatality; the remaining eleven had been relegated to the scrap heap since no one wanted to fly them.

Bell Airacuda. (US Air Force image.)

There is a bit of macabre comedy in the story of the Airacuda. Since the engines were in the rear, anyone exiting the aircraft in flight would be jumping into the teeth of a mammoth blender, ensuring instant death. The only manner of survival in the middle of a dogfight would require the pilot to feather the engines, thus allowing the gunners to exit the plane without being cut to pieces. However, with feathered propellers, the Airacuda would be a sitting duck for enemy gunfire. *Not a good idea.* A second emergency bailout system would allow the pilot to set off explosive bolts, blowing the propellers off their shafts and allowing the crew to escape. This action would, of course, make the Airacuda flightless—yet another miracle of clear thinking. Should the propellers be so jettisoned, there was every possibility that once they were blown loose, the errant props might spin through the fuselage cutting the Airacuda in two! And there was more: The airplane was heavy and slow, lacked maneuverability, and was fraught with cooling problems because of the positioning of the pusher engines. With even minimal power applied, the airplane was inherently unstable in pitch, roll, or yaw, and this instability made the Airacuda susceptible to incipient tailspins from which recovery was almost impossible.

The Airacudas were powered by several variants of the Allison V-1710 engine, all of which suffered from excessive heat buildup because of the reverse positioning of the engines. The overheating was so severe that while on the ground, the aircraft could not be operated under its own power. Instead, the Airacudas had to be towed to takeoff position, and once the engines were started, had to take off as quickly as possible to prevent engine overheating. Conversely, after landing, the aircraft's engines had to be shut down immediately to prevent heat damage. The plane was then towed back to the parking area to cool.

When the 37mm cannons were fired from the crewed nacelles, so much smoke was generated that the gunners/loaders couldn't see to aim their weapons; at the same time, they suffered every possibility of suffocating from cordite smoke. It is obvious that no serviceman in his right mind would ever willingly occupy either of the wing pods for fear of suffocation by cannon smoke or the possibility of being chopped into bits by the giant Mixmaster twirling on the trailing edge of the wing; and documentation[13] indicates that no human being ever left the ground occupying one of the Airacuda's nacelles.

As if the foregoing indictments were not enough to sentence the Airacuda to eternal damnation, the ill-tempered wretch didn't even have its own built-in electrical system. Indeed, the electricity for the aircraft was furnished by a separate auxiliary power unit (APU) located in the tail of the plane. This small gasoline-powered generator provided the major electrical power for the entire aircraft, an almost unthinkable option. To make matters worse, the APU was subject to frequent failure, an event that would leave the Airacuda with no power to fuel pumps, brakes, flaps, landing gear, or the engines. It's my understanding that there are several venerable Airacuda fan clubs still in existence nearly eighty years after this plane first took flight. I would be almost certain that few (if any) of these loyal fans ever flew the airplane.

Change was in the air. On the global front, Germany was riding roughshod over Britain and its allies, and the autumn of 1938 would witness Hitler's thugs strolling into the Sudetenland without so much as a slap on the wrist. The cardboard cutout that was Italian dictator Benito Mussolini was making noises in the Mediterranean, and the Far East stew pot was being stirred to a boil by a Japanese emperor who was chewing up China with intentions of making vast regions of the Pacific his personal feast. International strife covered the globe like a blanket, and there was a growing fear in just about everyone's mind that war was coming.

I was getting older and starting to like girls. My model building had slowed to a crawl, but airplanes—and the pilots who flew them—were still as important to me as ever.

Shining through the international gloom were some real highlights, and one of the brightest stars was a young pilot named Douglas Corrigan. It had taken only a single $2.50 ride in an old Jenny biplane to hook him on flying. He saved his money, took flying lessons, and worked for a time at Ryan Aircraft in San Diego. He actually did some of the welding on the *Spirit of St. Louis* and was proud that he had pulled the chocks from Lindy's wheels when he left for New York just before his fabled flight.

In 1933, while working on the East Coast, Corrigan pondered the question of how he could return to California. He located a trashed Curtiss Robin and purchased it for the grand sum of $310.00; then he threw his belongings in the plane and hopped, skipped, and jumped back home, giving demonstration plane rides to earn money for gas in what could best be described as "an absolute piece of junk."[14] At one point, the knob on the door handle had even broken off, and Corrigan used bailing wire that he borrowed from a local farmer to make the repair.

Upon his return to California, Corrigan again took up work as a welder and aircraft mechanic at Ryan Aeronautical Company, using funds to patch up and outfit the old Robin for long-distance flights. Incredibly, in 1935, he requested a permit to fly the six-year-old airplane nonstop from New York to London, but because of the condition of the aircraft, authorities denied the permit, terming the proposed flight suicidal[15] and finally telling him to "just stop asking."[16]

Eventually, Corrigan wheedled authorities into granting him a conditional permit to fly the plane from California to New York and return, "if the eastbound trip turned out alright."[17] On July 8, 1938, he and his *Corrigan Clipper* left California and, amazingly, flew nonstop to New York.

To keep himself awake, he had stuck his head out the window. He landed at Roosevelt Field on Long Island after a twenty-seven hour flight with only four gallons of gasoline to spare.

A week later, Corrigan topped off his fuel supply with slightly more than three hundred gallons of gasoline, for which he paid $62.26 cash. Then, at dawn on July 17, he propped the plane himself, climbed into the cockpit with some candy bars, and took off—ostensibly, for the return trip to California.

Strangely, after takeoff, he turned eastward.

A mere 28 hours, 13 minutes later, Doug Corrigan landed at Baldonnel Aerodrome near Dublin, Ireland. En route, the airplane's fuel tank (which was smaller than the one in the *Spirit of St. Louis* and carrying less gasoline) had begun leaking. As fuel puddled around his feet, Corrigan drove a long screwdriver through the fuselage flooring, allowing it to drain out. In interviews later with authorities, he claimed he had flown the wrong way due to foggy conditions and a "faulty compass."[18] As punishment for his illegal activities, the US Department of Commerce suspended his pilot's license for a period of eighteen days. He was also chided for not having a permit to land at Dublin's airport.

WHEN I SAW THE LAYOUT OF THE COUNTRY
AND THE LITTLE WHITE HOUSES
DOTTED HERE AND THERE,
I REALIZED IT DID NOT LOOK LIKE
WHAT IT SHOULD LOOK LIKE TO ME.

~ DOUGLAS CORRIGAN

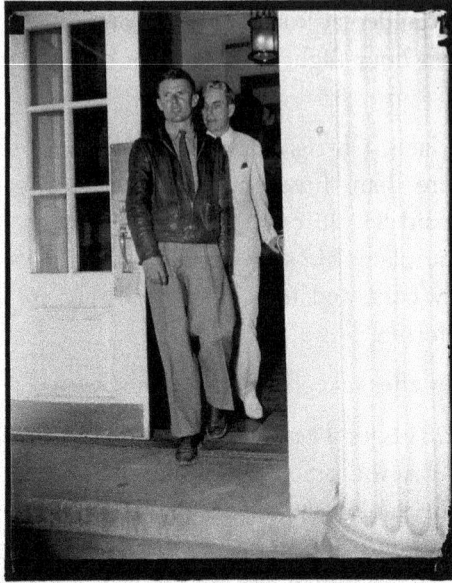

"Wrong Way" Corrigan visits President Roosevelt, August 31, 1938. (Library of Congress Prints & Photographs. Call Number: LC-H22-D- 4518 [P&P]. Photo by Harris & Ewing. No known restrictions on publication.)

He's "Right Way" Corrigan now! (Office of War Information photograph, Library of Congress Prints & Photographs. Call Number: LOT 9425 [item] [P&P]. No known restrictions on publication.)

Doug Corrigan and his plane were shipped home where he was greeted by President Franklin Roosevelt and a New York ticker-tape parade[19] with millions of cheering fans. Still lingering in the throes of the Depression and in a world staring at war, people everywhere had found a new hero and treated Corrigan as such. His celebrity status firmly assured, Corrigan and his now-revered *Corrigan Clipper* continued to draw crowds wherever he flew.

Corrigan's transoceanic journey would signal the end of an era of aviation freedom, and a bit of the fun of flying would soon forever vanish. Barnstorming and the two-dollar flight around the meadow were on their way out while rigidity and regulation elbowed their way in. Corrigan died in 1995 with the old Curtiss Robin stored in a shed beside his home in California. Although his parents had christened him "Douglas," to an admiring world, he would forever be known as "Wrong-Way" Corrigan.

There was considerable excitement in Seattle in June 1938. Another homegrown airplane was about to take to the skies; and I, like everyone else in town, was anxious to witness the test flight.

Boeing's new entry into the age of passenger flight was the 314 Clipper, a monstrous flying boat built to the specifications of Pan American Airways. Specifically designed to provide long-range, overwater passenger service, the airplane was immense, with a wingspan of 152 feet and a gross weight of 82,500 pounds. The Clipper was powered by four Wright Twin Cyclone engines, each producing 1,600 horsepower, and the aircraft had an astounding-for-the-time range of 3,500 miles. Seattle had a right to be excited!

The test flight was set for June 7, 1938, and a lot of Seattle lined the shores of Elliot Bay to watch. My grandparents took me to see the spectacle, and I was thrilled. I was as interested in the test pilot, Eddie Allen, as I was in the Clipper. Eddie Allen had been a long-time Boeing test pilot, and he was widely known in Seattle circles and highly regarded as a brilliant and practical engineer.

Boeing Yankee Clipper, ca 1939. (Library of Congress Prints & Photographs, digital ID hec. 26202. No known restrictions on publication.)

The great day was at hand, and with everyone watching, the engines built up to a roar as the immense aircraft rose from the surface of the bay and climbed slowly to the south. Allen then leveled off, executed a rather laborious turn to the left, and glided back to the landing area to the cheers of Seattleites. It was a wonderful experience, although perhaps a bit underwhelming—and with good reason. If one were even moderately familiar with airplanes, it was easy to detect a curious anomaly: the vertical fin and rudder seemed extremely small for the bulk of the aircraft; and apparently, there had been some concerns expressed about this by engineers at the University of Washington where wind-tunnel experiments on the 314 had been conducted.

Eddie Allen was a man of extreme talent and few words. When asked how the flight went, he replied, "The plane won't turn!"[20] The only way he was able to return the aircraft to the landing zone was to cut power to the port engines and give full throttle to the two engines on the starboard side. It had become abundantly clear to Allen and to all concerned that the vertical fin and rudder were *indeed* too small.

The single fin was replaced by two endplates, smaller rudders, on the ends of the horizontal stabilizer. Despite the modifications, flying the airplane still felt like herding a clowder of cats. Finally, the original vertical fin and rudder were again added to the mix, and the Boeing Clipper could make an acceptable turn to the right and left.

The wings of the aircraft were so large that a passageway was included inside to allow mechanics to work on the engines while in flight. In case of engine failure, the offending power plant could be shut down and its propeller feathered. The mechanic could then conduct repairs while the plane was thousands of feet in the air. In the history of the 314, such repairs were made a surprising number of times.

During the course of World War II, all the 314s were pressed into service as military transports, most of them flown by experienced Pan Am pilots. One of the 314s transported FDR to his important meeting with Prime Minister Winston Churchill at Casablanca.

Of the twelve 314 models built by Boeing, three were lost to accidents, only one of which resulted in fatalities. The remaining airplanes were sold to several different entities, then cannibalized or sold again as scrap. The day of the Boeing Clipper passed, but the sight of the monster creation scooting along and lifting from the waters of Elliot Bay is as clear to me today as it was seventy plus years ago.

One would think that after the fiasco of the Airacuda, the Bell Aviation Corporation would switch their production efforts from airplanes to lawn chairs, but such was not the case. Responding to the US military's request for a new single-seat fighter, in 1937, Bell jumped in with both feet. The specifications for the new aircraft were demanding: It was to have a top, straight, and level speed of at least 360 mph; carry 1,000 pounds of armament, including a cannon; and climb to 20,000 feet in six minutes or less. Bell's answer to the call for a new fighter was, without question, a revolutionary concept; and, oh my, she was a sweet one...a pretty girl you'd love to take to the prom!

The Bell P-39 Airacobra was tricked out with an Allison V-1710 engine placed to the rear of the cockpit, and it was the first fighter design in US history to be equipped with a rather handsome tricycle landing gear—indeed a beautiful set of gams! To meet Army Air Corps specifications, she also sported an Oldsmobile Model T9 37mm cannon, which fired through the propeller hub. Rounds for the Olds T9 were about one and a half inches in diameter and packed a powerful armor-piercing punch. The nifty little fighter also beat the prescribed performance numbers when she climbed to 20,000 feet in five minutes and stepped out at a smart 390 mph at altitude.

Bell P-39 Airacobra in flight at night with all weapons firing. (US Air Force photo.)

The prototype Airacobra was equipped with a General Electric turbosupercharger, which was responsible for the aircraft's superior performance. The turbine required an air scoop on the aft, left side of the fuselage, and that produced some drag. Meddling with parasitic drag components inherent in the Airacobra, the National Advisory Committee for Aeronautics, a federal bureaucracy, insisted the turbine components be completely housed within the fuselage. Because of the tightness of the airplane, there was no space available to meet this demand. Bell knuckled under and equipped production models with a mealy-mouthed, single-stage, single-speed supercharger, which effectively limited the Airacobra's fighting altitude to 12,000 feet.

These misguided actions nearly ruined her party dress and took away her corsage as an interceptor, but she didn't remain a wallflower for long. As production models advanced and modifications were made, the P-39D was decked out with an Olds 37mm cannon; two .50-inch, nose-mounted Browning machine guns; and four .30-inch machine guns mounted in the wings. The D model also featured self-sealing gas tanks and shackles for a 500-pound bomb or drop tank.

She was becoming a tougher lady.

Bell P-39 Airacobra center fuselage detail with maintenance panels open. (US Air Force photo.)

The unique design of the airplane called for a rather unusual cockpit and canopy. Entrance to the cockpit was through an automobile-like door on either side. The cockpit canopy, almost invariably a sliding structure in other fighters, formed a permanent roof over the cockpit of the P-39, causing some pilots concern over emergency ejection.

The doors were equipped with roll-down windows and were capable of being jettisoned for bailout. Another strange feature was the elongated propeller shaft running ten feet from the engine behind the cockpit to the tractor propeller at the front of the plane. The shaft ran through a raised tunnel on the cockpit floor and apparently caused no systemic problems in design or operation. The housing provided a fine gun platform, and the pilot sat very high in the cockpit with good visibility.

P-39 Airacobra. Drawing by Ed Larson, 2014.

The Airacobra was a tender airplane requiring attention to its weight and balance. Manuals covering the P-39 mandated ballast in the nose section in the absence of a normal ammunition load. In the absence of weight in the nose section, the P-39 exhibited a tendency to roll into a dangerous flat spin from which recovery was very difficult. The flat spin risk was vehemently denied by Bell until Soviet test pilots proved the aberration was valid and threatening. The Airacobra also tended to level out of a dive if the stick was not forcibly held in the forward position; nevertheless, maximum dive speed was a respectable 475 mph, and the

P-39's roll rate was better than the Grumman F4F Wildcat or the Mitsubishi A6M2 Zero.

The Airacobra's mid-engine placement and coolant system made the airplane particularly vulnerable to rear high-pass attacks or attacks from below and astern; and the altitude limitation of the single-stage, single-speed supercharger made the airplane unsuitable for high-altitude combat. However, the P-39 was ideally suited to low-level air-to-air combat and ground targets such as tanks, trucks, trains, and fixed installations since return fire would invariably come from below and ahead. Thus, the P-39 was a perfect fit for the needs of the Soviet Union waging war on the eastern front. The Russian Air Force received 4,719 P-39s during World War II—nearly half of all the models produced. Russian pilots loved the airplane because of its rugged construction, roll rate, and nose cannon, and the P-39s served well in combat against Bf 109s and Fw 190s. The plane also served with US forces in Alaska, Italy, and the southwest Pacific—specifically Guadalcanal. In all, 9,558 Airacobras were built. Production stopped in mid-1944. As of this writing, three Airacobras are still airworthy, and ten are in static displays around the world.

So the girl who came to the party stayed for the last dance. This was an airplane with a beautiful face and a figure that was easy to love, and even though they stole her turbocorsage, she was *still* one of the prettiest girls at the prom.

NINE

At the end of August 1938, my mother and I boarded the steamer *North Sea* for a trip to Alaska. This was a real turning point in my life. My mother and Oscar Larson had decided to marry in Juneau in early September as the salmon season was coming to a close. I recall standing by the railing and throwing rolls of confetti to my grandparents as the ship pulled away from its Seattle berth. I realized that my life was going to be a lot different from anything I had experienced before. I was, in effect, changing families, leaving my grandparents, who had been like a mother and father to me, and my uncle, who had always seemed like my brother. As a family, we had traveled the tortured pathway of the Great Depression and survived. My life now would be more affluent and filled with adventures that few kids had the chance to experience.

The journey northward through Alaska's Inside Passage on our way to meet Oscar was unforgettable. I stood by the railing for hours, constantly stunned by the beauty and wildness unfolding before my eyes. I had never left home before, and the sights and sounds of this wonderland through which I was passing were almost too much for me to comprehend. The small towns where we stopped were totally reminiscent of the Old West, complete with boardwalks, whorehouses, saloons, and false-front buildings. Alaska was a land of bearded men, rain, and frontier mentality. I loved it!

Each of the small hamlets we visited had its own collection of floatplanes. These light aircraft, tied to shaky log floats, lent an air of adventure and romance to every Alaskan town. Most of these planes had become too old and too raunchy to fly in the States. They had come up from Seattle, coughing, wheezing, and jumping like frogs from one backwoods pond to the next. The men who flew them could also fix them and keep them going, and the airplanes were as tough and utilitarian as the people and the towns they served. Old and unwashed Curtiss Robins, Fairchilds, and Lockheed Vegas squatted on pontoons in the murky waters, dripping oil from cylinder head gaskets that had flown too long and would fly even longer. In this place, airplanes were essential to get from one place to another. Mountains and weather were just stuff to fly over or through, and there were great pilots to do just that.

Oscar had flown into Juneau from the cannery, and he met us at the steamship dock when we landed. He and my mother were married the day after we arrived, on September 7, 1938. The wedding was performed by the United States Commissioner for the Territory of Alaska in the courthouse in Juneau. The next day, Mother and I again boarded the *North Sea* for a trip of about seventy miles to the cannery at Port Althorp with the man I now called Dad. Oscar Larson and I had developed a tremendously warm relationship, one that would last through all our years, and I was proud to regard him as my father.

We stayed at the cannery about three weeks while everything was being shut down for the winter. It was one of the most magical places I have ever known.

Cross Sound, the site of the cannery, lies at the northern end of Chichagof Island, one of the large islands that compose the Alexander Archipelago. Admiralty, Baranof, and Chichagof Islands run north and south along the coast of southeastern Alaska. They are known locally as the ABC Islands and renowned as the kingdom of the huge Alaska brown bear.

It is taxing to attempt a description of the cannery and its surroundings simply because it has always been so important to me. The cannery was, in truth, a small town that opened up for six or seven months each year for one avowed purpose: to can in the shortest possible time as many salmon as it was possible to catch. From late March to late September, a crew of hundreds of Chinese, Native American, Filipino, and Caucasian workers, each group offering specific talents with varying skills, worked twenty-four hour days, seven days a week in pursuit of that prime goal. The cannery was an ethnic hodgepodge, a peopled oasis, set in a magnificent land of vast wildness and unspeakable beauty. Each day at Port Althorp was an ongoing adventure, usually played out under gray skies and falling rain.

During what turned out to be the heyday of salmon fishing in southeast Alaska, the bulk of salmon were caught in elaborate fish traps. These traps were strategically placed along the shoreline and caught hundreds if not thousands of salmon each day. Trap fishing required a small fleet of towboats called cannery tenders, which emptied the traps and carried the fish to the various canneries they served.

I became totally enamored with these tough little boats that plied the waters around Chichagof Island in all kinds of weather. Life aboard them was always exciting for a teenage kid, and some of the best memories of my life are of these towboats and the men who operated them.

Doris E. Drawing by Ed Larson, 2008.

I spent many magnificent days aboard the *Doris E.* She was one of the cannery tenders owned by my dad's cannery, and she became my window on Alaska. I literally grew up working her decks while listening to the heartbeat of her huge diesel engine.

Fog, storms, wind, and rain were part of our daily regime. In the presence of storms, this world became a continuum of gray with glacial white at one end and black, timbered shadows at the other. There was impersonality about such colorless times, a drab sameness that left me truly longing for the sun. On those relatively rare days when it arrived, the transformation was at once dramatic and complete. Port Althorp and the straits that surrounded her were transfigured into a land of heart-stopping beauty.

I was constantly assailed by the sheer magnificence of this landscape: With a slight turn of my head, I faced towering, snow-covered mountains; immense glaciers; broad seas; untouched timbered mountains; granite crags; wide highland meadows; and quiet coves of such beauty they defy description. Being young, I easily became oblivious to such splendor, and it is only in memory that I can embrace the sheer scope and wonder of the place. Its immensity—the scale of earth structures here is virtually impossible to comprehend—and the sights, sounds, and smells of the land are what I remember best.

An old Bellanca mail plane was the only measuring stick against which I could gauge the vast surroundings about me. Each time it approached, I could hear the noise of its engine long before it was visible. The sound would emerge first as a faint hum, growing louder only after an interminable wait. The plane, an infinitesimally small speck in the sky, was totally dwarfed by the bastion of timbered peaks surrounding it, and there was so much space to traverse that the plane seemed to crawl across the blue void, leaving me with the feeling that, in fact, it was an illusion and would probably never arrive. At last, as the plane finally drew closer, it would assume its identity, displaying the unmistakable colors of wings and fuselage against the mammoth backdrop of timbered peaks. Descending, it would crease the waters of the bay with twin white slashes that disappeared as quickly as they were carved. Even after the plane reached the float and became full-scale, it still illustrated, somehow, the infinite expanse of earth and sea around me.

On fine mornings as the *Doris E.* headed northwest out of the bay, dead ahead and towering 14,000 feet above us lay the ramparts of the perpetually snow-laden Fairweather Range. Brady Glacier, ice blue and tarnished white, tilted toward us like a giant frosted meadow; its ice field ending abruptly in frozen cliffs that dropped into the intense blue green of Taylor Bay. Turning east, the world narrowed through North Inian Pass, and yellow light from the summer sun warmed the steep, crevassed banks rising from the shore to the forest's beginning. Stellar sea lions lounging on the massive rocks remained alert but unconcerned by our intrusion. At intervals through the pass, huge logs the color of chocolate bars were cast like jackstraws across boulder-strewn beaches. Massive tides and swift currents that were so much a part of Cross Sound and the straits had carried them there. In full sunlight, forested summits became almost lemon yellow; while below, havens of shadowy timber stood in near concealment.

As if this magnificence wasn't enough, it was doubled—cast back in a water mirror from the placid blue seas around us; erased only momentarily by the sparkling white bow wave of the *Doris E.*, it would swiftly reappear in the passing swell as an undulating counterpoint to the majesty above it. Even in feeble sunshine, the whole of the scene became texturally rich and intensely colorful—unfamiliar, suddenly new; and every time I witnessed this landscape, it was as if I was again seeing it for the first time.

Imagine then, the thrill of flying an aircraft through such a wonderland. I question the possibility of anyone, even the pilots who flew every day, ever becoming complacent or blasé. But there was a price to pay for the adventure; and as we shall soon learn, too often, the price was exceedingly high.

When the cannery had been buttoned up for the season, we again headed south to Seattle on the *North Sea*. My mother and Oscar were planning an extended vacation out East, and I was enrolled in a military school for the year.

The timing for a military school education couldn't have been better. There was a great trembling and groveling going on in Europe, and the world's maps were being redrawn in the face of savage aggression. Anyone with common sense could see the German-Italian-Japanese tripartition for what it really was: a group of jackals tearing apart their neighbors' populations to feed their insatiable greed for space and power.

In September 1938, Neville Chamberlain, the British Prime Minister, pandered and cowed before Adolph Hitler, attempting to appease the German's madness by giving him parts of Czechoslovakia. Then, in April 1939, in another disgusting exhibition of meekness, Britain was bullied by Benito Mussolini into recognizing Italy's brutal annexation of Albania. Emboldened by his success, Mussolini soon demanded Tunisia, Corsica, Nice, and Savoy from France.

Meanwhile, Hitler began an active pogrom against the Jews in Europe. Fueled by naked hate, Germany's Final Solution would become known as the Holocaust, that monstrous tragedy that will reflect for all time unending shame on those responsible for the murder of millions.

I did well in military school and enjoyed the somewhat Spartan existence. In addition to regular classes, we were taught to shoot, march, and take orders. This teaching would serve us well in the years ahead. At the same time, my interest in aviation and the political maneuvering in Europe increased. There were signs everywhere that the world was headed inexorably toward all-out war. It seemed no one could stop it.

As soon as school was out, I again headed north to Port Althorp with my folks. It was an idyllic summer at the cannery. My reunion with the men I had grown to admire was all I could imagine, and I spent weeks on the *Doris E.* as a part-time deck hand. The summer was a complete adventure, every day bringing some new, intriguing circumstance. In retrospect, I cannot imagine a better or more exciting venue for a growing kid.

The advent of Alaskan summer brought with it a sun not often seen, but a sun that barely set. It was easily possible to read a newspaper at 2:00 a.m. The summer also brought with it biblical rains that were an accepted part of Alaskan life. My mother counted fifty-four straight days of rain that summer, not a record, but nevertheless quite impressive. The rain bothered no one. I had long before adopted a daily uniform of tall hip boots, yellow slickers, and a sou'wester hat—pretty much standard outerwear for everyone at the cannery.

Needed supplies were delivered to our isolated location by steamboat, cannery tender, or airplane. Without the bush pilots and their stables of weary planes, the cannery would have been dead in the water. Once a week, there was a regular mail plane from Juneau; and two to three times a week, my dad's friends, Alex Holden and Shell Simmons, delivered essential cargo to us. Simmons and Holden had merged their bush pilot operations, and their company had served the various settlements and canneries in the area for many years. Holden was the quieter of the two men; but both he and Simmons were great pilots, and together, their years of Alaska flying experience had made them giants. If I were at the cannery, I never missed the opportunity to rush down to the fish float to check out the arriving or departing planes and talk with these two men, hanging on their every word.

Many of the pilots who flew into Port Althorp were famous; and in the years ahead, some would become legends. In 1938, Shell Simmons saved the crew of the cargo ship *Patterson*, which had run aground along Cape Fairweather, one of the roughest, most dangerous, most inaccessible bits of coastline in Alaska. Rescue attempts by the Coast Guard had proved futile because of vicious storms and bad weather; and as time was running out, the crew of eighteen faced certain death on the exposed beach. Simmons loaded a knowledgeable trapper into his plane and in a true act of heroism, landed in boiling surf near the stranded group. The trapper then led the bulk of the stranded crew to safety, and Simmons flew two of the weakest members back to Juneau for hospitalization. It was a rescue made possible only through Simmons's incredible flying skill.

In another act of bravery, Simmons ignored his own injuries to save one of his passengers from drowning following an accident off Chichagof Island. Savagely beaten in a collision with the plane's instrument panel during the plane crash, Simmons bore the disfiguring scars for the remainder of his life.

Toward the end of July, I complained one night to my mother about a persistent itching on my knee. I had noticed a small reddish patch about the size of a quarter, which was apparently the source of the trouble. For a week, I treated it with Lifebuoy soap—to no avail. It just wasn't getting any better. After a cursory examination, my mother concluded that I was near death from fish poisoning, or at least, about to lose my leg. My dad said that was nonsense; but Mother ruminated over it for a few days, longing for some contact with a member of the medical profession. Perhaps the outbreak was a manifestation of scurvy, the ancient mariner's curse. After all, I was working on a boat, wasn't I? Or maybe it was beriberi, or cholera, or how about a vagrant strain of malaria, or some other tropical disease that had worked its way from Uganda to Port Althorp? The die was cast; Eddie was going to the doctor.

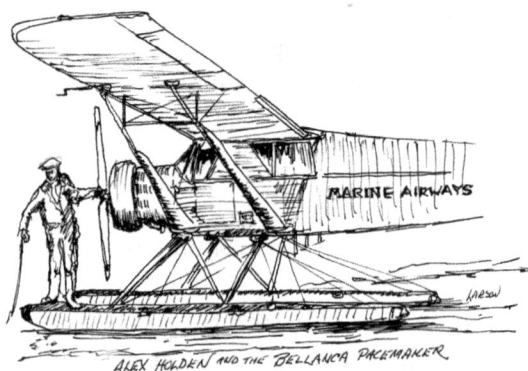

Alex Holden and the Bellanca Shakey Jake. Drawing by Ed Larson, 1996.

I have always suspected that the trip had a two-fold purpose. I'm sure my mother felt some concern about my knee. I'm equally sure she needed a little respite from cannery life. For her, a chance to see a doctor—any doctor—would be a high point in her summer.

A day or so later, Alex Holden flew into Port Althorp to pick us up. Naturally, I claimed the front seat in the old Bellanca Pacemaker high-wing monoplane. In minutes, I was asking questions.

The Pacemaker was like most aircraft that ended up in Alaska. Simply put, it was rode hard and put up wet. A huge, slab-sided machine, it had immense windows and an instrument panel that was dented and worn and covered with old compass courses written in pencil that had never been erased. It was nicknamed *Shakey Jake* because of its tendency to flap its wings in turbulent air; and even in 1939, it looked like a museum piece. There was some history to it, too. A year and a half before our trip, Alex Holden had taken a young, nondescript reporter from the *Washington Daily News* for a free ride over Taku Glacier. The passenger who had warmed the right front seat of the old Bellanca was Ernie Pyle, who later became the most famous war correspondent of World War II. Of the flight, Pyle wrote, "I have superstitions about airplane pilots. For instance, I have complete confidence in a pilot who is bald-headed, and practically none at all in one who has a mustache!"[21]

Pyle must have enjoyed the hell out of Alex Holden—he was as hairless as a cue ball.

Starting up and idling, the old Bellanca was as noisy as a threshing machine in a cane field. Holden shouted in my ear, explaining the procedures for takeoff. As I looked in the back, I saw my mother was white knuckling her armrest, and Dad didn't look that great, either. At the speed of a fast walk, we pulled away from the landing float leaving behind four or five cannery hands who had held on to the airplane while we got on board. After about fifty feet, Holden swung the plane into a slight breeze from the east and shoved the throttle open. The results were anything but electrifying. With the Bellanca, it took a little while for anything to happen. Finally, the plane made a reluctant decision to get going. As we picked up speed, Alex began moving the stick violently forward and aft. This action, of course, threw the passengers forward and backward in their seats as if they were on a hobbyhorse. He shouted something in my ear like, "Gotta shake her loose!"

After a moment, the floats got "on plane," and she finally broke free of the bay, shaking off saltwater like a wet Labrador. We climbed east over the salt chuck opposite the cannery; and in five minutes, the meadows and crags of Chichagof Island were flashing past us hundreds of feet below. This was a new, exhilarating adventure, and I was even more hooked on flying.

The trip to Juneau took about forty-five minutes. We flew beneath a cloud deck broken by bars of sunlight highlighting the sensuous yellow greens and acid blues of the solid spruce forests below. At cruising rpm, the Bellanca's engine felt like velvet, and the propeller spun a sunlit disk about four feet in front of our faces. The feeling was ethereal, almost spiritual. I would get to know it well in the years just ahead.

I talked with Alex Holden all the way, asking questions and taking in a new world. Holden must have liked kids; he pointed to the jiggling instrument panel explaining the message each needle was sending out and went on to explain the purpose of every switch and lever. There weren't that many; and before we got to Juneau, I knew them all by heart.

Holden was still talking as we let down over Gastineau Channel. As we flashed over the docks under a lowering sky, I looked down at the pontoons and waited; then in a moment, white feathers of spray flew out from the floats as we settled gently down on the water, a perfect landing.

We taxied up to the Marine Airways Terminal. Little more than a large unpainted garage on floats, its walls were lined with tools and airplane junk, and it was fronted by a wooden ramp extending out into the water so that aircraft could be pulled in and out for storage or repair. At the edge of the ramp, three men were fueling a Lockheed Vega with the hand pump from a fifty-gallon drum. One of the men was Shell Simmons, Holden's partner. I stood by the Vega while my parents chatted with him and the fueling was completed; then we moved a little away as Simmons cranked the engine for starting. Apparently, the mixture was too rich. Gas dripping from the cowling had run down the ramp and turned the water into a round rainbow, and when Simmons hit the starter again, the whole thing took off in flames. It was fairly spectacular until the prop blew out the fire.

Simmons shut down the Vega and climbed out laughing. My mother's face blanched white in fear. "My God," she reacted, "I'm glad that didn't happen to our plane!"

"Hell, Violet," Simmons chuckled in reply, "they *both* do that *all the time!*"

I assure you, that statement added immeasurably to Mother's white-knuckle flying syndrome.

As expected, my ailment was completely innocuous… a non-life-threatening case of ringworm. After spending a couple of days in Juneau at the Baranof Hotel, we met Alex Holden at Marine Airways and flew back to the cannery.

TEN

The return flight to the cannery captivated me even more. A midsummer sun lent a wealth of color and clarity to the forests, land, and sea; the day was simply unforgettable. Alaska flying is an experience not to be missed. It's true that the weather may turn sour at times; there is also an occasional bit of peril in the mix, but in this land, the sheer wonder of the scenery and the freedom of flight come together to stagger the imagination. One crosses whale-laden bays and immense meadows sprinkled with virginal, unfished alpine lakes. High crags reach up, covered with snow and ice that has not melted since the dawn of time. Even as a kid not given to much sentimentality, I felt my heart expand in the immense grandeur and freedom of that morning. The spell lasted from takeoff to touchdown. Too soon, Holden, our pilot, turned low over the cannery and set the Bellanca down flawlessly. We had become friends on this round-trip flight.

I continued to work on the cannery tenders after our return to the cannery, and the days wound down to late August. As isolated as we were, the noise of the coming Armageddon spilled out of the speaker of my dad's

Hallicrafters shortwave set. Hitler and the Nazis were implementing their sordid plan to wage war, and humanity would again be tragically assailed by overt German aggression.

On September 1, 1939, the Wehrmacht began its assault by invading Poland. Britain and France immediately declared war against Germany, and World War II had begun. Theater newsreels, daily papers, *LIFE* magazine, and other publications were soon filled with reports of the German *blitzkrieg* or lightning war on Poland. Nazi air and ground forces not only attacked Polish military installations, they also bombed and strafed innocent civilians fleeing in terror before their assaults. Polish roads and fields were soon scenes of total carnage. The Polish Air Force, a collection of old biplane fighters and other cast-offs, was wiped out in the space of a few days.[22] The Germans were enjoying an easy war.

In quick succession, like rubber ducks in a shooting gallery, other nations were soon ground under the heels of the goose-stepping Nazi war machine: First, Norway and Denmark, then France, Belgium, Luxembourg, and the Netherlands were invaded. In a ghastly retreat, tens of thousands of troops from Britain and victimized European countries fled to the French coast at Dunkirk seeking escape from the terror. They would be saved by a miraculous bridge of boats that carried them across the Channel to the safety of the "tight little island."

On June 14, 1940, the Germans entered Paris.

Refugees, ca 1940. (Office for Emergency Management, Office of War Information. National Archives Identifier: 535895. Local Identifier: 208-PP-93[2]. Unrestricted use.)

Evacuation at Dunkirk. (Scene from the 1943 film *Divide and Conquer* [*"Why We Fight #3"*] directed by Frank Capra and Anatole Litvak. US War Department film.)

From 27 May to 4 June 1940, 861 vessels evacuated 338,226 British, French, Polish, Belgian, and Dutch soldiers. During the nine-day operation, the losses were devastating: 243 boats were sunk, and the British left enough equipment behind to outfit nearly ten divisions of the German army. More tragically, in the wake of the battle, 11,000 Allied troops lay dead on the beaches, and more than 40,000 more were taken prisoners of war.

While in near-total sympathy with Britain, the United States still balked at actively entering the conflict. Memories of World War I were still fresh in the minds of an American public that had left too many bodies in the poppy fields of the Ardennes and the Argonne. Britain would, for a painful time, fight on alone against Adolph Hitler and his planned invasion of the British Isles under the Nazi code name *Unternehmen Seelöwe* (Operation Sea Lion).

Spitfire banking in the clouds. (US Air Force photo.)

As an impressionable fifteen-year-old, I was completely captivated by the drama of this war; and I identified with the desperate situation on the European continent and especially the Royal Air Force (RAF) pilots and planes, both of which stood badly outnumbered and alone against the frightening armada of German fighters and bombers. The Hurricanes and newly minted RAF Spitfires were as good as—and in some cases better than—their German counterparts; and the Battle of Britain and its successful outcome would eventually prove the words of the new Prime Minister Winston Churchill, who said, "If the British Empire and its Commonwealth last for a thousand years, men will still say, 'this was their finest hour.'"

Hawker Hurricane Mark I. (RAF photograph by S. A. Devon, 1940. Imperial War Museum, CH 17331. Public domain. [Her Majesty's Stationery Office has declared the expiry of Crown copyright applies worldwide.])

No. 1 Squadron RAF Pilot A. V. "Taffy" Clowes steps into his Hawker Hurricane Mark I (P3395, JX-B) in a revetment at RAF Wittering, Huntingdonshire, UK. Note the personalized wasp emblem below the engine exhausts. In October 1940, this aircraft was passed on to No. 55 Operational Training Unit and then transferred to No. 5 Flying Training School. Following a wheels-up landing at Ternhill in March 1942, the plane was written off.

Between the formal declaration of war and the near disaster at Dunkirk, the Allies and the Axis sparred for a time designated as the "Phoney War." It was as if two boxers were jabbing and punching at each other, trying to find the pattern for a knockout blow. In the meantime, Germany continued to move methodically across Europe, sweeping before it a horde of innocent and defenseless civilians seeking safety somewhere.

JU 87, ca 1943. (German Federal Archive [Deutsches Bundesarchiv] photo. Bundesarchiv, Bild 183-J16050/CC-BY-SA. [CC BY-SA 3.0 de http://creativecommons.org/licenses/by-sa/3.0/de/deed.en], via Wikimedia Commons.)

The SG 3 (Fighter-Bomber Wing 3) flying out of Yugoslavia terrorized regions of the Mediterranean for a time during the war.

If there was a way to terrorize and create chaos among the fleeing refugees, Germany had a weapon to do it; and if ever there was a Darth Vader of the skies, it was the Junkers Ju 87 dive-bomber, a bird of pure malevolence and a symbol of the unique evil of the Nazi cause. Nicknamed the "Stuka," it had the unmistakable appearance and demeanor of a vicious pterodactyl and truly performed as such. Its spotted undercarriage and inverted gull wings heightened its buzzard-like appearance, and the fang-like inverted exhaust stacks of its inline engine made the picture complete. Even its landing gear looked like prehistoric talons, and the bastard machine was equipped with a slipstream-operated siren called the Jericho Trumpet that, when activated during a dive, further panicked those on the ground. Once heard, its blaring scream was instantly recognizable and always terror producing.

First flown in 1935, the Stuka became operational as a dive-bomber with the Luftwaffe in 1936. It was widely used by the German Condor Legion to assault the populations of Spanish cities during the Spanish Civil War. The Condor Legion, which was formed to test drive Nazi war equipment, utilized expatriate German pilots and crews in its operations. Their main goal was to develop terror-bombing techniques that could later be used in the German aggression of World War II.

With a reluctant nod, I grant a bit of a tribute to German engineering in the design of the Ju 87. In addition to its siren, it was also equipped with an automatic dive-pullout system, which protected the aircraft and the pilot in case he suffered a blackout due to too many g's pulling out of a bombing run. Normal entrance to the dive was a 180-degree roll, then a pitch down toward the target. As the plane rolled on its back, two telltale tabs extended from the dorsal side of the wings indicating the automatic dive pullout had been activated. As the Ju 87 hurtled vertically toward its target, dive brakes were deployed to slow down dive speed, which was ordinarily about 350 mph. As the aircraft reached bomb-release altitude, a light on the ground-contact altimeter lit up, and the pilot would push a button on the control stick to release his payload. In turn, the automatic pullout procedure would initiate, and the control stick would automatically pull back to commence a maximum 6 g pullout. The aircraft's nose would begin to rise from the vertical; and when level attitude was achieved, dive brakes would retract, propeller speed would adjust to climb, and boost would be adjusted. It was a remarkably reliable system and a credit to aircraft engineering; but conceding the ingenious engineering of the Ju 87, the aircraft and the infamous pilots of the Condor Legion remain a hated symbol of the Nazi regime. In the course of the Spanish conflict, the Ju 87s of the Condor Legion flattened the small Spanish city of Guernica bringing massive death and destruction to its peaceful inhabitants. The artist Pablo Picasso, in turn, rendered a painting of the ravaged city, which quickly made the world aware of the cruelty and injustice of the Nazi war machine. It is my humble opinion that, in all probability, Picasso's painting *Guernica* will outlast the memory of Hitler, his Third Reich, and the Ju 87 Stuka. I hope by a thousand years.

Ernst Udet, an outstanding German fighter ace of World War I, was particularly fond of the Stuka. In a demonstration dive during the plane's acceptance trials, he barely escaped death when he waited too long to pull out of a dive-bombing run. Interestingly, Udet became an outspoken proponent of dive-bombing, staking his career on the bombing technique and its effect on civilian populations and military installations. Later variants of the Ju 87 became very effective ground attack aircraft and excelled in tank busting when equipped with two 37mm cannons. Continuing to champion the dive-bomber cause, Udet had a falling out with Luftwaffe Reichsmarschall Herman Goering; and during a troubled telephone call to his girlfriend on the evening of November 17, 1941, Ernst Udet committed suicide with a gunshot to the head. The manner of his death was reported to the German public as "the death of a hero occurring during Udet's testing of new weaponry."[23] It was yet another repugnant chapter in the history of the Junkers Ju 87 Stuka.

Beyond its ugliness, the Stuka possessed some critical faults. It was extremely vulnerable to enemy fighter attacks because of its slow speed and lack of maneuverability. It was seldom employed where enemy fighters were operational but became a staple on the eastern front where fighter presence was somewhat limited. One of my favorite schoolboy fantasies pictured a Hawker Hurricane with its guns blazing, stitching a line of bullet holes across the cockpit canopy of a diving Ju 87. In its demise, the evil dive-bomber would roll to the left and then spin and crash, blowing to bits in an open Polish potato field. This would happen, of course, only after the Luftwaffe pilot and gunner had safely parachuted to earth, waving a greeting to the Hurricane's pilot as he roared past overhead.

ELEVEN

We returned to a rainy Seattle the fall of 1939. My folks had enrolled me in prep school, and it took only a week to discover that I didn't like it there; and more importantly, I didn't like a lot of the kids who went there. My background had been a modest one, and I was proud of that. I complained enough about the situation that Oscar and my mother eventually pulled me out of the place and enrolled me at Roosevelt High School on Seattle's north side. Although I didn't know a single kid in the whole two-thousand-member student body, I loved it there and began making friends soon enough.

As the early days of the war rolled by, it was increasingly clear that Britain was outmanned and outgunned from the start; and in America, there was a growing difference of opinion on what we should do about the situation. On one hand, there were those entrenched in the belief that the United States should stay out of foreign wars; conversely, there were many others experiencing a mounting sentiment of support for Great Britain and a growing hatred for Germany and the Nazi demagogues that would lead it to disaster. Inevitably, it became clear that if the world were to remain free, America had to take a stand against the savagery of Germany and its Axis alliance.

A prelude to American involvement would occur on September 16, 1940, when President Franklin D. Roosevelt signed the Selective Training and Service Act—quite literally, a peacetime draft. The legislation required mandatory registration for all men between the ages of 21 and 35 (later expanded to all men aged 18 to 65 after America's entry into the war). Inductees were selected by local draft boards, and those notified would serve on active duty a maximum of one year, with a cap of 900,000 individuals in training at any one time. It would be the first long step down the pathway to war. The Selective Service Act would become increasingly inclusive and would largely govern the nature of United States military service until it finally expired in postwar 1947. During the time Selective Service was in effect, the various branches of the military would call up more than ten million men to serve for "the duration of the war plus six months."[24]

Like every kid I knew, I was caught up in the events leading to our involvement in the war. It never occurred to me to wait to be drafted. As soon as I could get permission from my folks, I planned to volunteer for the Naval Air Corps (NAC). All my life, I had been around water and boats, and I was absolutely passionate about flying, so the NAC was an ideal choice. In the meantime, there was high school to finish, girls to kiss, and a lot of jitterbug dancing to do.

My best friend in high school was a fun-loving guy named Johnny Condon. We were good kids. No hard liquor. No drugs. Oh, we'd sneak an occasional beer and leer at dirty comic books once in awhile, but that was about the extent of it. Johnny had a cute sister who I was interested in for a while, but my friendship with Johnny soon eclipsed any interest I had in his sister.

Johnny and I had both grown up around water; and whereas we both shared an interest in boats, Johnny wanted nothing whatsoever to do with airplanes. We both had dreams of enlisting. He wanted to go into submarines, while I, of course, wanted to be a flier. We picked up extra money working at the local yacht club by cleaning and shining boats for the more-affluent residents of Seattle. I didn't go overboard on the nautical scene, but Johnny frequently wore a red sock on his left foot and a green one on the right. He was a real waterman until the day he died—which was far too soon.

That fall, I bought a 1928 Chevrolet from my uncle for a dollar. The doors were falling off, and the upholstery was tattered. It was running, and that was about all. But it was a set of wheels, and for a fifteen-year-old kid, what could be better than that?

Pop helped me put some two-by-four doorposts in the frame of that old heap, and they worked very well. Then I bought a can of enamel paint, and with a brush, painted that car baby blue. It looked beautiful, and it was my pride and joy.

My first automobile—a 1928 Chevy—bought from my Uncle Charlie for one dollar. Drawing by Ed Larson, 2014.

I recall the first time I started her up, remembering not to put my thumb over the crank handle. In those days, that was an important first lesson: If the engine backfired and your thumb was over the crank handle, the crank could kick back hard and break your wrist. That never happened to me; although, I cranked the car a lot because I bought a lot of gas—one gallon at a time.

I drove her all through high school—rain and shine—on lots of double dates with Johnny and to lots of PTA dances on Saturday nights. It was the Big Band era, and I loved the music and the pretty little girls with corsages, fuzzy sweaters, and syrupy perfume that seemed at the time heaven-sent....

TWELVE

While I was working on my Chevy and dancing on Saturday nights, bad things were still brewing in Europe. The strange silence of the Phoney War held sway until the spring of 1940—it was as if everything was on hold for the moment—then May arrived...and with it, the fall of France and the beginning of war over Britain. For me, it was a poignant and thrilling time, but the events unfolding would determine the future of people worldwide.

To achieve victory, the Nazis determined to bomb Britain into submission, or at least batter it so badly it would be ripe for invasion by Germany's armor and infantry. The slender moat of the English Channel was a bastion against the Germans, but it became immediately clear it was not enough. To defend against the Nazi cancer bent on destroying Britain, the Luftwaffe would have to be driven from the skies over England. In short, the salvation of the British Empire would hinge on the wings of the defending Royal Air Force Fighter and Bomber Commands. The Hawker Hurricane and the Supermarine Spitfire would be their scepter and their sword. A few young men in a few fast and deadly aircraft would do battle against a superior force of fighters and bombers set out to destroy them. This clash of good and evil would be memorialized by Churchill when he proclaimed the battle in the skies over Britain would indeed become their "finest hour!"[25]

THE GRATITUDE OF EVERY HOME IN OUR ISLAND, IN OUR EMPIRE, AND INDEED THROUGHOUT THE WORLD…GOES OUT TO THE BRITISH AIRMEN WHO, UNDAUNTED BY ODDS, UNWEARIED IN THEIR CONSTANT CHALLENGE AND MORTAL DANGER, ARE TURNING THE TIDE OF THE WORLD WAR BY THEIR PROWESS AND BY THEIR DEVOTION.

~ British Prime Minister Winston Churchill
A tribute to the Royal Air Force,
House of Commons, 20 August 1940

In the early 1970s while on a trip to Great Britain, I stood in a field in East Anglia and imagined a fighter patrol arching back over this picturesque landscape following a sweep of the Channel. In an instant, it's World War II. Fighter pilots are doing battle with German Focke-Wulf Fw 190s and Messerschmitt Bf 109s in the skies over London; but out here, they are having fun: flying low, flat-hatting and cutting the grass over their beloved homeland. It is a beautiful morning. Come, stand beside me in this verdant field in East Anglia in the fading days of August 1939.…

It has been a warm summer, but the recent rains have greened the tall, mellow grass around us. We look out across the sea toward the beige coast of Normandy, now made frighteningly close by war. There is little wind, and toward the east, the blessed Channel rolls before us, glistening like silver in this soft and quiet dawning. Bits of ragged sea mist, like sky cobwebs, move and tear apart under the coaxing of the wind and coming day, while two hundred meters from where we stand, our coastal meadow plunges over the bastion of towering cliffs into the sea. To the west and down the twisted road from whence we came, one can see the rooftops of a tiny hamlet rubbing sleep from its eyes as it awakens to a circling chorus of raucous gulls seeking breakfast.

Suddenly, far off over the Channel, the quiet is breached by a rising wail from the east. As it grows closer, it sows a strange fear in us. Three small aircraft scream across the sea toward us, first in a shallow vee formation; then in the wink of an eye, they form a line astern and hurtle toward us like a single arrow. Instantly, we want to run and hide or dig for cover, but there is no time. They are very low; for a split second, our sight of them is lost beneath the brow of the chalk-like cliffs guarding this land.

Then they are upon us, soaring above the cliffs as we cower, dumbstruck under the deafening scream of their engines and stunning speed. At three hundred seventy miles an hour, they are barely thirty feet above our heads. Instinctively, in primal terror, we drop to our knees and cover our ears. Their sound is staggering—a hellish, snarling roar and sizzling counterpoint. The tall grass flattens around us in the tornado of their passing. Our senses reel under a cacophonous assault on our bent figures, spinning minds, and racing hearts.

In a second, they are past us by a mile or more—black silhouettes as we turn on unsteady legs in disbelief. They climb now, and we can see the roundels of England on the shining wings of three Hawker Hurricanes climbing toward the morning clouds.

We turn and walk slowly in near silence toward the village, lingering under the spell of an experience that will stay with us forever.

In the days ahead, our morning's terror would be washed away by the limitless courage and righteous fury of men like these three imagined RAF pilots. Remembered as "the few," they and their airplanes would become historic icons, and their collective gallantry would prompt Winston Churchill to proclaim, "Never in the field of human conflict was so much owed by so many to so few."[26]

The Hawker Hurricane and the Supermarine Spitfire are two fighter planes whose fame will forever be paramount in the annals of military aviation. It must first be recognized, however, that the wonderfully nimble Spitfire climbed to immortality on the wings of her slightly older and more durable sister, the Hurricane.

The Hurricane first took to the air in November 1935, and RAF squadrons began receiving production models in late 1937. The Hurricane Mk I was the first monoplane fighter in RAF service, eventually replacing the Gloster Gladiator biplane. Timing of the Mk I's arrival was heaven-sent. Britain had been at war with Germany for over two years, and the Hurricane would become the mainstay air weapon against British disaster. In July 1940, the RAF counted twenty-nine squadrons of Hurricanes and nineteen squadrons of the new Spitfires,[27] a total of 620 fighters. In the ensuing months as the Battle of Britain waged on, they would face a German Luftwaffe of 3,500 fighters and bombers bent on total destruction of the English way of life.[28]

The main targets of the Hurricanes and Spitfires were the Henkel He 111 and the Dornier Do 17 bombers, both capable of inflicting heavy damage. However, both also required close escort by Me 109[29] or 110 fighters, and such escort duty decreased the German fighters' aggressive potential. The Me 109 was most effective using the bounce attack—diving down from altitude to attack, and escort duties precluded this most effective fighting maneuver.

During the Battle of Britain,[30] which waged from mid-July to late October 1940, approximately 1,000 Fighter Command aircraft were lost; at the same time, British pilots downed nearly 1,900 Luftwaffe fighters and bombers.[31] The availability of 100-octane fuel to the RAF brought significant advantage to the Fighter Command. Better fuel allowed Hurricane and Spitfire pilots to boost their supercharger output, appreciably improving the performance of both aircraft. Years of complex modifications in supercharger efficiency, coolant design, and carburetion/injection systems paid off in the Rolls Royce Merlin's horsepower output, which climbed from 1,000 hp in its early models to an astounding 2,000 hp in the Merlin 66 engine.[32]

London is still "taking it." (Library of Congress Prints & Photographs Online Catalog. LC-USZ62-61239 [b&w film copy neg.]. No known restrictions on publication. No copyright renewal found in US Copyright Office, 2012.)

"LONDON, December 30, 1940 – Someday when peace has returned to this odd world I want to come to London again and stand on a certain balcony on a moonlit night and look down upon the peaceful silver curve of the Thames with its dark bridges.

"And standing there, I want to tell somebody who has never seen it how London looked on a certain night in the holiday season of the year 1940.

"For on that night this old, old city – even though I must bite my tongue in shame for saying it – was the most beautiful sight I have ever seen.

"It was a night when London was ringed and stabbed with fire..."

From "A Dreadful Masterpiece" by Ernie Pyle

It was not only the airframes that won the Battle of Britain, but the Merlin engine as well.

The Spitfire would soon eclipse its less glamorous sister. After a heroic RAF had won the critical Battle of Britain, the faster, more nimble Spitfire was a bright light in the troubling horizon. Its presence would dramatically influence the outcome of the expanding war between the Allies and Axis Powers. On August 4, 1938, the first Supermarine Spitfires were delivered to the RAF Nineteenth Squadron billeted at Duxford. Although the Hawker Hurricane was the real hero of the Battle of Britain, the Spitfire with its Rolls Royce Merlin engine would surpass the older Hurricane in speed and maneuverability as the war marched forward.

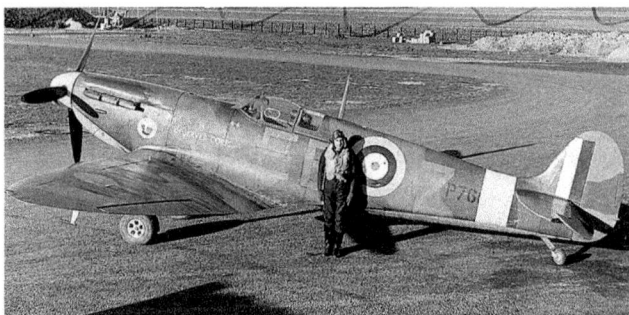

Supermarine Spitfire Mark IIA (P7666, EB-Z) with Squadron Leader D. O. Finlay, Commanding Officer of No. 41 Squadron RAF. (RAF photograph by P. H. F. Tovey, 1941. Imperial War Museum, CH 1890. Public domain. [Her Majesty's Stationery Office has declared the expiry of Crown copyright applies worldwide.])

The Spitfire would also create a legend of beauty and force in the skies above England and in the hearts of her countrymen. How could one not love the Supermarine Spitfire and its mother, father, and grandparents as well? The whole Supermarine family was composed of thoroughbred racers, descendents from a gene pool created by British engineer Reginald Mitchell, head designer of the Supermarine Aviation Works of Southampton, England.

While the Hawker Hurricane assumed a less vital role as a low-level fighter and ground attack plane, it continued to serve faithfully in the skies over North Africa, Malta, the Far East, and Russia. Its development was slowed, however, by concentration on the production of Spitfires. Thus, the Hurricane could not compete with the newer and more constantly improved Me 109s, which quickly surpassed the Hurricane's performance and effectiveness. The world should remember, however, that when it was needed, the Hurricane was there to gallantly defend an island nation in the worst of times.

THIRTEEN

The proving ground for seaplane racing was the annual Schneider Trophy Race. Inaugurated by Jacques Schneider, a financier and balloonist, this was a closed-course contest of pure speed held in such prestigious venues as Venice, Monaco, Hampton Roads, Cowes, and Chesapeake Bay. Attendance at some of the events topped 200,000 spectators—an indication of the interest in aviation in the 1920s and '30s, and the prize for the victor was £1,000 and the laurel of international celebrity. Various private interests and government agencies sponsored racing teams, and Britain's RAF was the angel lending heavy support to the Supermarine Aviation Works.

Supermarine, with Mitchell-designed racers, won the Schneider Race in 1922, 1927, 1929, and 1931, at which time, the trophy—after four victories and according to the rules—was permanently retired to British hands. All the victorious aircraft were beautiful, but the loveliest of all was the 1931 winner, the Supermarine S.6B. It seemed to have emerged from a cocoon of tomorrow, setting a new speed record of 340.08 mph.[33] More importantly, the lovely S.6B was the unmistakable mother of the stunningly beautiful Supermarine Spitfire.

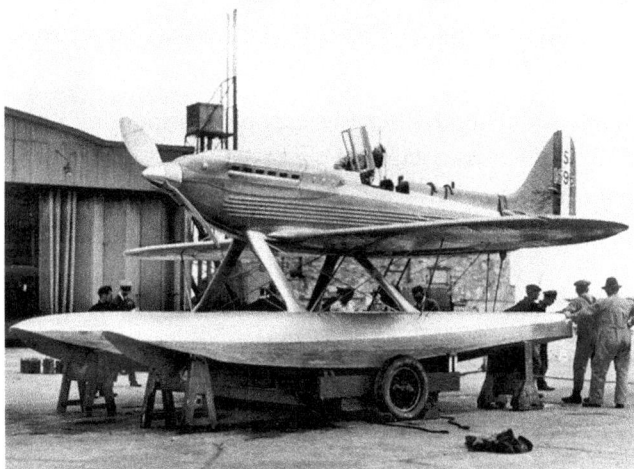

Supermarine S.6B seaplane, ca 1931. (Public domain. [Her Majesty's Stationery Office has declared the expiry of Crown copyright applies worldwide.])

It has been said that if the Hawker Hurricane was a workhorse, then the Spitfire was an act of genius. Mitchell was the genius, and his designs would culminate in arguably the most beautiful fighter plane ever to take to the skies. In 1932, the British Air Ministry put out feelers for a new fighter plane and invited Supermarine to propose a design. Up to that point, Supermarine had been entirely engaged in the design and production of racing seaplanes, and neither Reginald Mitchell nor Supermarine had ever even built a land plane, let alone a fighter. No matter, Mitchell's brilliant conceptions and racing prowess breached the chasm between racer and fighter plane with revolutionary results. On its maiden flight in June 1936, Mitchell's airframe, designated Type 300, was powered by the newly designed

Rolls Royce Model PV-12 engine. The marriage of the two magnificently designed entities exceeded all expectations of weight-carrying ability and speed. The Air Ministry, totally impressed, immediately ordered 310 Supermarine aircraft[34] and designated the fighter the Spitfire, a name Mitchell considered "silly."[35]

The production fighter was capable of mounting not four machine guns, but eight, with a commensurate increase in ammunition. Early production models used a wooden, two-blade propeller made by De Havilland, but later models were fitted with a three-blade De Havilland prop, increasing the top speed by five miles per hour. The demand for the airplane was desperately and dramatically increased by the deteriorating relations between Britain and Germany, and other manufacturers began licensed production almost immediately. The Nuffield Group received an order for 1,000 Spitfires and built an entire factory dedicated to the production of the aircraft.

Reginald Mitchell died on June 11, 1937, of the cancer that had plagued him throughout the development of the Spitfire. He lived just long enough to see the triumph of his tremendously beautiful aircraft—an airplane that would serve in every theater of war as a fighter and fighter-bomber, shipboard fighter, and reconnaissance plane. There would be over forty manufactured variations, and its speed would be increased by twenty-five percent as its weight doubled. Its service would be terminated in the mid-1950s after more than 20,000 of these aerial icons had been produced.

In spring 1940, the critical days of the Battle of Britain still loomed ahead, but everyone seemed aware that England was on the ropes, and the world trembled as the German juggernaut rolled over western Europe, pushing Allied forces to the beaches at Dunkirk and stranding over 338,000 British, French, Belgian, Polish, and Dutch troops on the tidelands facing annihilation. What occurred next was a miraculous rescue mounted by British forces and a courageous citizenry who joined hands. From May 27 to June 4, nearly every floating vessel on the east coast of England traversed the Channel carrying back as many troops as could be crammed on board. Some rescue ships were huge; most were small; the smallest vessel, *Tamzine*, was only fifteen feet long.[36] A devastating defeat was transformed into a pageantry of bravery and sacrifice that will be celebrated forever in chronicles of British history.

In a much less heralded event that spring, I awoke one morning with a really bad bellyache and ended up in the hospital for an emergency appendectomy. Even though the world was falling apart, we still had to get ready to go to Alaska for fishing season.

My mother and I departed Seattle on the *North Sea* in late May. I was looking forward to life in Port Althorp and to getting back to work on the cannery tender. By now, I had developed into a pretty good deck hand on the *Doris E.*, and the skipper let me stand night watches at the wheel.

One afternoon as I was standing on the dock looking to the east, I noticed the *Sally S.*, sister ship to the *Doris E.*, heading up the channel toward the cannery. Black smoke was pouring from her stack, and she was throwing a hell of a bow wave. As she got closer, I was really surprised that they didn't back her down a bit. My dad didn't like them pushing the big diesels that fast, and I figured somebody was going to catch hell. When the ship got within three hundred yards of the float, the skipper gave three blasts on the air horn and swung her into the dock. This was highly unusual, and as I started to walk down the ramp toward her, one of the deck hands came trotting up the ramp and said, "Ed, don't go down there!" By this time, my dad brushed past me walking very fast, and I noticed something on the afterdeck covered with a tarp.

The skipper and my dad talked for a minute; then they raised the tarp, and I could see a pale body, obviously dead. It was a young man named Leonard Johansen. I knew him well. He had been working as a deck hand on a pile driver the company used to set fish traps. At lunchtime, a bunch of the guys had been sitting around, and somebody had dared him to dive from the top of the driver's gin pole, a tall structure like a crane that held the driving hammer. Len took up the dare, climbed the gin pole, and dove into the water. He paddled to the edge of the driver and seemed OK; but a few seconds later, he went into cardiac arrest and died in minutes. It was a shocking blow to everybody in our small, isolated community and especially for my dad who figured it was his responsibility to oversee everyone's safety.

About a week later, we lost an expensive anchor in the rocks in a small cove some miles from the cannery. Things weren't going that great, but there was a lot more hell to come....

FOURTEEN

When I wasn't working on the boat, I stayed with my folks in the apartment and made models to while away the time. About the only things I read were newspapers, *Pacific Fisherman*, and *Flying* magazine. My fascination with airplanes and flying was ever increasing, fueled by reports of legendary air battles between the RAF and Luftwaffe, which I faithfully followed as best I could.

My interest in the contemporary fighters was not limited to the good guys. With the exception of the Ju 87 Stuka, which I found repulsive, Luftwaffe aircraft were not only operationally effective but beautiful as well. Most Luftwaffe planes had a sort of Teutonic squareness about them, but there was one notable exception: the quite stunning Focke-Wulf Fw 190 Würger—a lovely combination of Butcher Bird and ballerina and a worthy partner to Willy Messerschmitt's masterpiece, the Bf 109.

The years between 1936 and 1940 saw an epiphany of fighter design on all fronts by all nations. Many dramatic changes were due to improvements in metallurgy techniques and engine design, but one cannot overlook the impact made by the genius of individuals like Reginald Mitchell, Willy Messerschmitt, Kurt Tank, Alexander de Seversky, and Edgar Schmued, designer of the incomparable North American P-51 Mustang.

Focke-Wulf Fw 190D-9, National Museum of the United States Air Force. (US Air Force photo.)

Messerschmitt Bf 109G-10, National Museum of the United States Air Force. (US Air Force photo.)

In May 1935, Germany first flew the Bf 109. Designed by Messerschmitt, it would be the mainstay fighter of the Luftwaffe during World War II. Ironically, no production engines were available for the prototype; however, German and British relations were such that British authorities traded four Rolls-Royce Kestrel VI engines to Germany for an operational Heinkel He 70 model to be used for testing purposes.

The Bf 109 was a well-designed and ultimately practical frontline fighter. Its modular construction would serve the Luftwaffe equally well in the killing cold of Russia and the most cruel conditions of North Africa. However, like every aircraft ever built, its design was a compromise that would result in admitted shortcomings. A major weakness was its landing gear. The narrow, lightweight track design carried with it a drastic reduction in control while taxiing and during takeoffs and landings. Another salient fault was a cockpit canopy that opened from the side but could not be opened during flight. In addition, the framing of the canopy itself cut down on critical pilot visibility.

But there were plusses in this aircraft as well. Since the wing loading of the Bf 109 was rather high, the plane was equipped with automatic leading-edge slats and camber-increasing flaps that greatly improved stability in low-speed flight control. Its engine was equipped with dual coolant tanks so that if one was punctured by gunfire, it could be closed off, and the aircraft would continue flying, and this capability was of tremendous importance. A personal friend who flew the Bf 109 on contract with the Israeli Air Force following World War II described the airplane to me as "highly responsive, a joy to fly, and a beast to land."[37]

Focke-Wulf Fw 190. Drawing by Ed Larson, 2014.

Nicknamed the "Butcher Bird," this plane was a ballerina of consummate, long-limbed beauty. With frightful speed, she was capable of shattering pirouettes; in the sky, she was Anna Pavlova's Sleeping Beauty. *But in haste, she had donned the shield and sword of the truly evil, and she fell in flames from a tearful sky—a broken flower, crushed by the righteousness of avenging justice.*

The Focke-Wulf Fw 190, first flown in late 1939, was developed as a backup for the Bf 109 under the same Reich Air Ministry provisions. The Fw 190 was simply a beautiful airplane; and from all reports, it was a total delight to fly—light on the controls with astounding roll and climb rates. Nicknamed the "Butcher Bird," it was equipped with a 14-cylinder BMW 139 radial engine, which presented more frontal area and incurred more drag. Its designer, Kurt Tank, described it as "not a racehorse, but a cavalry horse."[38] Tank, a design genius, fabricated a close-fitting cowling to minimize the adverse effect of increased drag; however, with the tight-fitting engine cowling came yet another big problem: excessive engine and cockpit heat. A special ventilating fan was then incorporated into the engine cowling to alleviate the risk of overheating. With its wide-stance landing gear, ground handling of the Fw 190 was said to be excellent. In contrast, the Bf 109's narrow, knock-kneed landing gear accounted for ten percent of all Bf 109 aircraft being lost in landing and takeoff accidents. Over time, the Fw 190 had many variants and turned out to be an able and intimidating aircraft, giving the Luftwaffe two very menacing fighting machines.

While examining the sinister beauty of the aforementioned fighter planes, one must not forget there were also clowns in the crowd. The United States Navy was still prowling about in search of a shipboard and land-based fighter plane. In the course of this intense search, June 1939 witnessed the testing of the Brewster F2A Buffalo, a product of the Brewster Aeronautical Corporation.

Brewster was engaged in making carriages and some minor aircraft components, and like the proverbial shoemaker; they should have "stuck to their last." In addition, the company was rife with mismanagement and even outright fraud. But with war approaching and a frightful impatience, the Navy selected the Buffalo because the Grumman F4F Wildcat, a much superior airplane, was not quite ready for flight tests.

The Brewster Buffalo was a true lemon that would plague its builders till the end. The machine was underpowered, outgunned, and referred to with such names as "beer barrel," "suicide barrel," and worse. Fighter pilots take great pride in pulling up their landing gear as soon as they lift off the runway—there's something beautiful about doing that. This did not happen with the Brewster Buffalo. The landing system was madness: The process for raising or lowering the undercarriage involved a complicated sequence of opening and closing various hydraulic valves to pressurize the system. Should the pilot err in the sequence, the gear would not lower if it were in the up position, nor would it retract after taking off—the pilot had to fly somewhere to hide while he was retracting his landing gear!

Brewster F2A-3. (US Navy photo.)

Training flight from Naval Air Station, Miami, Florida, on 2 August 1942, piloted by Lieutenant Commander Joseph C. Clifton.

Some of the Buffalos served with the RAF after being shipped to the United Kingdom; and it's obvious the RAF also considered the aircraft a dog. The Brit's opinion can be summed up by remarks made by Lieutenant Commander Alan Black, 805 Squadron CO, RN Fleet Air Arm, RAF, "The Buffalo was a delight to fly—very maneuverable....It would have been an excellent fighter, but the guns could not be fired because the ends of the wires, which were part of the interrupter gear, failed; and 805 did not have the necessary spares."[39] The United States procurement authorities and the Navy pilots who flew the Brewster Buffalo shared the "exulted" opinion of this misshapen creature; and so, like its western plains namesake, the Buffalo just faded away.

Amazingly, forty-four of these aircraft were unloaded on the Finnish Air Force, whose pilots seemed to like them. But even these few Brewster F2As finally died due to lack of available parts. It was a fitting, dodo-bird ending for a richly deserving recipient. In all, just over five hundred Brewster F2As were built.

One should have been quite enough.

FIFTEEN

Autumn 1940 was in full swing, and we were in the process of closing down the cannery. Most of the cases of canned salmon had already been dispatched to Seattle on steamships, and the fish traps were being towed into the bay to anchor out the worst of the winter weather. I didn't work on the boat for a few days because my help was needed to get our stuff ready for the trip home. It was a slow time; most of the cannery staff was just hanging out, picking up bits and pieces to be stored away for the upcoming spring while waiting for steamer passage south.

Our second-floor apartment was located above a small company store, only about twenty feet from a huge, three-story warehouse, which held all the canning machinery on the first and second floors and a large web loft on the third floor. The top floor was filled with tarred fish netting, stored there to be used on the fish traps. On the other side and equidistant from our apartment was a similar huge, three-story warehouse that was used to store cases of salmon waiting for shipment to Seattle.

Port Althorp Cannery. (From *Spring Tides: Memories of Alaskan Towboats* by Edward C. Larson, 1996.)

We lived in the superintendent's quarters on the second floor of the center building.

One evening shortly before our departure, I was sitting in the living room with Dad, reading something and listening to the Hallicrafters shortwave radio spilling out news about the air war over Britain. Suddenly, there was a huge explosion in the web loft, and an immense fireball blew two fifteen-foot-wide doors off the front of the warehouse. The explosion was followed by the shrill sound of the cannery's steam whistle blowing repeatedly.

FIRE!

Dad rushed out of the apartment and down the stairs leaving the door wide open. I pulled on a pair of cord pants, shoes without socks, and a sweatshirt and jacket and quickly followed. A couple of minutes later, my mother had finally dressed, and she joined us on the dock outside our apartment. As a growing group gathered around us, smoke poured out of the third story of the cannery building where the loft doors had been blown out. It was still dark inside the web loft when Bill Lester, the storekeeper, came up and put his arm around my shoulders. I was just a kid, and I was scared. "Maybe the fire's all out," I said in a voice not quite my own.

"Eddie," he replied, "I think it's just the damn smoke hiding the flames; it's a tinderbox up there!"

Someone had begun playing a fire hose across the ridge top, and a quiet descended on the night. We stood there for perhaps three or four minutes, and it seemed maybe it was over. The group was now getting quite large, but the talk was in low tones filled with anxiety. Then suddenly, bright orange flames broke out across the roof ridge, completely overpowering the several fire hoses now reaching the roof. Bill was right. The place I loved was dying in front of me. That night would be the first of several hells I've suffered in my life.

The huge warehouse buildings were in such close proximity that they burned almost as one. Some of my mother's Native American friends had time to run into the apartment and grab some of her clothes. I had no chance to retrieve anything. Now people were running back and forth in a sort of disfigured chaos, not knowing what to do. A machinist dashed by, asking if I'd help him roll out some acetylene and oxygen tanks from the welding shop before they went off and killed somebody. We rolled about a dozen tanks to the edge of the dock and pushed them into the bay. The little *Eagle*, the smallest of our cannery tenders, had left her moorage and was beginning to play seawater from her pumps onto a 20,000-gallon fuel tank farther out on the dock. A lot of gasoline was stored there in fifty-gallon drums; if the fuel dock went, it would be a disaster. At about that same time, the flue, which supplied all of the fresh water to the cannery, burned through.

In minutes, the fight was over. The roar of the inferno was deafening.

The cannery building, with its treated seine nets, burned like a Roman candle. In short order, there was catastrophic collapse. The supports of the cannery's second floor, with its heavy canning machinery, dropped first—taking with them the first floor and the dock—plunging everything into the bottom of the bay. Within thirty minutes, the small company store and our apartment followed, crashing into the black tidal wash. As flames roared skyward, the adjoining storage warehouse, filled with 33,000 cases of canned salmon, exploded fiery projectiles into the air, eventually burning through the dock support timbers and tumbling the whole mass into the water with a great steaming growl. The conflagration illuminating the cool green of the surrounding forest could be seen by villagers of Elfin Cove ten miles away. The spectacle was awesome.

People stood in small groups watching and saying nothing, seemingly unable to comprehend the destruction that was all about them. Rain filled with ash and carried horizontally by the fire's wind streaked our faces and clothes. Tremendous heat accompanied an incessant roar punctuated by gigantic hissing sounds and explosions of unknown things.

Half of the cannery structures were situated on piling above the tidal waters of the bay. The Oriental and Caucasian bunkhouses, radio shack, cookhouse, Alaska Native quarters, and a couple of other outbuildings were located on the beach and connected to the cannery by a wide-planked walkway about a hundred yards long. This would be the only avenue of retreat as the docks and buildings that were the cannery were consumed by flames.

And then it was over. As the flames died down, the whole of the destruction was thankfully, for some little time, cloaked by the darkness of night and falling rain. We were in desperate need of assistance now. The few buildings beyond the shoreline had survived. They were, however, totally inadequate to house the number of people stranded by the fire. For the balance of the night, people sought refuge from the rain wherever they could. In an incredible stroke of good fortune, a passenger ship of the Alaska Steamship Company was cruising near Juneau and immediately responded to our desperate plea for help. Under forced draft, they headed to the cannery, indicating they would arrive the following afternoon to rescue as many of our personnel as they could crowd aboard.

Dawn usually comes with a gray wetness to Port Althorp. The morning following the fire was no exception. The cold light of day brought a smoldering scene of complete devastation. The oil dock and main dock face, both saved by the *Eagle*, were the only things left. What had once been the large dock area was now only blackened piling. The concrete steam plant pillars rising in the middle of the huge burned mass were like headstones wreathed in a dirty, black haze. Lifted by the morning wind, gray ash swirled about covering the jet-black of burned timbers and painting the whole scene the color of the lowering sky. Here and there, wires, pipes, and strange bits of iron and steel poked up. These were the tools and machines we'd lived and worked with. In many ways, it was impossible to tell what they had once been. The remains of our apartment lay collapsed in a charred mass on the rocky beach. Between tides, I found the blackened barrel of my rifle, the remnants of a few pots and pans, and the twisted, burned steel of my dad's shortwave radio set.

Port Althorp generators fifty years after the fire. (From the author's collection.)

The steamer arrived that afternoon and evacuated everyone who wasn't absolutely essential to the task of closing down what was left of the cannery. Food and supplies were dropped off for the skeleton crew that remained. My parents and I stayed on so that Dad could supervise. We took up temporary residence in a tiny room over the radio shack and ate at the small cookhouse—a far cry from the "Blue Room" where we had taken our meals during the season.

It was a sad and depressing time, and there was a profound and abiding gloominess about the place now. My dad had been intensely involved for a number of years with the operations at Port Althorp. The place was a source of pride for him, and its loss was personally devastating.

He carried on in his usual competent fashion, attending to all the details of the canning year and the subsequent fire, but there was a change in him—as if the fire had made him suddenly older. We had all lost more than a cannery that night, but it was a bitter disappointment for him and a life-changing experience from which he would never recover.

A salvage company contracted to remove the cans of salmon, repackage them, and market the result as pet food. I worked for this contractor for a short time. Between the tides and amongst the blackened piling, I slogged about on tidal rocks picking up thousands of discolored and burned cans; it was true stoop labor. Overhead, remnants of charred docking from which ashes and soot mixed with ever-falling rain sifted steadily down on those of us working below. The reclaimed cans were thrown into a cooler tray, which was then lifted to the dock where they were stacked for shipment. It was a filthy task, and I hated it.

The contractor was later accused of selling the reclaimed cans for other than the specified pet product. If such were the case, I could have personally assured the purchasers that the cut-rate salmon they selected was not only cooked, it was in fact well done!

Salvage work was a far cry from the job I had as deck hand on the *Doris E.*, and I complained constantly. I was saved from further abuse by the arrival of the *North Sea*, which took us home. I returned to Seattle and high school very late as usual but caught up with my C average and dancing soon enough.

SIXTEEN

The year 1941 was, of course, a fate-filled year, and it started out rather poorly. Since the cannery was gone, my dad's job with the parent company was also gone. I was in my junior year in high school, and I plugged along as usual, but the war was increasingly on everybody's minds. Europe was fast becoming a disaster with German ground forces and the Luftwaffe running roughshod over everything in sight; and although it sounds like an excuse, it was hard to concentrate on algebra when I thought of Allied forces with their backs to the English Channel. Newspapers, magazines, and radio news correspondents detailed the progress of the war, but everyone knew the Germans had the hammer.

The draft was beginning to change the color of America into shades of olive drab and navy blue. Suddenly, young guys from every neighborhood and hamlet were being transported to training camps all over the country. They would be gone a long time…some never to return. The war was coming, and it was hitting very close to home.

That summer, I drove a car for a wealthy local family. I didn't make much money, but it was a neat job. The work brought in enough dough to keep me in gasoline for my Chevy, and cleaning boats in my spare time with my buddy, Johnny, paid for dance bids and late-night hamburgers. My dad went north with another company as a bookkeeper, and Mother and I held down the fort at home. Around the country, people were contributing old pots and pans to aluminum drives and volunteering with their local Red Cross chapters. Looking back, it's apparent—we were all getting ready for war.

In September 1941, the United States transferred fifty US destroyers to a desperate England in exchange for permission to use British bases for American troops and planes. The mindset of America was becoming increasingly clear: Germany and the Axis forces were enemies that threatened people everywhere, including our own shores.

Dad came home from Alaska in mid-October, and we were a family again. My folks had purchased a home in Viewridge, an upscale neighborhood in Seattle where homes overlooked Lake Washington and the Sand Point Naval Air Station. It had become quite a bustling place for all kinds of naval air traffic. It would become busier than hell in a very short while.

December 7, 1941, began as any other Sunday. I washed my old Chevy, which I seldom did—probably because I had a date, about the only conceivable reason I had for cleaning my car. Dad was working in the yard, and I flipped on the radio in the garage.

It was in that instant that World War II began for us.

*DECEMBER 7, 1941, A DATE WHICH WILL LIVE
IN INFAMY, THE UNITED STATES OF AMERICA WAS
SUDDENLY AND DELIBERATELY ATTACKED BY
NAVAL AND AIR FORCES OF THE EMPIRE OF
JAPAN...NO MATTER HOW LONG IT MAY TAKE US
TO OVERCOME THIS PREMEDITATED INVASION,
THE AMERICAN PEOPLE WILL IN THEIR
RIGHTEOUS MIGHT WIN THROUGH
TO ABSOLUTE VICTORY.*

~ PRESIDENT FRANKLIN D. ROOSEVELT
FIRST DRAFT TO SPEECH BEFORE CONGRESS, DECEMBER 8, 1941

Within moments, we were very still, listening in disbelief to reports of Japan's sneak attack on Pearl Harbor.

The news was mind-boggling. Utter chaos followed. Rumor is the feedbag of panic, and there were plenty of rumors as the ensuing days rolled by: reports of Japanese submarines in Puget Sound; a Japanese invasion force off the Northwest Pacific Coast; and local Japanese, acting as fifth-column spies and activists, were seen everywhere. There was even a rumor claiming that Japanese-American traitors had cut arrows in their hay fields directing incoming Japanese bombers toward the site of the Boeing Plant. It was all crazy and untrue; but it was a time when reality, objectivity, and common sense were hammered into submission by prejudice and fear, and "Remember Pearl Harbor" became a national mantra as a massive flood of men rushed to enlist and "pay back the bastards!" If accurately portrayed, Naval Marshall Admiral Isoroku Yamamoto's statement regarding the Pearl Harbor attack was not only wholly accurate, but prophetic as well: "I fear all we have done is to awaken a sleeping giant and fill him with a terrible resolve!"[40]

Some twenty-plus years ago, on a rainy afternoon, my friend, Charlie Taylor, a Pearl Harbor survivor, sat with me in the cabin of his small sailboat. We had a specific purpose: I wanted to visit with him about his experiences on perhaps the most fateful day of his life.

Charlie vividly painted the chaotic violence of that early December morning when he and some of his shipmates met horror and tragedy with uncommon valor. Following the deadly events of that fateful Sunday, the US Pacific Fleet, with the exception of its carriers, lay in virtual ruin on the harbor bottom, and more than 3,500 Americans[41] lay dead or wounded—their future hopes and dreams drifting away on the winds of war across the cordite-smoke-blackened skies of the Pacific. This is Charlie's story....

It had been a very warm fall. The USS Honolulu *returned from maneuvers off the north coast of Oahu on 5 December 1941. Berthed first beside a finger pier in the southern section of Pearl Harbor, she was later flanked on the starboard side by the light cruiser* St. Louis. *The next day, December 6, dawned bright and warm—the type of day that made the islands a paradise of sun, surf, and sand.*

Tired from rough days at sea, Gunner's Mate 3rd Class Charlie Taylor and some of his buddies decided to hitch a ride into Honolulu for a day of sightseeing, restaurants, Chinese bars, and girl watching—a day any young sailor had a perfect right to enjoy. Since they were on Cinderella Liberty, they were due back to the ship by midnight—0000 hours.

Charlie, by his own admission, had wobbled up the gangway close to midnight with "a pretty good load on." He rolled into his bunk without even taking off his whites and slept until 0745 when he awoke with a raging headache and the heartfelt wish that he'd downed a few less Black & White Scotch whiskies the night before. Going to the head, he washed his face and plastered down his short, dark hair with a splash of cold water. Still in the uniform he'd slept in, he made his way slowly down to the mess deck where he knew he could grab a cup of hot joe to put out the fire in his brain.

Entering the small dining area two decks down, he grunted a gruff "good morning" to a couple of shipmates, poured a cup of coffee from a stained aluminum pot, and sat down and tried to focus. Four or five sailors also recovering from liberty were sitting on a bench talking amongst themselves about the constantly impressive subject of girls and sex. At that moment, Charlie was not particularly interested—his head splitting, he could only wonder how long it would take to recover.

Three sips of hot coffee later, the raucous sound of a gong signaling general quarters broke through the small room like shattering glass. Charlie and his shipmates sat in silence, staring at each other for five or six seconds. Then, one young sailor shouted out, "Sunday morning is a hell of a goddamn time to have a GQ drill!" Topside, a bugle blown in fear and off-key filled the intercom speaker. Now the small group, knowing something was terribly wrong, raced to the companionway to see what was going on.

Charlie Taylor's war had begun.

Before he could clear the open hatch, Charlie spied a line of black-bodied Japanese torpedo planes roaring in from the southwest; they were set to strike the moored battleships along Ford Island, a half mile away. At full throttle, torpedo bombers raced across the harbor while their pilots toggled release triggers in perfect broadsides. At point-blank range, they couldn't miss.

As Charlie watched for perhaps thirty seconds, he experienced a moment of extreme satisfaction. From the destroyer Bagley, *moored a hundred yards to the north, a 5-inch/38 cal gun roared, and he saw an incoming torpedo plane disintegrate. The shell, which vaporized its target, hadn't even travelled far enough to arm itself.*

But this small triumph was short lived; and soon, frustration set in. To prevent accidents, Navy peacetime regulations mandated that firelocks for deck guns be kept under lock and key. Firelocks were stored in a small shed on deck. These mechanisms were like firing pins—without them, the 5-inch guns could not fire and were completely useless. Incredibly, the keys to open the door of the Honolulu's *firelock shack were in the pocket of a petty officer serving elsewhere on board.*

Charlie raced to the shed, grabbed a spanner wrench, and began angrily smashing the thick padlock barring access to desperately needed supplies. As he swung the heavy wrench, it glanced off the padlock severing the end of his thumb. There was blood everywhere, and it would be the last time Charlie Taylor ever wore that set of whites. With three other frantic crewmen, he continued smashing at the shack handle all the while screaming for someone to locate the keys.

The USS *Arizona* (BB-39) burning after the Japanese attack on Pearl Harbor, 7 December 1941. (Franklin D. Roosevelt Library, Public Domain Photographs, 1882–1962. National Archives Item number: 195617. Unrestricted use.)

Finally, keys arrived; and Charlie, suffering excruciating pain, began the critical process of cocking the firelocks—placing them one-by-one in a vise and forcing them against a heavy spring. After what seemed an eternity but was actually about ten minutes, the first of the Honolulu's *5-inch guns fired.*

Meanwhile, incoming dive-bombers and torpedo planes raced from every quarter, and all hell had broken loose with heavy explosions everywhere along Battleship Row. The USS Arizona was the most heavily damaged, suffering three near misses and four direct hits before a 1,760-pound armor-piercing bomb crashed through her decks, exploding her magazine, and sending her to the bottom of the harbor with catastrophic loss of life—the blast so thunderous, it sent shockwaves back and forth across the entire surface of Pearl Harbor.

From the bridge of the Honolulu, orders directed the onboard crew to get underway. In response, sailors with axes rushed to the dock to cut mooring lines and release her. Someone accidentally severed the shore power cord, which provided hydraulic pressure to the moored ship, thus leaving it with no hydraulic power whatsoever and crippling the vessel. With the loss of shore power, all shells had to be lifted from the magazine by hand crank—a painfully slow and laborious procedure. As sailors sweated and strained to deliver each shell to the gun placements, Japanese bombers hammered ships in the harbor, and flyby Zero fighters strafed everything that moved.

Looking aloft, Charlie saw a dive-bomber separate from a group and aim itself at the Honolulu. As it screamed downward, he watched the bomb wobble a bit in the shackles during its release. The missile hurtled toward them but missed the deck by about ten feet before plunging through the heavy concrete finger pier and exploding underwater against the powder magazine of the ship. Charlie felt the bow of the vessel rise slightly, shudder, and then settle back as if tired of the struggle. The explosion tore a huge hole in the Honolulu's *hull but miraculously did not set off the powder magazine located directly adjacent to the blast site.*

View from a Japanese plane during the torpedo attack at Pearl Harbor. (Reproduced by authorization of the Navy Ministry. US Navy photo from the collections of the Naval Historical Center. Photo #: NH 50930.)

View is from the west of the island with the supply depot, submarine base, and fuel tank farm in the right center distance. "A torpedo has just hit USS West Virginia *on the far side of Ford Island (center). Other battleships moored nearby are (from left):* Nevada, Arizona, Tennessee *(inboard of* West Virginia*),* Oklahoma *(torpedoed and listing) alongside* Maryland, *and* California. *On the near side of Ford Island, to the left, are light cruisers* Detroit *and* Raleigh, *target and training ship* Utah *and seaplane tender* Tangier. Raleigh *and* Utah *have been torpedoed, and* Utah *is listing sharply to port. Japanese planes are visible in the right center over Ford Island and the Navy Yard to the right. US Navy planes on the seaplane ramp are in flames." (Source: US Naval Historical Center.)*

In most battles, there is a fateful moment when one knows whether he will live or die. It's something you never forget. For Charlie and Gunner's Mate Slick Walker, that moment occurred as they were on their knees passing 5-inch shells from the ammunition hoist to the gun emplacement on the upper deck. Charlie looked aft and aloft in time to see a dive-bomber roaring toward the Honolulu's *midship section with him, Slick, and the gun crew directly in its sight. It was as if everything happened in slow motion: Heavy fire from the* Honolulu, St. Louis, *and* Bagley *centered on the diving aircraft but left it totally untouched. The fate of the crew and ship seemed sealed...then, inexplicably, after a perfect approach, the deadly ordinance aimed directly at them did not release As the bomber shallowed out in its dive, it flashed over them at better than 200 mph and was lost from sight.*

It's likely that mechanical failure made the bomb hang up in the shackles, but whatever happened, the fate of every man on board the Honolulu *changed forever. "I looked at Slick, and he was bug-eyed and white as a sheet," related Charlie. "His lips were trembling and purplish; I suppose I looked the same way. We were both still on our knees, but I don't remember praying." Charlie continued, "The first thing Slick said was, 'God, I'm glad he didn't drop that thing!'"*

Thick black smoke surrounded them in every direction, and the raw smell of cordite filled the air. Charlie and Slick continued feeding ammunition to the gun crew who by now were encircled in brass shell casings. With a 5-inch shell in hand, Charlie looked toward the bow of the ship just as a Zero fighter roared up alongside them, strafing the finger pier with machine gunfire. "His canopy was open, and I could see a white bandana tied around his forehead," related

Charlie. "I got a perfect view of him. He was laughing at us as he flashed by. I'll never forget that face!"

As the Zero roared past, it banked over the stern of the Honolulu *and was lost from sight. Machine guns crackled in constant counterpoint to the roaring flames of burning aircraft, ships, and fuel oil. It was a scene from hell that would be permanently etched in the minds of every man fighting there on that fateful day.*

Then, as quickly as it had begun, it was over. At 1000 hours, the last of the attacking Japanese aircraft turned north and disappeared. In their wake, destruction and death lay everywhere. It was a total holocaust, which could only be viewed in open-mouthed amazement. Charlie remembers only pervasive quiet, excruciating fatigue, and disbelief at what had happened...feelings that would be shared by the American public...feelings that would quickly transform into a seething rage that would burn within the loins of the nation until long after Japan was decimated by destruction and defeat. If one listens closely, you may still hear the rallying cry, "Remember Pearl Harbor," that was triggered over seventy years ago on what President Franklin D. Roosevelt called "a date which will live in infamy."[42]

Ten years later, Charlie, now a chief petty officer, saw his old buddy Slick in the recreation hall of a DC naval building. Slick was shooting pool and intent on his game when Charlie came up behind him and whispered softly, "God, I'm glad he didn't drop that thing!"

Without turning around, Slick laid down his pool cue and said, "By God, that's Charlie Taylor!"

There is a poignant epilogue to Charlie Taylor's story. During one of the last Pearl Harbor Survivors Association meetings that he attended, he encountered a crewman from the *St. Louis*. Charlie asked his fellow sailor if he remembered the Zero that had strafed the finger pier beside the *Honolulu* on that fateful Sunday morning. Charlie said he could "still see the face of that Japanese pilot laughing as he flashed by," continuing, "I've been lookin' for that sonofabitch for more than fifty years!"

Chief Petty Officer Charles L. Taylor. (From the author's collection.)

His Navy buddy looked at Charlie with surprise. "Didn't you see what happened?" he asked. "After he banked over the stern of the *Honolulu*, he headed right at us...his plane wavered for a second; then we saw him catch a wingtip in the water and cartwheel into a million goddamn pieces that sank to the bottom while we watched. He never knew what hit him!"

At last, Charlie Taylor's war was finally over.

The nation's hatred for Japan following the sneak attack at Pearl Harbor was accompanied by a subliminal but legitimate fear about what the "Japs" could actually do to us. Following the December 7 attack, high school became somewhat less important. Schools and communities were transformed into forums of war preparation and survival. There was a growing anxiety about what the future might hold for an America now completely involved in a monumental struggle against evil. Soon on, we experienced blackouts, blood drives, bandage seminars, gas rationing, commodity shortages, and recapped tires; and every day saw more blue and gold stars hanging in neighborhood windows—blue indicating a member of that particular family was now serving his or her country; gold signifying a family member had paid the last full measure of devotion for our country with his or her life.

Ten weeks after the bombing of Pearl Harbor, on February 19, 1942, President Roosevelt signed Executive Order 9066. This would be the overture action that physically excluded individuals of Japanese ancestry, regardless of American citizenship, from living near US coastlines. Japanese were regarded as a threat, something to be dealt with. Thus, the pages of American history opened a dismal chapter on civil rights. Sadly, the very first individuals of Japanese ancestry to be expelled to relocation centers were those living on Bainbridge Island in Puget

Sound, in my home state of Washington. Their farms and fields would soon be gone and their culture trampled as they were transported to a place of arid land and tarpaper barracks totally alien to their nature and way of living.

I recall a Japanese kid in my high school whose name I believe was Toshi. He sat in front of me in English class. He was quiet and unassuming, and we made only occasional eye contact; I don't think we ever actually spoke. In those tenuous days, I saw him as totally different from me. I was immature and unwise, derelict in compassion, and prejudiced against our enemy. I came into class one Monday morning, and the seat in front of me was empty. Toshi had gone somewhere. I never saw him again. At the time, I was pretty much unaffected by his absence. In retrospect and old age, I think surprisingly often of him and of the friends we might have become in some other, gentler time. It is a humbling thing to remember…bothersome and brushed with a pale coat of sorrow and regret.

SEVENTEEN

T he face of the American fighter plane was about to change. Just a few years before Pearl Harbor, there were still Boeing P-26s in the inventory of the US Army Air Corps. But the handwriting was on the wall. Despite its beauty, the P-26 Peashooter with its fixed gear and open cockpit was a thing of the past. Biplanes were fast giving way to sleeker, more unified, monoplane-configured aircraft—innovative, different in beauty, and better capable of serving the demands of new-age air war. The United States had to catch up to the rest of the world by developing homegrown Army and Navy fighters that could truly compete in the battlefield skies emerging all over the world.

If ever there was a family of fighting planes that a kid could love, it was the generations of Curtiss Hawks that were bred through the 1920s and '30s. Arguably, these fighters constitute some of the most beautiful airplanes ever to serve a growing nation. The Curtiss line finally flowered into the Curtiss P-40 Warhawk, a single-engine fighter/ground attack aircraft that was introduced in 1938.

The P-40 did not hatch from a newly laid egg; rather, it was the result of a lovely genesis of flying machines built first by the Curtiss Aeroplane and Motor Company of Buffalo, New York, and later, the Curtiss-Wright Corporation. The company was first organized in 1916 by Glenn Curtiss, a giant in the history of American military aviation. Curtiss actually founded the American aircraft industry and is widely recognized as the pilot of the first officially witnessed aircraft flight in North America, for which he was issued US Pilot's License #1. (Interestingly, Orville Wright received license #5.[43]) Curtiss was instrumental in the development of naval aviation in the United States during the period between the First and Second World Wars.

My affections for the last of the Curtiss and Boeing biplane fighters stems from the fact that they were simply beautiful, highly complex aircraft. The early Curtiss Hawks and Boeing F4Bs were among the last of the wind-through-the-wires era of American military fighters. I built models of them because I loved their stocky, strong, compact configuration and the fabulous detail and decorative touches that enhanced them, transforming them into true industrial art forms. Even their interplane struts and wires added to their exotic beauty.

In the long list of Curtiss fighters, I suggest the most beautiful models were the little F9C Sparrowhawk and the P-6E Hawk, first ordered by the Air Corps in 1929. A single, 600-horsepower Curtiss V-1570 Conqueror engine gave the handsome P-6E its high-performance capability and placed it in the 200 mph category—very adequate for its time. The undercarriage was beautifully painted, and the wing strutting and empennage made the whole machine simply a delight to the eyes. There was much of the Curtiss racers in all of the Hawks, and it showed to wonderful advantage.

USS *Akron* (ZRS-4) launches a Consolidated N2Y-1 training plane (Bureau #A8604) during test flight near the Naval Air Station in Lakehurst, New Jersey, 4 May 1932. (US Navy photo, National Archives. Item #: 80-G-463185. Unrestricted use.) Note the airship's trapeze handling gear below the hangar bay.

The F9C Sparrowhawk was a tiny machine, just twenty-one feet long with a wingspan of slightly more than twenty-five feet. Although it was a real midget in the world of fighter aircraft, its small size belied its capability and contributed to its beauty and grace. The Sparrowhawk was diminutive for a reason: The airplane was designed to be transported within an aerial aircraft carrier. The USS *Akron* and USS *Macon* were helium-filled airships designed for long-range reconnaissance in support of Navy fleet operations. Their duties included transport of the Sparrowhawk. Described as a "parasite fighter," the F9C was suspended from a large hook and could egress by lowering on a cable through a large door on the airship's ventral surface. Once its engine was started, the F9C could then disconnect from its tether directly into the slipstream of the flying airship. Rejoining the mother ship, however, was a dicey maneuver. The pilot had to fly close to the bottom surface of the airship and snare a trapeze with a hook situated on the top wing of the airplane. The aircraft's engine was then shut down, and the little Sparrowhawk was lifted into place within the belly of the whale.

The elfin Sparrowhawk was powered by a Wright R-975, 400 hp radial engine (top speed 176 mph) and armed with two fixed .30-caliber, forward-firing machine guns;[44] however, she never saw combat, which, because of her size, was perhaps a good thing. Both the *Akron* and *Macon* were cursed by ill fates.

In 1932, the *Akron* was damaged during removal from her hanger in Lakehurst, New Jersey. Extensive repairs were required before she was once again airworthy. On May 8, she began a flight to the Pacific Coast. Three days later, she attempted a mooring with an inexperienced ground crew at Camp Kearny near San Diego. In the process, she became unmanageable, and her mooring cable was cut to prevent damage. As she began a rapid ascent, three of her ground crew sailors failed to let go of the trail lines and were carried high into the air. Two fell to their deaths; a third managed to secure himself to the line and was saved an hour later by being drawn up into the interior of the airship. The whole macabre scene was caught by photographers and widely viewed by the public. I first saw the newsreel at the impressionable age of eight and was strongly affected by the terrible scene of the two sailors falling to their deaths. I have never forgotten the incident.

USS *Akron* (ZRS-4) in flight, 1931. (US Navy photo #: NH 63070.)

Despite this tragedy, the West Coast tour continued. I remember standing in the schoolyard at John B. Allen Elementary with my second-grade class, watching in wonder as the USS *Akron* sailed over our heads. In the midst of the Great Depression, she was a fabulous sight. Kids from every classroom suddenly flooded the schoolyard waving, screaming, and shouting up at the huge wonder as she floated above us, virtually filling the sky. In a time of deprivation and in a nation deeply troubled, she stood as a source of pride and wonder...a symbol of a better time to come. I have never forgotten the tragedy that befell her, but I recall with joy, the exhilaration of seeing her that day in flight.

Following her West Coast tour, the *Akron* returned to fleet operations and in conjunction with her three F9C aircraft undertook numerous training flights and widespread scouting missions from her base in Lakehurst, New Jersey. All proved effective, and the mechanical trapeze arrangement for launching and retrieving the tiny Sparrowhawks apparently performed with complete success in all of the *Akron's* operations.

On the evening of April 3, 1933, the *Akron* set off from her New Jersey hanger on a mission to assist with calibration of radio direction finders along the New England coast. Through human error, the airship was flown into an area of vicious thunderstorms. As she passed over Barnegat Light, New Jersey, at about 10:00 p.m., she was struck by heavy downdrafts, which forced her lower and lower. Despite all attempts to regain altitude, she was forced down in the sea with a loss of seventy-three passengers and crew. Rear Admiral William A. Moffett, the first chief of the Bureau of Navy Aeronautics, was among the casualties. Only three survived the accident.

In a like scenario, the USS *Macon* was lost in a storm off Point Sur, California, on February 13, 1935. *Macon* had suffered some structural damage in a flight previous to her final trip. Close to Point Sur on Monterey Bay, she encountered severe wind shear, which tore off her top rudder, the support girders of which had been dislodged in an earlier flight. A massive discharge of ballast caused her to rise above her permissible pressure altitude, and she vented sufficient gas to cause her to lose lift; she slowly descended from about 5,000 feet before gently settling in the bay. Two lives were lost out of a compliment of seventy-six, but the era of the grand dirigibles had come to an end. Sadly, the *Macon* carried four Sparrowhawks to the bottom with her. In 1939, the US Navy retired the last aging Sparrowhawk and transferred it to the Smithsonian Institute. Today, only three F9Cs remain. A fully restored

Sparrowhawk resides in the Boeing Aviation Hanger at the Steven F. Udvar-Hazy Center of the Smithsonian Air and Space Museum in Chantilly, Virginia.

The Boeing P-12 and its Navy version, the F4B, are fine examples of the beautiful, short-coupled biplane fighters that spanned the years between the wars. First flown in 1928, the P-12 had a long operational history with both the US Army Air Corps and the Navy. During its active service, many variants using different engines were produced. The P-12 remained in service as a first-line fighter until it was replaced by the P-26 Peashooter in the mid-1930s.

The history of the Curtiss Hawks is made even more impressive by the production of the revolutionary P-36 (Hawk 75/Mohawk), which was first flown in May 1935. It would be a contemporary of the Hawker Hurricane and the BF 109, an all-metal monoplane of clean design powered by a radial engine. But more important, the P-36 would morph into the apex of the Curtiss fighter line—the beloved Curtiss P-40 Warhawk (United States designation for all models)— which would serve for some time as the icon of American fighter-plane power.

The Warhawk was somewhat modular, making it easy to maintain. In addition, it was exceptionally rugged and capable of operation in extreme conditions. As quickly as these aircraft left the assembly lines, they were grabbed by the Soviets and British who referred to the B and C models as Tomahawks and all models after D as Kittyhawks.

The first model, XP-40, was actually the tenth Curtiss P-36 built. In a revolutionary transformation, an Allison V-1710 inline engine equipped with a single-speed supercharger replaced the R-1830 radial, and the smaller frontal area of the V-1710 provided less drag and more speed than the radial engine that had previously graced the same airframe. The engine change brought level flight air speed to about 315 mph. Further redesign of the front cowling covering the glycol and oil cooler radiators produced a deep "chin" on the P-40 and increased its air speed to 362 mph. The larger cowling and deeper chin not only made the airplane fly better, its radical form was fear inspiring—particularly when the shark's mouth motif was applied.

The P-40 was one of the tightest-turning fighters of World War II. Clive Caldwell, the leading Australian air ace, described it as "faster downhill than almost any other airplane with a propeller"[45] and with "almost no vices." This lovely airplane would see combat in every corner of the globe and make history as a midaltitude fighter and ground attack aircraft of monumental importance.

In April 1939, the United States government placed its biggest aircraft production order in history, purchasing 524 P-40s and praying they'd get them as soon as humanly possible. American military circles were aware of the existence of the Messerschmitt Bf 109 and the Mitsubishi A6M Zero, and we were already way behind the curve and running scared. The P-40 would be a godsend: capable of fighting in every theater of war and serving twenty-eight nations, including Japan, which flew a captured P-40 to identify her capabilities.

Curtiss P-6E Hawk, National Museum of the United States Air Force.
(US Air Force photo.)

Curtiss P-36 Hawk in flight, National Museum of the United States Air Force.
(US Air Force photo.)

Curtiss P-40E Warhawk, National Museum of the United States Air Force.
(US Air Force photo.)

I loved the P-40 from the first moment I saw it; and before long, I knew its configuration like the back of my hand, doodling countless sketches of it, oft times, on the lined pages of my notebook in French class. There was just something romantic and exotic about it. Obviously, the British and Soviets agreed, and the aircraft performed for them equally well in the withering North African heat and in frigid Russian winters. However, the P-40's most fabled association was with the First American Volunteer Group (AVG)—the "Flying Tigers." While flying for underdog China against the Empire of Japan, the escapades of the Flying Tigers created adventure stories of air combat that I believe will live as long as people love fighter planes and fighter planes fly. Stories of the AVG P-40s and their crews were told and retold in magazines, comic strips, military journals, newsreels, and motion pictures. Coverage of the war in China, "Vinegar Joe" Stillwell, and Claire Chennault thrilled the American public at home and served as a real morale booster in the gloom of early 1942.

Milton Caniff's comic strip, *Terry and the Pirates*, did a whole story line on the Flying Tigers. Caniff even used some of the actual AVG pilots as characters in the strip. Caniff's drawings were exquisitely rendered and technically accurate graphic recreations of the men, the airplanes, and the topography of Western China, Burma, and India. Also depicted was the famed Hump of the Himalayas, over which converted B-24 Liberator Bombers, Curtiss C-46 Commandos, and the ever-faithful Douglas C-47 and C-54 transports delivered badly needed cargo. Flying in all kinds of weather, these workhorses carried gasoline, bombs, and ammunition to the beleaguered Chinese and American bases in free China.

One would like to think the famous shark's mouth motif started with the P-40s flown by the Flying Tigers, but such is not the case. Shark's mouth nose art first appeared on other aircraft, including the Messerschmitt Me 110; but as images of the war in China filtered in, the distinctive shark's mouth motif became synonymous with those P-40s flown by AVG contract pilots serving under the direction of Claire Chennault.

Despite all my affection for the P-40, I was acutely aware that she had a hard time climbing stairs. Upwards of 16,000 feet, she was left gasping for air due to the single-stage supercharger with which she was cursed. Spitfires, Hurricanes, and the Me 109 could run and play at 30,000 feet—but at that altitude, the P-40 was left breathless. No thinking person could fault her below 16,000 feet, but the lack of a robust supercharger on her Allison V-1710 made her a wallflower at altitude.

The same was true of the P-39 Airacobra: Poor performance at high altitudes made the aircraft an also-ran. It would seem that a supercharger for the Allison V-1710 could have been successfully designed and incorporated into the airframe configurations of both the P-40 and P-39, but a litany of problems crippled this effort. Trouble with fuel-air mixtures, excessive heat buildup, engine detonation, and the design of ducting made the supercharger addition impractical. The Rolls Royce Merlin engine was already waiting in the wings, and it would provide the lungs needed to solve this high-altitude problem in fighter performance. But closer to the ground, the fact remains that the P-40 acquitted herself with grace and aggression against the German Me 109, and at ground level, she was a bit faster (an advantage that dropped off with increasing altitude).

Of equal importance was her capability against the Japanese A6M Zero. The two airplanes were as different as night and day. The A6M was a handsome, lightweight fighter with none of the protective features of the P-40. The A6M had no armor for the pilot or critical areas of the airframe and no self-sealing fuel tanks, which made it very vulnerable to fire and explosion. However, the absence of these protective factors also made the aircraft extremely light and maneuverable with a tight turning radius and an enviable high rate of climb. Because of these advantages, Chennault instructed his P-40 pilots to steer clear of turning with a Zero. Instead, the Fighting Tigers developed a "boom and zoom" attack strategy whereby the P-40s would dive on enemy aircraft and attempt to down them in single passes. The single-pass technique utilized the Warhawk's higher dive speed, superior strength, and ruggedness of the lane to its best advantage.

New and better fighters were on the drawing boards, and they would eventually eclipse the P-40 legend. In my opinion, however, the Curtiss Warhawk was truly a savior in the early, dark days of the war, serving in every clime imaginable and in conditions that could only be described as mechanically appalling. Of the more than 14,000 Curtiss Warhawks produced between 1939 and 1944,[46] only nineteen are reported airworthy at this writing. But in a time of fear and vulnerability, they were the very best we could do, and there is a simple nobility about them and about those who flew them that sets them apart in the gauntlet of air combat.

EIGHTEEN

The days of our lives were now filled with war. During the ARCADIA Conference of December 1941, Roosevelt and Churchill determined the course of America's early war efforts: "Europe first"[47] would commit most of our military resources to Britain and the Soviet Union over response to Japanese imperialism in the Pacific.

The Japanese response was swift. Invasion of Burma in January 1942. February found Japanese forces capturing Singapore and making the western Pacific a Nipponese lake. Then April brought with it the tragic surrender of US forces on the Bataan Peninsula and the cruel beginnings of an era of Japanese-imposed savagery. Treatment of prisoners and civilians by their Japanese captors created tremendous hostility in those of us who fought against them. Many will never grow old enough to completely forget the atrocities or forgive the criminals who committed them.

To offset the traumatic defeat at Bataan, the United States military devised one of the most daring and dangerous plans of the war: a secret bombing raid on the Japanese homeland.

IF WE SHOULD HAVE TO FIGHT, WE SHOULD BE
PREPARED TO DO SO FROM THE NECK UP
INSTEAD OF FROM THE NECK DOWN.

~ JIMMY DOOLITTLE[48]

On April 18, 1942, after weeks of practicing short-field takeoffs from two secluded airstrips in Florida, Lieutenant Colonel Jimmy Doolittle led a group of sixteen B-25B Mitchell bombers from the deck of the aircraft carrier USS *Hornet* on an unbelievably audacious raid on Japan. The plan was for the *Hornet* to take the bombers close to the Japanese coast, launch them, and then retreat eastward toward safety at flank speed.

Picture yourself sitting in the left seat of a B-25, waiting for takeoff. It is a half minute before your turn to go...time is an eternity of seconds laid end to end. Outside the streaked windshield, there is only a moving violence, a dismal grayness, falling rain, and the heaving deck of the Hornet. *She has already turned into the wind giving you fifty knots over the deck. Ahead of you—less than 500 feet away—is the plunging bow of the carrier. By the time you reach it, you must be airborne or you'll meet a blackness and cold that will last for your particular forever.*

The Wright R-2600 Double Cyclone fourteen-cylinder engines are short stacked, roaring on each side just a few scant feet from your head. The airplane shakes and shudders inconsolably, like some tortured living thing, held only by your feet pushing viciously on the brakes. The cockpit is cold and alive with drafts of frigid wind. Your hands on the throttle are sweating as your eyes sweep the instrument panel for rpm, cylinder head temperature, boost, fuel pressure, oil pressure, any sign of weakness. Then it's back to the view through the rain-streaked windshield.

View from the island of the USS *Hornet* (CV-8) en route to the Doolittle mission launch point, April 1942. (US Navy photo # NH 53421.)

Eight of the mission's sixteen B-25B bombers are lined up for launch from the carrier's flight deck. The USS Nashville *(CL-43) is visible in the distance.*

The instant has come...it's a GO! Feet come off the brakes and now embrace the rudder pedals as the plane half leaps, half lurches forward. Throttles are pushed to the breaking point against the stops.

Then there is focused silence: Your mind is oblivious to everything save for steering and feeling the airplane move forward. Slanted figures on the deck hunker down against the frigid wind, their shapes blur as you move faster, ever faster....The nose wheel lightens and responds to the elevator pressure that has become second nature...the brow of the flight deck looms closer, ever closer as the control column inches back toward your belly. Then there is the instant of communion with the wind. You are flying on the bitter edge of an incipient stall; meanwhile, the carrier is now the pursuer. The shout of "GEAR UP" is absolutely integral with the copilot's upward jerk of the handle...the air speed indicator is stuck at four knots above stall speed, and the airplane mushes along over the violence of the sea like a too-small child without training wheels.

You cannot breathe...you have no breath...you will the airplane into flight, in futility tightening your ass muscles to make them ounces lighter. The gear is halfway up as the air speed adds another three knots, then ten, then twenty, and the incipient stall is only a rotten memory. Your baby is climbing through the mists toward the others of her kind that, by now, are far ahead on a mission of stupendous proportion.

Just hours ago, on the block where I live, I paced off the 810-foot takeoff distance[49] available to Doolittle, his crew, and their B-25s. When I looked back, I thought again about those aboard the planes that day. The distance that I paced off is appallingly short. My deepest respect goes out to those who braved that distance, lifted off, and headed for immortality.

The last of the Doolittle Raider planes taking off from the USS *Hornet*. (Department of Defense, Department of the Navy, Naval Photographic Center. National Archives Identifier: 520603, Local Identifier: 80-G-41196.)

Aerial view of B-25 Mitchells in formation. (US Army Signal Corps photo.)

Good luck did not prevail for the mission. The *Hornet* and its task force were spotted by a small picket boat, which radioed Tokyo of an impending attack. Under the circumstances, the *Hornet* was forced to launch the Raiders about 700 miles off the Japanese coast, making the planned safe landings in western China impossible.

The Raiders would have to fly out their fuel in hopes of bailing out or landing just out of reach of Japanese forces on the Chinese coast.

The B-25s approached Japan, arriving over their destinations about noon. Ten military and industrial targets were struck in Tokyo, two in Yokohama, and one each in Nagoya, Kobe, and Osaka. The Raiders met with antiaircraft fire and fighter opposition, but none was badly damaged.

Sixteen aircraft continued west where their crews bailed out or crash-landed at various locations in eastern China. One of the bombers landed in Russia where the plane was confiscated and its crew interned. Jimmy Doolittle's crew and most of the other Raiders escaped to safety with the aid of local Chinese. Two Raiders drowned following the crash landing of their aircraft; one was killed on bail out after the mission was completed. Eight were captured at or near their crash sites; of those, one died of beriberi and malnutrition, four survived forty months of torture and imprisonment, and three of these heroic airmen were executed by firing squad in a disgusting disregard of international law.

The heroism of those who participated in the raid stands as an achievement that forever changed the course and history of the war. While minimal damage was done to the Japanese, the effect on our nation was monumental.

US Army Air Forces Lieutenant Robert L. Hite (blindfolded) is led by his captors from a Japanese transport plane after he and seven other Doolittle crewmembers were captured. Hite was copilot of Crew 16 (B-25B s/n 40-2268, *Bat out of Hell*, 34th Bomb Squadron). (US Air Force photo 050607-F-1234P-021.)

After 45 days of captivity in Japan, Hite and the seven other captured Doolittle airmen were returned to China for imprisonment. On 15 October 1942, Lieutenant Dean E. Hallmark, Lieutenant William G. Farrow, and Corporal Harold A. Spatz were executed; Lieutenant Robert J. Meder died in captivity. Hite and the other surviving airmen were finally liberated on 20 August 1945.

The courageous efforts of the Doolittle Raiders renewed the spirits of the American people after the black and fearful days following Pearl Harbor...and in the process, our nation found a new confidence. I vividly recall the satisfaction of knowing that at least a few bombs had fallen on what had become a truly hated enemy. I also remember hoping and praying that it was only a precursor of what was to come.

NINETEEN

In the few short months since Pearl Harbor, it seemed as though the entire nation had created a new sense of itself. We were moving from a Depression economy into the new, vigorous, and vital role of manufacturers—makers of everything from canteens to aircraft carriers, and no longer did the nation sleep. Factories and small production shops were running twenty-four hours a day, every day of the week, and everywhere, companies were looking for more employees to fill out the rosters of their constantly increasing payrolls. Seattle was booming, too. No one stopped by the house anymore looking for a handout; everybody was working somewhere and producing stuff with which to win a war.

My family was a part of the action. My dad hung in with the salmon company and was declared "essential" because of his connection with food production, and my mother took a job with an outdoor sign company called Foster and Kleiser. With the ever-present rumors about Japanese attacks on the northern Pacific Coast, Foster and Kleiser, along with my mother in tow, was assigned the formidable task of camouflaging the Boeing Airplane Plant so that it could not be seen from the air by any passing Japanese bombers. The Boeing plant, located on the south side of Seattle, covered a land area of nearly twenty-six acres.[50] The assignment involved covering the entire property, as well as the plant itself, with a walk-on camouflage landscape, complete with houses, cars, trees, and some cardboard cows. The job was tantamount to wrapping Montana in gift tissue.

To make a long story short, they did it, and in record time. My mother was as proud of the accomplishment as if she had built it all by herself. It was another example of America's commitment to winning the war. There were some misgivings about the project, however. The actual Boeing Airport adjacent to the plant was still readily visible from the air, as was an adjoining waterway and several highways. Unless Japanese bomber pilots and bombardiers were entirely blind, these visual clues were a dead giveaway as to the plant's true location. Had there been any photos taken of the plant prior to its camouflaging, the whole project would have disclosed the phony suburb as an admirable but ineffective exercise in city beautification. Fortunately for all concerned, there were no attacks by Japanese bombers, and the aircraft plant under the tent remained productive, cranking out B-17s, B-24s, and eventually B-29s that ultimately destroyed the Germans and the Japanese as well.

My mother did a hell of a job!

American and Japanese fleets entered the ring in early May 1942 to begin a four-day slugfest known as the

Battle of the Coral Sea. Japan was intent upon strengthening its hold in the South Pacific by invading Tulagi and setting up a base at Port Moresby, New Guinea. This would be the first naval battle in history in which opposing carriers struck each other with aircraft.

In the ensuing battle, the United States lost the USS *Lexington* (CV-2) and several support ships, including a fleet oiler. Seventy US aircraft were also lost. The operation cost the Japanese one light carrier, a destroyer, several small ships, and ninety-one shipboard aircraft. A Japanese carrier, a destroyer, and several small support vessels sustained damage.

Retiring to lick their wounds, the Japanese called off the planned invasion of New Guinea. Their advance in the South Pacific was turned back.

The damage inflicted on the Japanese carriers in the Coral Sea severely cut their offensive capabilities. More importantly, it greatly contributed to America's decisive victory in the monumentally important Battle of Midway—which was scarcely a month away....

PHOTOGRAPHS

My grandparents, 1902.

Ed Garrett, my dad.

My beautiful mother, Violet.

Me, at 7 months.

My childhood home in Seattle,
built by my grandfather.
Mom and I moved in with my grandparents
and Uncle Charlie after my dad split.

Mrs. Hall's Kindergarten class, 1930.
I am the kid on the far right.

Pop, Gram, me, Mom, and Uncle Charlie at the start of the Great Depression.

Gram, Mom, and me as the Depression continued.

Family picture during hard times.

Working as a deck hand on the *Doris E.* in Alaska.

Mom, after she
married Oscar.

Me
at military school.

Oscar Larson,
my stepdad.

Oscar Larson, my stepdad,
at Bushman's Cannery, Port Althorp, Alaska,
where he was superintendent.

Me with Captain Phil Hastin and Harold "Jorgy" Jorgensen
on the afterdeck of the *Eagle*.

On deck the *Doris E.*

The *Hazel H.*

Me and my 175 lb. halibut.

My graduation photo, 1942.

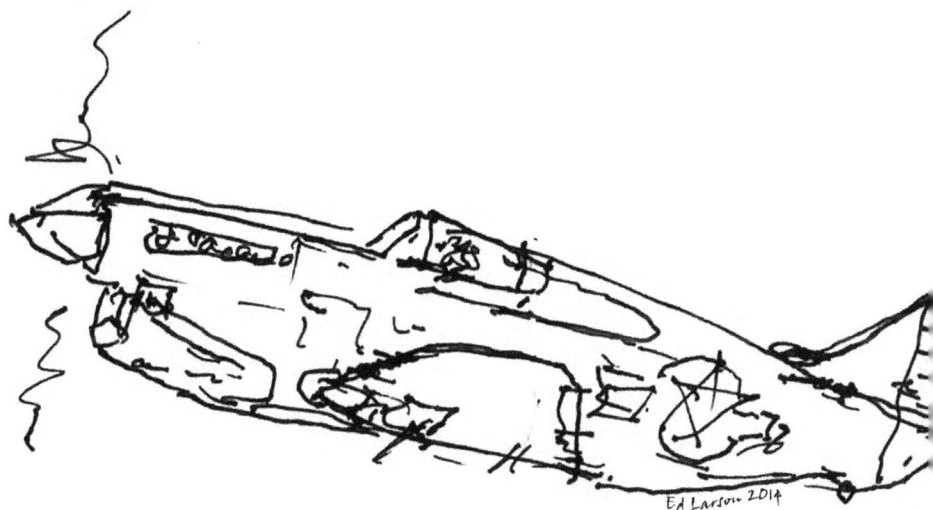

Ed Larson 2014

PART TWO

TWENTY

*I HAVE SEEN WAR. I HAVE SEEN WAR ON LAND
AND SEA. I HAVE SEEN BLOOD RUNNING FROM
THE WOUNDED. I HAVE SEEN MEN COUGHING
OUT THEIR GASSED LUNGS. I HAVE SEEN THE
DEAD IN THE MUD. I HAVE SEEN CITIES
DESTROYED. I HAVE SEEN TWO HUNDRED
LIMPING EXHAUSTED MEN COME OUT OF LINE—
THE SURVIVORS OF A REGIMENT OF ONE
THOUSAND THAT WENT FORWARD FORTY-EIGHT
HOURS BEFORE. I HAVE SEEN CHILDREN
STARVING. I HAVE SEEN THE AGONY
OF MOTHERS AND WIVES. I HATE WAR.*

FRANKLIN D. ROOSEVELT
ADDRESS AT CHAUTAUQUA, AUGUST 14, 1936

I magine a book titled *WAR*. Seemingly benign and innocuous, it is black-bound and filled with a litany of human conflicts. Its flyleaf should bear a warning label: BEWARE WHEN OPENING. Turn only one page of this volume's list of inescapable tragedies, and one may neither reach the end nor close the cover on pervasive sorrow. It is inevitable that as time passes, wars become remembrances and battles become chronicles, but for those of us who have lost a loved one, the pain haunts us for the remainder of our days.

Some years ago, I sat for lunch with Captain Jack Reid, USN (RET), and Lieutenant Commander Brian Foss, USCG helicopter pilot and former port director for the Santa Cruz Small Craft Harbor. It was a sunny and quiet afternoon, and our table overlooked the harbor entrance and an ever-present gathering of gulls. We spoke of many things, mostly about our war experiences, and more specifically about Reid's scouting flight in his PBY-5A on the fate-filled morning of 3 June 1942....

Jack Reid's patrol squadron, VPB-44, had been deployed to the Midway Islands to conduct a series of extended combat patrols north, west, and south of the atoll. The United States had intercepted and decoded Japanese transmissions and was aware not only that a naval and air attack was imminent, but also of the planned date of the attack and relative strength of the Japanese forces that would be used to launch the assault.

In response, the US Navy had hurriedly dispatched to the area three carriers: the USS Yorktown *(CV-5), USS* Enterprise *(CV-6), and USS* Hornet *(CV-8), along with support vessels. Meanwhile, the atoll itself hosted an airfield and a sketchy group of US fighters, scout planes, torpedo and dive-bombers, and a contingent of B-17s and B-26 Marauders ready to defend against the invading enemy. The stage was set—but one critical fact remained: To hit the enemy, we had to find them first! That was then-Ensign Reid's mission: to detect Japanese naval presence in the vicinity.*

Although the assigned search area on the morning of 3 June 1942 was at the extreme range for the fuel capacity of Reid's aircraft, he and his crew agreed to "stretch things a bit" and fly a longer search pattern in hopes of locating the Imperial Japanese Navy. At the edge of a sixteen-minute extension, Reid and his copilot suddenly identified a large number of ships far to the west and heading toward Midway. It was Japanese forces bent on invading the islands and eliminating the US threat in the Pacific—a victory that would decisively answer the Doolittle Raid and Battle of the Coral Sea and cast a severe psychological blow to our nation.

Reid immediately radioed Midway: "Sighted main body, Bearing 262 Distance 700."

Midway Radio immediately responded: "Amplify."

Unaware of Japanese code disclosures known only to United States Navy top brass, Jack Reid assumed the invasion vessels he had spotted constituted the main Japanese attack force; but beyond the horizon, there were several Japanese attack groups approaching Midway. Also mistakenly assuming there were carriers in the group he'd spotted, Reid expected an attack from their shipboard fighter cover that would down his clumsy PBY like a lame duck in a shooting gallery.

In response, Reid dove to a low altitude and remained at a distance using sparse cloud cover as he shadowed the Japanese force, all the while relaying definitive information to Midway. Finally, Command ordered Reid and his crew to return home. It had been nearly two hours since they'd first sighted the enemy force, and it was a flight that would change the course of history.

We lingered over a final cup of coffee that sun-kissed afternoon while Reid finished his story: He'd made his final approach to Midway that fateful day with both fuel-pressure warning lights burning and a prayer in his heart. After he landed, the launch ramp crew checked his fuel tanks. The stick came out dry—the tanks had completely drained. This was an unforgettable luncheon with a truly historic figure.

On 3 June 1942, Japanese vessels covered the sea around the Midway Islands like fleas on a homeless 'possum. Kaigun Taishō[51] Nagumo's four carriers, *Akagi, Kaga, Hiryū,* and *Sōryū,* were the four aces in Emperor Hirohito's poker hand—quite possibly, the winning hand that would pick up all the chips.

> *WE ARE ACTIVELY PREPARING TO GREET*
> *OUR EXPECTED VISITORS*
> *WITH THE KIND OF RECEPTION THEY DESERVE,*
> *AND WE WILL DO THE BEST WE CAN*
> *WITH WHAT WE HAVE.*
>
> ~ ADMIRAL CHESTER W. NIMITZ[52]
> COMMANDER IN CHIEF, US PACIFIC FLEET

At 1230, land-based US military aircraft were launched from Midway. Their attack, which included Army Air Forces[53] Boeing B-17s, was ineffective, inflicting only light damage on the Japanese fleet.

Before dawn the next day, Nagumo answered with a sizeable attack force of carrier bombers, Nakajima B5N torpedo planes, and A6M Zero fighters. The sortie resulted in considerable damage to Midway's defense installations and to aircraft on the ground. In addition, the attacking Zeros shot down three F4Fs and thirteen of the obsolete and ineffective F2A Buffalos.

Midway Atoll, 24 November 1941.
(US Navy photograph. National Archives #: 80-G-451086.)

View from southwest across the southern side of the atoll. Naval Air Station Midway Islands is in the foreground. Sand Island, location of most other base facilities, is across the entrance channel.

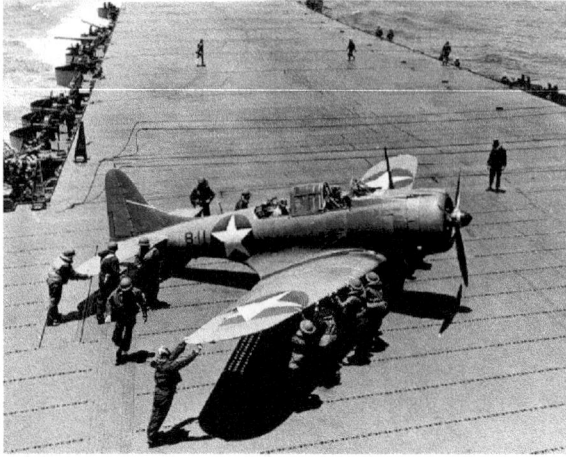

An SBD-3 Dauntless dive-bomber of Torpedo Squadron 8 prepares for launch from the USS *Hornet*, Battle of Midway, 4 June 1942. (National Naval Aviation Museum photo No. 1996.253.648 [1].)

By 0600, US scouting planes had located Nagumo's carriers; and at 0800, two squadrons of fighters, five squadrons of dive-bombers, and three squadrons of torpedo bombers were on their way to destroy them. On this morning, a "Divine Wind"[54] would blow, and it would propel American forces. Before the sun set, there would be tragedy and triumph in the Pacific...and I would suffer a personal loss that I have yet to forget.

Even as our aircraft were closing the gap between our carriers and the Japanese flattops, Nagumo was in a quandary. Midway had not been neutralized, and a second attack was essential to allow his planned invasion to proceed. Nagumo considered the possibility there might be American carriers in the vicinity, but that issue was not confirmed by Japanese scouting reports. *Should he plan for a strike against US carriers or neutralize Midway?*

USS *Yorktown* (CV-5) is hit on the port side by a Japanese Type 91 aerial torpedo during the midafternoon assault by planes from the carrier *Hiryū*, Battle of Midway, 4 June 1942. (US Navy photograph #: 80-G-414423.)

SBDs from the USS *Hornet* over the burning *Mikuma*, early afternoon, 6 June 1942. (United States National Archives #: 80-G-17054.)

Nagumo's decision was fateful: strike the islands a second time. He ordered all of his reserve aircraft to be armed with contact-fuse land bombs to further destroy Midway's capability to resist invasion.

The rearming of reserve aircraft was well underway when Nagumo received communication from one of the Japanese scout planes indicating they had sighted a "...sizeable American naval force to the east."[55] There was no mention of carriers in the initial report, but a subsequent message sent from the scout plane mistakenly stated that one carrier was detected in the force. Now frantic, Nagumo countermanded his own orders, directing all aircraft be rearmed again—this time with torpedoes. The attendant confusion of this effort, coupled with the need to refuel and spot aircraft for takeoff, filled the decks of the four Japanese carriers with a spaghetti-like labyrinth of fueling hoses; torpedoes; bombs; and running, bewildered men: a recipe for disaster.

Meanwhile, Nagumo's carriers were a far reach for attacking US aircraft. The fighters, whose escort was essential for the protection of the torpedo and dive-bombers, were decimated by lack of fuel. Ten F4F Wildcats from the USS *Hornet* had to ditch after running out of gasoline. Fighters from *Enterprise* and *Yorktown* also had to ditch or turn back. Now, a coordinated attack by US forces was only a broken dream, and it would be up to the torpedo and dive-bombers to cripple or kill Nagumo's ships.

In one of the most dramatic incidents of the war, three squadrons of Douglas Devastator torpedo bombers attacked the four Japanese flattops. Without fighter protection, the slow and clumsy Devastators were fair game for Japanese fighters. It was, in all aspects, a suicide mission.

Hornet's Torpedo Squadron 8, under the leadership of Lieutenant Commander John C. Waldron, was the first to attack. The entire squadron of fifteen Devastators was shot down either by shipboard fire or Zero Fighters from Nagumo's combat air patrol. More tragically—with the exception of Ensign George H. Gay Jr.—every man in Squadron 8 was killed.

Following Gay's torpedo run, his Devastator pancaked into the sea. He floated for hours, witnessing firsthand the ensuing battle.

Among the dead on that fateful day was Aviation Radioman 3rd Class Robert Kingsbury Huntington, gunner in the rear cockpit of Gay's Devastator. He died in the run-in attack on *Kaga* as he and Ensign Gay experienced intense machine gun fire from five pursuing A6M Zeros.

Bob Huntington had just turned twenty-one.

Half the world and an entire lifetime away from the riddled gunner's cockpit of Gay's Devastator lay Parsons Field at the Lakeside School where Bob Huntington and I played football during the 1939–40 school year.

Bob was a rugged kid, a senior, and one of the stalwarts of the team. I was new to the prep school, a very poor athlete, and a terrible football player. Being lightweight and very slow were not attributes for football success; and I contributed nothing to the Lions' lineup during my short tenure at Lakeside, except to turn out every day in the rain and cold in the futile hope of somehow becoming something better.

Despite my self-perceived ineptitude, Bob always treated me with kindness and made me feel a part of the team...it was a brand of kindness that a teenage kid never forgets. I was deeply grieved by Bob Huntington's death, and it is a feeling that has stayed with me the duration of my life.

The USS *Robert K. Huntington* (DD-781), Puget Sound Naval Shipyard, 30 May 1945. (Official US Navy Bureau of Ships photo 19-N-84107. Public domain.) Photo of Bob Huntington from the Lakeside yearbook.

Bob Huntington was posthumously awarded the Distinguished Flying Cross for heroism and extraordinary achievement for his service at Midway; and in a singular honor, Destroyer DD-781, the USS *Robert K. Huntington*, was christened in his name. An Allen M. Summer-class destroyer, she was commissioned on 3 March 1945, and like her namesake, served her nation well. She was decommissioned on 31 October 1973, after earning two battle stars for service in Vietnam.

The narrative of the battle at Midway draws only the Xs and Os, the strategic field positions and first downs of this historic conflict. But let us consider the massive emotional drama—the terror experienced by those who actually fought and lived or died there. Let us climb into the front cockpit with Ensign George Henry Gay Jr....

This Devastator has become a refuge for me...like the tree house in the backyard where I grew up...and the sky is filled with warm sunshine on this tropical Pacific morning. There's great beauty here amongst the misty sea clouds—but today, my mouth is dry, and I know not whether in the next hour I will live or die....

My hand is sweaty on the throttle quadrant; behind me, Bob is sweating, too. My stare constantly returns to the cold-faced fuel gauges, hovering lower and lower and lower, telling me that even now, the flight deck of home may be forever just beyond our reach. Manifold pressure, cylinder head temperature, oil pressure all check out...fuel gauges again...lower.

Now, I see the Jap carriers below...gray, flat-backed rats with long white tails, slithering across the ocean blue; in search of crumbs, they sully this sun-filled day with their smoke...nemeses of evil....

Zeros EVERYWHERE! Dropping on us like flies, two TBDs splash on my right. Machine gun bullets through the canopy sound like gravel on a tin roof...rear view: Bob—stretched over the flex mount...all red...all blood...Jap carrier closer now, I'm flying down a gun barrel toward a wall of hell fire....I will die here...Instrument panel shot out...BASTARD ZEROS...cordite stink and hydraulic oil...over the deck...SOBs running helter-skelter...fuel hoses...roll left...level out...

Formation of US Navy Douglas TBD-1 Devastators from Torpedo Squadron 6 (VT-6) operating in the Pacific off the aircraft carrier USS *Enterprise* (CV-6). (National Naval Aviation Museum photo No. 1996.253.1000.)

Launched on the morning of 4 June 1942 against the Japanese carrier fleet during the Battle of Midway, the squadron lost nine of fourteen aircraft during their attack.

Gunner's compartment. (From the author's collection.)

NO GODDAMN AILERONS... NO RUDDER... CUT THE THROTTLE... STICK BACK... HERE COMES THE DITCH! Water is cold—I'm still alive....

As the attack advanced, other squadrons faired nearly as badly: the USS *Enterprise*'s Torpedo Squadron 6 lost nine of fourteen aircraft; *Yorktown*'s Squadron VT-3 lost ten.[56] Massive casualties and loss of aircraft had made this a devastating run...and not one torpedo had struck a Japanese carrier.

In truth, the Douglas TBD Devastator was not a bad airplane, only an airplane that was made deficient by virtue of newer, faster, and better naval aircraft. Its dismal performance at Midway was partially due to lack of coordinated attack, utilizing fighters to protect the torpedo and dive-bombers. It was quickly withdrawn from service following the Battle of Midway to be replaced by the newer and more effective TBF Avenger.

Locating the Japanese carriers had been a fuel-costly and difficult endeavor. Five squadrons of US dive-bombers were running low on fuel when *Enterprise* air group commander C. Wade McClusky Jr. spotted the four Japanese carriers and their attending vessels underway. The dive-bombers began their attack immediately at 1022 hours on 4 June 1942, with three squadrons simultaneously attacking the Japanese fleet.

The Divine Wind had begun to blow.

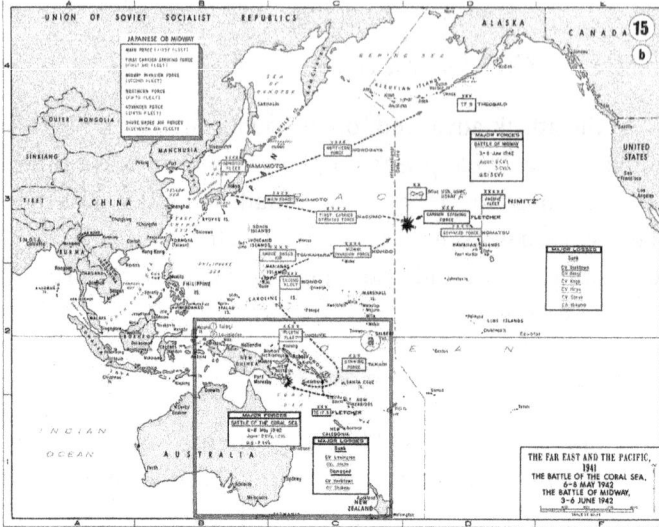

Map showing the vast area of the Pacific covered during the battles of the Coral Sea and Midway Islands. (United States Military Academy, Department of History.)

Screaming down, McClusky's unit scored hits on *Kaga*. Meanwhile, another bomber group pierced *Akagi's* hanger deck, igniting a catastrophic fire and series of explosions—a near hit badly damaged her flight deck and disabled her rudder. *Sōryū* took three lethal hits to her hanger deck at the hands of *Yorktown* bombers, and in all, *Kaga* took four to five. Within minutes, three of the four Japanese carriers were burning like blowtorches.

As the American dive-bombers turned away from their attack, the besieged carriers were quickly abandoned and scuttled. The battle had been joined. Japanese domination of the Pacific was history.

Hiryū, the remaining enemy carrier, launched an immediate counterattack against USS *Yorktown*.

In the ensuing battle, the US carrier took several hits and was gravely damaged.

Hiryū in turn was set ablaze in a final strike by dive-bombers from *Enterprise*. The Japanese carrier was so severely crippled she was unable to land or launch aircraft. Desperate attempts to stop raging fires were unsuccessful, and she was spotted the next morning abandoned and sinking. Shortly afterward, she vanished beneath the sea. Her commander, Kaigun Shōshō[57] Tamon Yamaguchi, who had attended Princeton University, went down with his ship.

In a poignant postlude, *Yorktown* suffered an attack by Japanese submarine I-168, which scored two torpedoes hits while the carrier was under tow. Though valiant efforts were made to save her, the USS *Yorktown* sank on 7 June 1942.

In the days that followed, the opposing ships that were still operational snapped at each other's heels like wild dogs. But on this Divine Wind, American forces had decisively defeated the Japanese, and their victory would ultimately lead to triumph in the Pacific.

TWENTY-ONE

While Bob Huntington and his squadron mates were dying at Midway, I was preparing to graduate from Roosevelt High School. All the pomp and circumstance surrounding commencement seemed out of step with the marching feet now covering most of the globe. Kids my age were going to war everyday in places that were not even in our geography books.

In the six months following Pearl Harbor, there had been a staggering change in the attitude of our country. We had been lifted from the depths of the Great Depression, a war of want, to the drama of a war of survival. It was as if America had been dropped into a crucible of malevolence and annealed into a terrible sword of righteousness and retribution, and there was in everyone a consuming unanimity of purpose—a magnificent obsession for victory. Old and young, pauper and prince, the able and feeble joined hands in a pledge of vengeance against the dark forces of the evil Axis. The spirit of American freedom never burned brighter. It was both a beautiful thing to see and daunting in its intensity.

Graduation Day came and went, and my buddies and I put our futures on hold while we awaited the call for military service. I was only seventeen and not yet eligible for the draft, so I began working with Johnny Condon and Frank Nolan at Pacific Marine Supply Company as soon as school was out. Pacific Marine was a staid old company located on Seattle's waterfront. The company furnished items of all kinds to Northwest marine interests and the Alaskan fishing industry; and like everyone else, they had taken on defense contracts to assist in the war effort. Their specific contribution was the manufacture of portable pumps designed for use aboard naval vessels and at on-shore installations, mostly for fire protection. Johnny, Frank, and I assembled the pumps and packed them for shipment. It was a great job, and that summer cemented our camaraderie into a lifetime of abiding friendship.

Frank Nolan was the funniest guy I had ever met. His humor was both instinctive and swift. I always thought his brilliance ran on two tracks across his mind. One track he used for ordinary communication while the other track ran on ahead searching for and always discovering something funny to say. Frank's wit is a priceless gift. I am blessed. He still shares it with me today.

Johnny Condon and I had been friends for a long time, and early on, I'd had a crush on his sister. Johnny was the consummate waterman: sailor, navigator, mechanic, and deckhand…the finest I have ever known. Together, we had fun shooting pool and messing around with our cars and girls. We smoked too soon and drank beer too soon. The war would make us grow up too soon.

As a trio, we worked well together—we were productive, but at the same time, we still had fun. Since Pacific Marine was close to the waterfront, we had as coinhabitants of our workplace a surprising number of rats scurrying around in search of such goodies as may have fallen from our lunch boxes. In an effort to diminish their population, we each kept a small cardboard box nearby filled with nuts and bolts that became ammunition in our own private war on rodents. Collectively, we fired hundreds of missiles at the creatures; and to the best of my remembrance, we never scored a kill. Our failure to reduce our enemy's numbers was a deep concern to each of us considering the fact that we would soon be defending our country against people who could shoot back.

Volunteering for military service formed a major part of the daily thinking of everyone eligible and able to serve, and I was no different from the rest of my peers. Growing up as I did around planes and boats, I was obsessed with becoming a Navy fighter pilot; and since I was fully conversant in all types of planes, I was naturally convinced that a couple of days of cockpit time would sufficiently qualify me for carrier landings.

Since I was only 17 years old, I needed my parents' permission to join up. With their signatures in hand, I went to the Navy Recruitment Center. The day was lengthy and involved. I first had to pass the required mental exam. That was immediately followed by a rather intense physical exam. By 2:00 p.m., I had passed both examinations and was now ready to complete the final papers. I recall the ensuing few minutes with a lifetime of regret.

"Keep 'em flying" WWII recruiting poster. (Office of Government Reports, 1932–1947. National Archives Identifier: 513525, Local Identifier: 44-PA-37.)

I was seated in a chair in the office waiting to sign my final papers when, after looking at my responses to questions on the physical exam, a yeoman at the desk said to me, "Better look over the list of diseases you've had and be sure to check all of them."

I took the paper, looked it over, and remembered some years before when my mother had taken me to an allergist who ascertained that I had a slight hypersensitivity to grasses. I checked the box labeled "Hay Fever/Allergy" and returned the form to the yeoman. That simple act changed my fate and my war. I was immediately rejected and left the recruiting office in a state of stunned regret. My dream of becoming a Navy pilot was over.

Goddamn it, I'm going to fly!

The next day, I made an early morning trio to the Army Air Forces Recruiting Office and picked up the application for entrance into the Aviation Cadet Program. The day after that, with the application bearing my parents' signatures in hand, I underwent the required mental and physical exams, and by 5:00 p.m., I was officially enlisted in the United States Army Air Forces Aviation Cadet Program. Needless to say, there had been no mention of hay fever or asthma. I was advised that I would not be called up until at least late spring 1943, so now I just had to wait.

The halcyon days of the summer of '42, Pacific Marine, and transient rat packs ended in early September. As yet, Johnny and Frank had not committed to military service, and the Army Air Forces (AAF) had assured me there would be no call-up for at least six months, so we enrolled at the University of Washington. Frank and I pledged the same fraternity, although, for me, it was all pretty meaningless. It was difficult to concentrate on blue books and quizzes when the local papers delivered want ads for workers and obituaries of kids, many dying before they were old enough to drink beer. Like Kirby Ryan, killed on some goddamn island in the western Pacific; Bob Huntington at Midway; Arlo Wells, dying in the explosion of a B-24 near

Albuquerque; Ken Jensen, dead in the crash of a C-47 off Kenai—these were only a few of the early casualties. There would be many more. These valiant young men vanished more than seventy years ago; and yet, I still remember their names and their faces....

I left the university at the end of the fall quarter. My folks had moved to San Francisco where my dad's job had taken him, so I figured I'd go south for a little sunshine. While I was there, I signed up for a few short art classes concentrating on aircraft illustration, and I remember the rendering of a new P-39, which turned out well; but after a week or two, I dropped out. The only compass in my head pointed toward the AAF and active duty, and I vegetated on the back burner of impatience and ennui.

TWENTY-TWO

About the third week of January, I decided to return to Seattle and find work until my number came up. Mother and I drove up, and we stayed with my grandparents. Frank had gone to boot camp in Farragut, Idaho, and Johnny was training in the Great Lakes. In the space of a few months, they would be a hell of a long way from Puget Sound. So would I.

The first full day back, I was at Pacific Marine's front door again looking for a job. The company desperately needed help in any way, shape, or form. The assistant manager, who had rather taken to Frank, Johnny, and me, proudly led me to the main floor and advised me that I was now manager of the outboard motor department. It was a job guys would sell their souls for in peacetime, and I couldn't believe my good fortune. I worked a couple of days and was warmly welcomed. It was on the second day that I took a few minutes to wander up to the third floor where my buddies and I had worked the previous summer.

The pumper contract had run out, and only concrete emptiness remained where we had waged our war on the rats. It was a crushing experience just standing there. The summer of '42 was gone, and I felt a cloying sense of overwhelming loneliness. I was glad when I turned and left that space. I would not see Frank or Johnny again for years. Frank would become a radioman and gun crewmember on a tanker bound for every hot spot on the globe. We lost Johnny a few years ago. He made it through several Pacific patrols on a submarine but spoke little about it. War changed him, as it changed us all.

I clocked out that day and went home to the familiar little house on Queen Anne Hill. I had a big date planned for that night with Miss Edie Bond, a pretty little blond who was eighteen and athletic in track and field. She was also the proud owner of a red Ford convertible that rather rounded out her personality. We were classmates together at Roosevelt, and I had always liked her, sort of like a school buddy—well, not *quite* like that.

Edie and I caught a movie and followed up on Broadway with burgers and Cokes. We had a lot of fun, and the time just sort of whizzed by. It was close to midnight when we turned the corner on my grandparents' street. I was a little alarmed to see all the lights still on in their house, and I told Edie that I'd better check things out, and I would call her in the morning.

When I entered the house, I was met by Gram and Mom, who were rushing around making funny little noises. When I asked what was up, they told me Dad had called. I was supposed to be on a train in forty-eight hours, bound for a basic training facility in Lincoln, Nebraska. And there was another hitch: The train I was supposed to be on was departing from Oakland, California—eight hundred miles away! The induction letter advised that if I missed the transport train, I'd be shot or suffer something equally dire. There was only one way to meet the deadline: I had to fly to San Francisco the next day.

The following morning, I contacted Pacific Marine Supply to advise them their new outboard motor manager had been grabbed by the armed services and that they could send my paycheck, small as it was, to the little house on Queen Anne Hill. I then, of course, called Edie Bond to tell her what had happened. She bade me goodbye with what I hoped was a wistful sigh, and I told her we'd catch another flick after the war.

I regret that I never saw Edie Bond again.

In this day of sophisticated travel, a little flight of eight hundred miles on a commercial airliner is so mundane as to beg mention. Not so in January 1943. A commercial flight still reigned as an adventure complete with beautiful young stewardesses, white linen doilies, an individual ashtray in the armrest of each passenger's seat, and other amenities designed to make flight a patrician experience. To avail myself of this service, I plunked down fifty-five dollars, the going fare to San Francisco. It was a princely sum of money at the time, and in spite of numerous letters and complaints, Uncle Sam never saw it clear to reimburse me.

The flight to San Francisco was uneventful and at an airspeed of about 140 mph took several more hours than a contemporary flight that distance requires. Dad met me at the airport and delivered me to the appointed spot on the Oakland Pier. It was early afternoon, and a motley crew of young guys from all walks of life was gathering, many with cardboard suitcases that were a hallmark of Depression days. Small gaggles of people surrounded the new, would-be warriors—mothers crying and fathers chain smoking and leg staring at young girls who were, with their sobs, telling their boyfriends goodbye. With all of this tearful bleating, there was ever so much of a sheep-shearing quality about the humble scene, and Norman Rockwell could have well used this setting for a cover of the *Saturday Evening Post.*

A couple of commissioned officers and numerous noncoms were shouting periodically for the new recruits to get in line so we could be properly counted and tagged. Herded with guttural, four-letter profanities, four hundred of us fashioned a jagged line. I shook Dad's hand, and with the ragtag flock in front and behind me, stumbled forward to board the aged Pullman cars lining the pier. I was dressed in a light gray suit and tie and wore a three-quarter-length, light, reversible raincoat. It was ineffective cover against even the chilly breeze brushing the harbor that afternoon.

A hissing and leaking steam engine, barely visible ahead, would provide the power to pull us to Nebraska over some of the toughest mountain passes in America. From the way the unkempt old engine looked, I doubted it could pull us out of the yard. Black smoke, carrying a goodly mix of soot would mark every torturous foot of our four-day exodus. We would follow a classic route: Leaving Oakland, we would head east over the Sierras, cross Nevada, Utah, Colorado, and Wyoming. The town of Laramie would greet us with a temperature of fifteen degrees below zero. Fortunately, we wouldn't be there long; but en route to our destination, it would be a cold journey all the way.

A WHOLE LOTTA GOODBYES...

IN THE TWELVE-MONTH PERIOD BETWEEN
31 DECEMBER 1942 AND 31 DECEMBER 1943,
776,833 AMERICANS BECAME ACTIVE MEMBERS OF THE USAAF.

Source: AAF Statistical Digest, Table 4 – Military Personnel in Continental U.S. and Overseas, By Type of Personnel.

Images from Scene from *Report from Nebraska, North Platte Canteen, August 1945.* (Department of Defense. Department of the Army. Office of the Chief Signal Officer. Online Public Access of the National Archives. Identifier: 20069. Local Identifier: 111-ADC-6284.)

I lost sight of Dad in the crowd. I'm sure he merely went back to his car and headed for home. The wait stretched from minutes to an hour, then two hours, then longer. The crowd of well-wishers finally ran out of tears, blown kisses, and goodbye waves, and reluctantly dribbled away from the scene to return to their respective homes and hearths. The rain was intermittent through the afternoon, and darkness came early. The night-lights of the pier came on, illuminating the persistent, somehow annoying, wind-driven rain. Still we waited. There was some minor grumbling, but all was beyond our control, and absolutely nothing happened as time stretched to a point of near revolt.

Finally, at 9:00 p.m., musings about our fates and futures were suddenly jolted by a solid jerk forward, followed by cheering. This action was in turn answered by cars backing up perhaps four or five feet before coming to an abrupt, jarring halt. Belching steam sounds from the engine and agonizing screeching from the ancient wheels accompanied each movement. Perhaps five minutes went by; then the whole contraption began to move slowly forward. Without drama or doughnuts, our individual wars had finally begun.

At this time, it might be interesting to direct your attention to the conveyance and rolling stock that made up our caravan.

Passenger and freight cars were in notoriously short supply due to the war, and our particular Pullman had been resurrected from a railroad graveyard outside of Baltimore, Memphis, Peoria, or some point unknown after having languished in a state of decomposing rust. The sage green mohair seat covers had long since worn into a ruin of tears and grubby stains created by years of food spillage or worse. There were still intricate rococo designs etched into the dirty mahogany plywood panels surrounding the ancient interior; and unbelievably, the gaslight fixtures of another era still remained affixed to the walls, although electric lights now made them obsolete. It appeared the windows had never been washed; one could gain only the foggiest of outside images through the panes, some of which were cracked and broken. And due to the patina of dirt, dust, and rust that had permeated every corner and surface of the car as it whiled away the decades, the longer we rode in it, the more these surroundings left an odd taste in my mouth—it actually *tasted* old.

Furthermore, the archaeological character of this Pullman was not limited to its interior appearance. We soon discovered that the running gears were in an equal state of disrepair. Long ago, wind and weather had morphed the wheels into shapes no longer truly round. They were not square, of course, but surely somewhat flattened from the original castings, and the noise and constant clicking of the flat spots would punctuate any activity or thought on our journey across more than half the country.

As for my fellow travelers, an observer might predict violence or trouble from a group of young men thrown together by circumstance and confined for days cheek to jowl in a moving metal box. But such was not the case. Even as an indifferent teenager, I was struck by the quiet, benign demeanor of the men around me. From the first rolling start, there was only the low hum of quiet conversation. No raucous laughter. No overt behavior.

Surely, some of this was the result of the emotionally draining farewells to family and friends left at Oakland Pier; but that said, I am sure there was a more compelling reason: Deep down, we were all a little anxious and fearful about what lie ahead...and most of us realized that whatever the future held for us, our lives would be indelibly changed forever.

TWENTY-THREE

The miles clicked by as the days moved forward, and the trip to Nebraska became a blur. Even now, specific details are shored up only by some of the hundreds of letters I sent to my family through the course of the war. These communications are, in fact, a journal in shoeboxes, saved with loving care by my mother and grandmother. Without these chronicles, the rail trip to Nebraska would fail to exist. There are skinny remembrances of clanging bells at railway crossings, the eternal click and clack of the wheels, and the ceaseless swaying of the ancient cars; but beyond that, my recall brings to mind only the peculiar behaviors of my caged companions.

There are a few immutable, universal rules that everyone should always adhere to: Never cheat at cards, don't steal other people's stuff, and keep God in a pocket that's easy to reach. Another is this: Don't go to Nebraska in the wintertime. It's damn cold. When we finally arrived at our destination—in varying stages of disbelief and discomfort—we alighted from our Pullman cars to blowing snow, only to be loaded onto unheated buses for transport to Lincoln Army Air Field, the haven of rest that would house and care for us during the first weeks of our new military experience.

The facility was a shambling creation of disparate buildings cobbled together by sheer necessity around a former municipal airport. After Pearl Harbor, it was essential to build large training facilities to train millions of young guys on how to win a war. Construction of the base had only begun six months or so before we arrived. The results of such haste were readily apparent as we stood shivering in frigid temperatures, awaiting our assignment to barracks that were little more than chicken coops, built without concrete or metal components because those materials were essential to the war effort. Thus, the exterior of the buildings were covered only with tarpaper, which made them terribly hot and dry in the summer and terribly cold in the winter.

We were put at ease by the sergeant who allowed us the latitude to move a bit and stomp our feet to ward off the bitterness about us. Then one of our platoon members, speaking out of despair, voiced the question: What about some warm uniforms to replace the San Francisco civvies we'd worn since leaving Oakland? Some low-level verbal exchange passed between the noncoms in charge, and the reply was not good. We were advised that there had been a screw up, and no uniforms would be available for about a week.

The truth is the wind and cold were close to unbearable, and the announcement that we were not to be issued uniforms for at least seven days was incredibly bad news that struck every man in our platoon as a death sentence. We immediately pictured ourselves dying in the snow, unheralded and forgotten—and we would not die as uniformed soldiers, but as poor unfortunates dressed in varying bits of civilian clothing totally unfit for Nebraska winter.

We encountered several more setbacks as we stood waiting on the frozen turf. It would be one depressing announcement after another—beginning with the fact that our day would end with lights out at 2130 (9:30 p.m.) and would commence the following morning at 0530 (5:30 a.m.). The next shock to intrude upon our shivering senses was the introduction to our drill instructor. Sergeant Maddox, or "MAD-OX" as he was irreverently called, was everything his hyphenated nickname suggests. He exhibited absolutely none of the attributes of a revered leader who would mother us for the coming months, and even after seventy years of treasured hatred, his name still strikes terror in my heart.

While other noncoms addressed our group, MAD-OX stood glaring at us with disdain and ill-concealed contempt. He was a man whose body resembled nothing so much as a badly weathered fireplug, with a skin texture to match. He was surly, cynical, and sarcastic with all the grace and compassion of a junkyard dog. With a couple of profane comments, he proceeded to march us a block or so down the snow-filled street where we were dismissed and allowed to enter one of many new tarpaper barracks. My particular residence bore the identifying number T-917.

The wooden-floored barracks were about seventy feet long by thirty feet wide and featured coal-burning stoves at the ends of the structures. Plain, iron bunks were arranged perpendicular to and along the lengths of the buildings. Footlockers for personal storage were placed at the ends of the bunks, and bare bulbs hanging from the open-raftered ceilings illuminated the interiors. It could be said the accommodations were "basic."

The stoves were the subject of almost constant ridicule. While they were sturdy, rather large, and burned a lot of coal, they heated only themselves. It was futile to expect warmth from them since they emitted only a thin halo of heat, and then only inches from their surface. We quickly learned to expect nothing of comfort from them. Our latrines were several buildings away and were equally spartan. The mess hall, whose name was amazingly descriptive, was a march of a couple of blocks away.

While the stove in T-917 burned merrily on its futile mission, we were directed by a stringy corporal (obviously one of MAD-OX's lackeys) to make up our sacks, which consisted of a couple of dun-colored sheet blankets and a single GI blanket tucked in with square corners. Following a settling-in period, we were marched to the mess hall for evening chow. Flavored by the spice of genuine hunger, the evening's meal was OK, contrary to many others in our future.

There was always a long line waiting in the snow to enter the mess hall and chow down, and our outfit always seemed to be at the end of it. We ate out of mess kits—another staple of Army life—and after each meal, we again fell in line to wash down these utensils. This procedure was a classic exercise that became more repugnant as the days went by. The wash-down line snaked slowly past two GI cans filled with lukewarm water. When one's turn came, he dipped his mess kit by its handle down into the vile, greasy mix, swished it around to remove the solids, and then dipped it into the second GI can containing what was laughingly called the rinse water. It must be stated that the water in the second can was just as foul as that in the first, and both GI cans were located just outside the mess hall on a frozen porch; so as the mess kit was withdrawn from the second can, the mixture clinging to it was almost instantly frozen into a disgusting coating that would remain until the next meal. Such was the routine for breakfast, lunch, and dinner. That this practice never inaugurated a full-blown cholera epidemic is something none of us could ever quite understand.

Following the evening meal, we were free until 2130 when taps was blown, and it was lights out. I vividly recall climbing into my bunk fully clothed and pulling the single GI blanket over my head. I can, to this day, recall exactly what I said to myself that first night of terribly cold, fitful, and broken sleep...the phrase has never left me: "There will be no heat in the world again...forever."

In preparation for this story, I researched the ambient cold temperatures that prevailed in Lincoln, Nebraska, during my tenure there in 1943. During January, February, and March, there were only nine days in which the temperature dropped below zero degrees Fahrenheit. This is encouraging until one realizes that for the remainder of those winter days, the temperatures ranged from slightly above zero to a high of around freezing.

The days progressed, and our enmity toward Sergeant Maddox increased exponentially following each of his transgressions. His surliness seemed to mount with each passing day, and many of us in the platoon discussed various operations by which we could kill him and get away with it. He marched us constantly, most of the time at double time. With cynical laughter and constant profanity, he ran us until we bent over from raw fatigue. Physical training sessions were filled with cruel and prolonged exercises that brought us to the brink of corporeal and mental exhaustion; and we began referring to him as "the goddamn maniac," "sonofabitch," "Japanazi," and worse. As the platoon gathered in increasing hatred toward him, everything became his fault. If the weather got colder, it was MAD-OX. If the chow was bad, it was MAD-OX. If we caught KP (kitchen patrol) or the flu, it was MAD-OX. And all the time we spent condemning his soul to endless hell, we were too myopic to see the changes that were emerging in what was once a disparate gaggle of grunts.

Friendships were being forged in the face of adversity. Under his constant, profane criticism, we were jumping higher, running faster, marching farther and better, just to prove he was a damn liar. Each of us would do anything to exceed his demands and shut him up; and in the process, we were turning into a cohesive unit that began casting credit on our barracks and on ourselves. We developed a crack drill team and basketball team. As for MAD-OX, he seemed happy to be living in his own skin, profaning and abusing his poor charges, while all the time laughing at us and getting loaded every night at the soldiers' club.

If there was a bright spot in the ongoing melancholy that was basic training, it was the soldiers' club. Located about three snow-laden blocks from our barracks, it was a huge barn of a building offering such pleasantries as the base commander would allow. We loved the place. It was always warm, and the 3.2 beer was cheap and cold. There were pool tables, a snack bar, jukeboxes, and comfortable lounge chairs with girlie magazines to peruse. The place was always filled with GIs of varying shapes, sizes, and degrees of drunkenness, and it was a simple oasis of fun in the midst of a forsaken land. On many nights, my buddy Don Spangle and I tripped our way home in the snow and the dark. With bellies full of beer and the promise of hangovers, we were unconcerned by whatever miseries the first notes of "Reveille" might bring. We were loaded, life was sweet, and MAD-OX was only a bovine buffoon to be endured and forgotten once we took to the skies.

The snow came and went, but the Nebraska cold never left us. During the last week of March, a rumor began circulating that we would be moving on ahead of schedule. It was great news and brought some figurative sunshine to the gray skies of late winter. On 28 March, we were directed to gather up our gear and prepare to move on as aviation students to a College Training Detachment in Des Moines, Iowa. Physical and mental exams had pared down the size of our group, and many of those who had aspired to pilot, bombardier, or navigator positions would now be relegated to radio or gunnery schools or to aircraft mechanic training. It was only one step of many designed to eliminate those who seemed less apt.

Our last day at Lincoln AAF featured a large parade and addresses by various officers wishing us well in achieving our goals. One final time, we would fall in before Barrack T-917, but this time, as a uniformed and disciplined group who wanted to fly.

As closing instructions were given, the persistent Nebraska wind harassed us for the very last time. Sergeant Maddox stood aside as the cadre called us to attention. I watched him, as did probably every man in our unit. His face was implacable, unreadable, without a hint of goodbye. The order was given: Left Face! With the execution of that order, we marched down the windblown street, and Maddox vanished from sight.

I never saw him again.

The train we boarded in Lincoln was a far cry from the "Toonerville Trolley" that had carried us halfway across the continent. Its most important feature was its wheels—they were round. We traveled the two hundred miles to Des Moines in relative comfort, absent the mind-blowing clicking of flattened wheels and screech of bearings wanting grease.

The number of aspiring airmen in our platoon had been drastically reduced from the hopefuls that had so long ago peopled the rainy Oakland Pier. Upon our arrival, we were warmly welcomed by a host of local well-wishers and transported to the campus of Drake University, a respected institution of higher learning.

A group of about fifteen of us was assigned quarters in what had been the Sigma Alpha Epsilon fraternity house, now commandeered by the AAF. I recall throwing down my barracks bag on a bunk next to that of a blond-haired kid who seemed somewhat indifferent to my attempts at exchanging pleasantries. I found out soon enough that his name was F. P. Mignin Jr. He was from Galesburg, Illinois, and a couple of years older than I was. In a twist of fate occasioned by the alphabetical listing of our last names, we would share our lives and our airplanes until we shook hands and parted one final time at the end of the war.

TWENTY-FOUR

*YOU WERE SELECTED FOR PILOT TRAINING FOR
JUST ONE REASON: BECAUSE THE AIR FORCES
WHOLEHEARTEDLY BELIEVE THAT YOU POSSESS
THE BASIC QUALIFICATION TO BECOME A PILOT
AND OFFICER. IF THAT WERE NOT TRUE, YOU
WOULD NOT BE READING THESE WORDS....*

~ *PRIMARY FLYING STUDENTS' MANUAL*
ARMY AIR FORCES TRAINING COMMAND, 1943

T he distance between Des Moines, Iowa, and Lincoln, Nebraska, is just under two hundred miles, but my training experiences at these two camps were as vastly distant as the stars in space. The College Training Detachment (CTD) was designed to pour knowledge into us as quickly as it was humanly possible to assimilate. It was information still largely military flavored, but textbooks and incessant study now absorbed our waking hours. We were dropped into advanced studies in higher math, physics, theory of flight, meteorology, and world geography. The courses were college level and had to be completed at lightning speed. An aspiring aviator was expected to master his studies or wash out trying. And in addition to our educational responsibilities, we faced constant drilling and physical training. In short, it was a tall pole to climb, but at the top was a wonderful carrot: The last week of our College Training Detachment, we would receive ten hours of flight training in one of thirty Cub Cruisers sitting patiently on the ramp at the Des Moines Airport.

"O'er The Ramparts We Watch. United States Army Air Forces," 1941–1945. (Office for Emergency Management, Office of War Information. National Archives Identifier 515097. Local Identifier 44-PA-1434.)

In my youth, I had shunned math as a scourge for others to suffer. That lunacy nearly did me in. I struggled to keep up with the math offerings and had to seek constant help. I handled the other courses with comparative ease, but every free moment on weekends was filled not with fun and frolic, but with math studies. It was perhaps best that I spent my time on math. The Des Moines area was unique in that it was the site of Fort Des Moines, an ancient military post that was now serving a singular purpose. It was, in fact, the basic training installation for twelve thousand eager young Women's Army Corps recruits who were undergoing their initial military training just as we had at Lincoln.

The prospects inherent in this auspicious situation were, for an eighteen-year-old, simply mind-blowing. We were four hundred aviation students out-womaned at a ratio of thirty-to-one, and we often joked about what would happen to us if the WACS as they were called ever escaped from their stronghold and came after us. There was much fantasizing and not a little bit of wistfulness attached to the contemplation of being torn limb from limb by a horde of sex-crazed young women. To our great disappointment, it never happened.

About two weeks into our CTD experience, our billet was changed from the Sigma Alpha Epsilon House to the top floor of a Methodist church several blocks from frat row. The billet was very satisfactory save for Sunday mornings when the bells were tolled to summon the faithful to worship. For those of us who had heavily indulged in beer the previous night, the bells were highly distressing, and we reported the problem to our commanding officer. He resolved the situation in typical CO fashion by mandating that we who had complained "get our asses out of the sack" and attend church services every Sunday. My bald-faced lie about being Buddhist fell on deaf ears, and my barracks brothers and I could be found each Sunday morning in a front pew before the adoring gaze of the local Methodists.

With my math skills improving, my entire academic outlook brightened in the closing weeks of CTD. Worry and concern were replaced with the great expectation of flight training. Everything we had endured was pointing us to the moment when we would strap ourselves into Cub Cruisers and, with our instructors, take to the skies. *How would we react to the aggressive handling of an airplane? Would we puke our chance away in a brown paper bag? Would we succeed or fail?* Admitted or not, these questions bedeviled each of us. No one was exempted from the threat of washing out, and the prospect of watching dreams we had pursued like some sort of Holy Grail slip through our fingers was heart stopping.

The magic day arrived on 30 June 1943. It was a sunny morning, and the bus ride to the field seemed endless. Each of us reported to an instructor waiting close to his particular Cub Cruiser. In the next three days, we would receive ten hours of flight instruction designed to discover any deficiency that might diminish our prospects of flying.

The Cub Cruiser was a benign little thing. Composed of aluminum tubing and skin-tight fabric, it was built like a buxom ingénue in a too-snug sweater. Before beginning, we were given a rather extended explanation of this little puddle-jumper's parts and particular flight characteristics, along with a concentration on the importance of the preflight check.

No aircraft should ever be flown without a preflight check. It is simply as basic as fastening a seat belt. The preflight check assures the pilot that the nuts and bolts essential to the aircraft's structure are present and accounted for. The complexity of the preflight will vary from airplane to airplane. In some cases, the items to be checked may seem innocuous; others can mean the difference between life and death.

Piper J-5 Cub Cruiser. (Ahunt photo, public domain.)

The instructor explained the basic controls universal to all aircraft: a rudder controls yaw, an elevator or horizontal stabilizer controls pitch, and ailerons control roll. These three flight controls, appropriately coordinated, make an airplane dance. Misused or improperly applied, these same three controls can result in a flight ending tragically.

Climbing into an airplane cockpit heightens one's focus and alerts the senses. There is the smell of aviation fuel, sweat, hydraulic fluid, ethylene glycol, rubber, plastic, leather, the high-cut residue of lacquer, old cigarette smoke, and lurking trepidation. For me, it's like the faint scent of perfume behind a pretty girl's ear—a bit erotic, a bit evocative, and totally engaging. The first moment I climbed into the little Cub Cruiser, I knew it was a place I should be.

We began with shallow turns, maintaining level flight, establishing the airplane's proper attitude for climbing or descending, and practicing recovery from power-on/power-off stalls. A stall occurs when the aircraft is forced into a condition in which it can no longer maintain the lift required to stay in the air. The stall is analogous to the lack of power an automobile experiences when it is forced to climb a hill that is too steep. In a stall, the aircraft becomes unstable and invariably falls into the legendary tailspin of fact and legend. There is no question that my first intentional tailspin was the most significant maneuver of the entire flight-instruction experience, just as the first accidental spin is very likely to be a pilot's last significant flight experience.

A STALL IS A LOSS OF LIFT AND INCREASE IN DRAG THAT OCCURS WHEN AN AIRCRAFT IS FLOWN AT AN ANGLE OF ATTACK GREATER THAN THE ANGLE FOR MAXIMUM LIFT. IF RECOVERY FROM A STALL IS NOT EFFECTED IN A TIMELY AND APPROPRIATE MANNER BY REDUCING THE ANGLE OF ATTACK, A SECONDARY STALL AND/OR SPIN MAY RESULT. ALL SPINS ARE PRECEDED BY A STALL ON AT LEAST PART OF THE WING.

~ US DEPARTMENT OF TRANSPORTATION
FEDERAL AVIATION ADMINISTRATION, 1991

After explaining the mechanics of a spin, the instructor cleared the area by circling to ensure no other aircraft were in the vicinity. The next three minutes were special. From level flight, the instructor pulled up the nose of the little plane, and our airspeed began to drop off dramatically. Something was going to happen. There was a sudden hollow sound as the prop gasped for air and the wing lost its life-giving lift. Buffeting and shaking became all too pronounced as if we were riding over a very rough road; then, without warning, the left wing suddenly dropped, and we were in a tailspin that would continue until we effected recovery or slammed into the ground.

I suddenly found myself forced sideways in the cockpit, disoriented and scared, grabbing for anything I could hold on to, with the nose of the Cub Cruiser pointing straight down and spinning like hell towards some farmer's cornfield. In the early days of aviation, this spin would have been a death sentence. It's impossible to reckon how many early pilots died trying to recover from an accidental tailspin. The first recorded tailspin recovery—in 1912—was made purely by chance. The lucky aviator was English Navy pilot Lieutenant Wilfred Parke. Out of the depths of his panic, the mystery was finally solved.

At this very moment, however, I wasn't terribly interested in the history of spin recovery—only in how to stop this machine from spinning into the landscape and killing us both. From over my shoulder, I heard the instructor shout in my ear, "OPPOSITE RUDDER" as the rudder bar slammed over to the right; then, "FORWARD STICK" as he jammed the stick aggressively forward; and finally, "NEUTRALIZE" as he pulled the stick gently back. The little Cruiser stopped its wild gyrations, and we resumed normal flight. Those three control movements, aggressively executed and in that precise order, have virtually ended the menace of tail-spinning aircraft.

Despite my momentary terror, the spin in the little Cub Cruiser had been totally predictable and equally harmless. In some aircraft, namely those with a concentration of weight toward the rear of the fuselage, recovery from a tailspin can become not only very difficult but, at times, impossible. In such cases, the airplane exhibits a flat spinning characteristic. Such was the case with the Bell P-39 Airacobra, where the center of gravity was far aft because the engine was situated behind the pilot. Should the P-39 enter a spin, the manufacturer's spin recovery procedure was simple and direct: BAIL OUT!

Bell P-39F-1-BE Airacobra. (US Air Force photo.)

Before the ten-hour flight instruction phase was over, I was entering and recovering from spins strictly on my own, with complete confidence and without wide-eyed terror and ill-suppressed screams.

Our College Training Detachment session was completed on 3 July 1943. We boarded a train for Santa Ana, California, for the next phase: preflight training and classification. I found myself thinking less of home and much more about stick, throttle, rudder, and the airplanes that I was now sure I could fly.

There would be many tailspins in my future, both literally and figuratively. Some recoveries would be simple; many would be very difficult indeed. In the meantime, I had scored a lot of college credits in my three months in Des Moines. No WACs had molested me or any of my flying colleagues, but I was on my way back to California, and best of all, I was getting paid a dollar and ten cents a day to pursue something I loved.

I felt myself to be the luckiest guy in the world.

In retrospect, after seventy years, I still do.

TWENTY-FIVE

*ABOUT FOUR HOURS FROM LOS ANGELES,
IT IS HOT, AND WE'RE DAMN TIRED OF
RIDING, RIDING, RIDING ON THE TRAIN
FOR THREE FULL DAYS AND NIGHTS...*
~ FROM A LETTER WRITTEN HOME TO MY FAMILY, JULY 6, 1943

It's about 1,600 miles from Des Moines, Iowa, to Los Angeles, California. Unlike the trip from Oakland to Lincoln, the train ride west was less arduous, and the rolling stock was in far better condition than the rattler that took us east. There were many stops along the way: at sidings where priority freight sped past and in towns where local girls and young women offered coffee, doughnuts, and smiles under the watchful eyes of their mothers. At times, the hospitality was passed out in sunshine, at other times, in falling rain. Every stop we made, someone turned out to greet us—just another example of a nation welded together by determination, pride, and graciousness.

Scene from *Report from Nebraska, North Platte Canteen, August 1945*. (Department of Defense. Department of the Army. Office of the Chief Signal Officer. Online Public Access of the National Archives. Identifier: 20069. Local Identifier: 111-ADC-6284.)

We reached Los Angeles on 6 July 1943. Pete Mignin and I sat at a café table outside the LA train station while we waited to be loaded on buses for transportation to Santa Ana. The warm sun reminded us both that we were about as far as we could get from Lincoln and Des Moines. But as Pete and I were sipping coffee, a deadly drama was playing out in near total darkness on the other side of the world....

The New Georgia Sound approximately bisects the Solomon Islands. It was nicknamed "the Slot" because of the heavy warship traffic (Allied and Japanese) that coursed through its waters. It was also the site of ongoing critical naval battles between the combatant navies. The Japanese used it to supply their forces on Guadalcanal. It was the job of the allied navies of the United States, Great Britain, Australia, and New Zealand to stop and destroy any Japanese vessels transiting its waters.

USS *Helena* fatally damaged in combat at Kula Gulf. (US Navy photo from the Naval Historical Center, Collection of Vice Admiral Walden L. Ainsworth. Photo #: NH 76496.)

On this particular night,[58] three United States light cruisers, *Honolulu*, *St. Louis*, and *Helena*, intercepted a group of Japanese destroyers intent on a supply mission to Guadalcanal. In the ensuing battle, three torpedoes struck the USS *Helena*, fatally damaging her. One torpedo hit the forward engine room—the battle station of my dear friend Ray Paddock.

Ray was killed in the blast along with fifty of his shipmates.

My mother received a poignant letter from his widow following the sinking of Ray's ship, a copy of which she forwarded to me. I was deeply touched by its content and how she expressed her sorrow about the loss that had suddenly assailed her life. She spoke of fate and of the terrible, weighty cloak of grief that she'd been forced to wear.

The letter from Ray's widow reflected the monstrous sadness that blanketed nearly every town and hamlet on the globe. Brought about by the unspeakable evils of Germany, Japan, Italy, and their small herd of evil doers, death, grief, and mourning had become a way of life that would infect souls and cities everywhere. I saved and now hold Ray's widow's letter in my hand. It has been over seventy years since its writing, but the anguish and grief it expresses are timeless.

Santa Ana Preflight School was a sweatshop of constant physical and mental exercises designed to probe and poke at our bodies and minds and discern what made us tick. We were informed that the results of the classification process would be posted on Saturday, 24 July. These results would determine whether we would be pilots, navigators, or gunners; and of course, those results were constantly on our minds. We arose every morning at 0500 and drilled, picked weeds, or took tests all day long. This was our daily routine, and there seemed to be no end to it. I wrote a letter home a couple of days before the classification notices were posted and told my family, "If I wash out, it won't be because of lack of effort…I've put everything I have into this thing, and I'll take my chances."

I pulled sixteen hours of KP on the big day, so I couldn't check the board until late that night. Nobody was around; and standing in the dark, I recognized this was a day of destiny in my life. A single bare bulb illuminated the bulletin board as I stepped up to check the list. Almost immediately, I picked out my name with those classified as pilots. I'd come a long way since the days when Art Nelsen and I flew our balsa models off his back porch.

Santa Ana Army Air Base gated entrance. (From *Army Air Forces Training Command Manual*, ca 1943.)

I wrote home several times after the classification notice went up. My letters were filled with empathy for friends who hadn't made the grade. Some of the guys I'd started out with on the train to Lincoln had washed out, and their future was now Gunnery School. Most would become proficient as waist or turret gunners on B-17s and B-24s. And while I was entering Primary Flight Training, they would be receiving orders assigning them to heavy bomber units in Europe or the Pacific. We all had started with the same hopes and dreams. Knowing how desperately I wanted to succeed, I could imagine the pain and disappointment that would affect many of them for the rest of their lives.

Flying Fortress (B-17F)		Liberator (B-24D)	
Length	74'9"	Length	66'
Wing span	103'10"	Wing span	110'
Vertical fin height	19'	Vertical fin height	18'
Gross weight	60,000 lbs	Gross weight	60,000 lbs
Bomb load (average)	5,000 lbs	Bomb load (average)	8,000 lbs
Cruising speed	211 mph	Cruising speed	225 mph
Horsepower	4800	Horsepower	4800
Armament .50 cal. machine guns	12	Armament .50 cal. machine guns	10

Airplane configurations and locations of crews in heavy bombers. (From *Target Germany: The U.S. Army Air Forces Story of the VIII Bomber Command's First Year over Europe, 1944.*)

There was little time to dwell on the results. For those of us who were at last classified as Aviation Cadets of Squadron 44-D, the drilling and studies were endless, utilizing every hour to move us ahead. Our classes ran from 0700 till 1200. Physical training (PT) was from 1300 to 1400, drill from 1400 to 1530. Retreat was from 1600 until 1700, then mess and study until lights out. The courses were steeped in practicality for an aspiring military pilot: Aircraft and naval recognition that required instantaneous identification of friendly and enemy aircraft and ships, more advanced math as it pertained to navigation computations, and Morse code rounded out the curriculum, with a bit of theory of flight and examination of various aircraft engine types thrown in.

Although demanding and fast paced, my studies came on rather well. While my weakness in math still required extra effort, two areas of study were pushovers for me: aircraft recognition and Morse code. The countless airplane sketches I had done over the years allowed me to recognize different aircraft at once with only minimal details, and learning Morse code also was effortless. I attribute this to my experiences as a drummer in a dance band during high school and college—there's a rhythmic correlation between beating a drum and tapping a telegraph key. We were required to receive and send messages at a rate of fourteen words per minute—a very moderate rate of speed but complicated for some to achieve, and many of the new cadets had difficulty. Toward the end of Preflight, it became known that some cadets had paid instructors to change their scores. It was an ugly situation that resulted in the disqualification of those individual cadets involved and demotions for their instructors.

Two of us in our squadron were recognized as the top guys in aircraft recognition. My rival was not one of my favorites. He was a bit of a posturist, if there is such a word, and he bragged about his many areas of knowledge. It was decided that the two of us should go head to head in what came to be known as "The Mother-of-All-Aircraft-Recognition Showdowns."

For classroom purposes, photos of aircraft and ships were flashed on a screen for a period of a tenth of a second. For our competition, the time was reduced to a

Grumman F4F Wildcat fighters in tactical formation, mid-1943. (US Naval History and Heritage Command photograph #: NH 97484 [Rear Admiral Samuel Eliot Morison files].)

General Motors FM-2 "Wildcat" fighter undergoing flight-testing, late 1943. (US Naval History and Heritage Command photograph #: 80-G-224669.)

rather phenomenally short flash of light that was totally demanding and challenging.

The moderator, who was our instructor, began flashing images of aircraft on the screen in a darkened room; and we responded by writing the name of the aircraft, the manufacturer, and the wingspan of the particular aircraft as it flashed onscreen before us. The duel continued for some time until the last slide was projected and the room lights turned on. Our lists were identical until a crucial slide about halfway through the program. My opponent identified the aircraft pictured as a Grumman F4F Wildcat. That had been my original impression, but I had picked up an aberration that Gordon had missed.

In the flash of an instant, I noticed that the vertical fin and rudder seemed a bit out of scale. The minor variation revealed to me that the aircraft was not a Grumman F4F Wildcat, but was indeed the almost-identical FM-2 "Wildcat," a product of General Motors. I had won. There was no prize—only the monstrous satisfaction I felt in winning, and at the time, it was immensely important to me. Quite obviously, it still is.

Gordon and I never talked much after that. I had punctured his balloon, and it was pure triumph.

Advancement to Aviation Cadet status meant an increased in my monthly pay rate to the lofty sum of eighty-five dollars a month, most of which I sent home.

My academic progress continued to be a checkerboard of success and mediocrity. Typically, one of my letters reported a math score of 70...barely passing, along with two scores of 100 each in aircraft recognition, a subject in which I continued to excel.

SECTION III

NOMENCLATURE, CARE AND CLEANING, AND SAFETY DEVICES OF AUTOMATIC PISTOL, CALIBER .45, M1911

■ 64. The automatic pistol, caliber .45, M1911, is a recoil-operated, magazine-fed, self-loading, hand weapon. The magazine holds 7 rounds. The pistol weighs about 2½ pounds. (See fig. 13.)

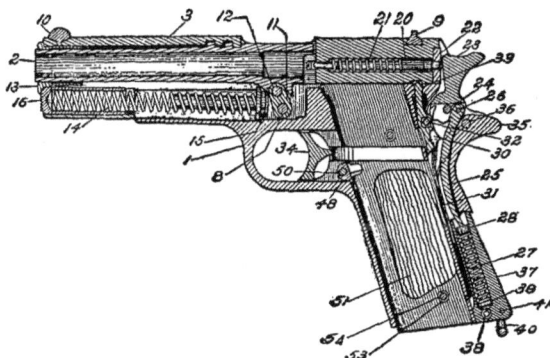

FIGURE 13.—Longitudinal section of pistol, showing component parts in assembled position.

a. The method of disassembling your pistol given below is sufficient for cleaning purposes. You should not attempt more detailed disassembling until you have received instruction from your officers or noncommissioned officers.

Automatic Pistol, Caliber .45, M1911. (*Basic Field Manual, Soldier's Handbook.* United States War Department, 1941.)

Marksmanship training at Santa Ana involved instruction in the nomenclature and firing of the Browning .30-caliber machine gun; the Thompson submachine gun; the small-bore rifle; and the Automatic Pistol, Caliber .45, M1911.

Early on, Pop had taught me how to handle a rifle and a Colt revolver; and I had been on the small-bore rifle team at Hill's Military Academy under the tutelage of Sergeant Jennings, a regular Army Infantryman and renowned sharpshooter. At Lakeside School, I had joined the rifle club and shot competitively with the Winchester Model 52 (the premier target rifle of its time), so a trip to the firing range was not a new experience for me. I qualified as Marksman with the small-bore rifle and was top qualifier in our squadron with the .45 automatic pistol.

For all of my accomplishments at Preflight School, the one that gained me lasting fame was a competition to design a Squadron 44-D Insignia. The honor included painting the winning design on a large piece of plywood to be hung outside the orderly room. During this artistic adventure, I was relieved of all drill exercises and PT, which of course delighted me. Painting very slowly and with an extremely small brush, I worked this gig for all it was worth. My CO finally determined that I wasn't painting the *Mona Lisa* and insisted I speed up the process so I could do more drilling and KP; but in a rare stroke of good fortune, we got a new CO, an art lover who appreciated me for what I was: a "Leonardo in khakis."

The Squadron 44-D Duck Insignia looked great when it was unveiled on the exterior tarpaper wall of the orderly room. Not exactly *The Last Supper*, but it worked well for me. After that, the new CO set me to work painting numbers on the barracks and landscaping the area around the orderly room. Then there was some light carpentry to be done in the barracks and in the office. In all, it was a bonanza of special duties that kept me from pots-'n-pans hell and hated PT. My special detail would last until nearly the time we left Santa Ana; and until this day, I am truly grateful for the change of command, which made it possible for my artistic skills to flourish.

Toward the end of August, I obtained a weekend pass to meet a buddy in Los Angeles. Gil Schaller and I had been friends at Roosevelt High School, and he was in the infantry and stationed at Camp Roberts.

We did LA properly. Since we both loved Big Band music, we hit some famous venues like the Palladium, where Jimmy Dorsey was playing; Earl Carroll's, which featured Stan Kenton and his orchestra; and the Coconut Grove at the Ambassador Hotel. It was a great evening; and for a while, we forgot about PT and close-order drill. We had also forgotten about planning on a place to sleep that night and only by chance checked the desk at the Ambassador for the possibility of getting a room. There was one room available: a deluxe suite.

The manager looked at us and said we could have it for eleven bucks a night; however, when we explained that we were just a couple of poor GIs and asked if he could give us a break, he let us have that beautiful suite, fit for a king, for six dollars and seventy-five cents! It was probably the best deal in the whole state of California.

Preflight School was coming to a close. We got word that we'd be leaving for Primary School about the first of

October, so a bunch of us got together and planned a big squadron party and dance for our last full weekend in Santa Ana. The squadron raised $2,000.00 to rent the Biltmore Bowl and hire a dance band for the evening. It was all money we'd made the hard way—out of our paychecks—and there were a lot of days spent dreaming about the big blowout. A cadet friend lined me up with his sister as a date. She was beautiful in the black-and-white photo he'd shown me. I talked to her a couple of times on the phone, and she sounded just as good as she looked. Obviously, it would be a great party.

A lot of hostility had begun to surface between service personnel and local Hispanic men in Los Angeles, and 1943 was a bad year for race relations. It was also the year of the zoot suit craze. These suits, characterized by baggy, peg-bottomed pants and wide, padded, very long suit coats, had become a fashion statement for many young Hispanic and African-American locals. They had also become a red flag for soldiers, sailors, and Marines. By late spring, the situation was very tense, particularly in downtown Los Angeles. As a result, on 7 June 1943, military commanders declared the city of Los Angeles off limits to all service personnel.

The ban remained and effectively cancelled the possibility of our squadron party. To rub salt in the wound, the booking agent declared bankruptcy and took off with all the dough we'd raised to put on the gig. It was a real downer for everyone.

I never got to dance with the pretty girl in the black-and-white Kodak glossy.

Too bad. We would have made a lovely couple.

TWENTY-SIX

On 28 September, we got word that we would be transferred to the small valley town of Visalia for Primary Flight Training. Everybody rushed for a road map, and we discovered it to be about 240 miles southeast of San Francisco. Further investigation showed that the place was equipped with the Ryan PT-22, a low-wing monoplane that I would grow to love. About that same time, I received a note from my birth father. He wanted to know how I was doing. He was off somewhere, flying and fixing aircraft engines. I got in touch with him, we exchanged pleasantries, and that was about it.

We left Santa Ana on Friday, 1 October. Before departing, we stood at attention in front of our barracks. For the last time, I looked at the orderly room. That work detail had bought me three and a half solid weeks of escape from close-order drill and KP. For the first time, I noticed the squadron insignia—my Squadron Duck—was hung crooked. It didn't bother me at all. Somebody in the next bunch could fix it. I was going flying!

Invariably, I had been the youngest serviceman in any group of my peers. To keep up, I was forced to fit a mold that was older than my years and experiences. It was not an easy role to fill. Somehow, I muddled through. Lincoln, Des Moines, and Santa Ana had provided an arc of learning opportunities for me. Through the bifocals of my ninety years, I look back on these experiences as being not only places in time, but also as powerful triggers that soldered me irrevocably into the man I have become. When I left Santa Ana, the weld bead had been fired. I would be forever removed from a close affiliation with family and home. The world and our nation expected extraordinary things from us, and I was joined in a new bond with a Band of Brothers.

We arrived in Visalia on 4 October, just sixteen days before my nineteenth birthday. The little town and its adjoining airport were as far from Government Issue as one could get. Air Force Primary Schools were run on cost-plus-ten-percent contracts with private enterprise companies. Under the provisions of these contracts, the more the operators spent, the more they profited. This practice was not good for the American taxpayer, but it often provided a paradise for participants in the flying programs.

Our "barracks" were small individual dorms, very much like what one might find in a private school setting. Each dorm was a separate entity containing space for twelve occupants in air-conditioned comfort. We slept on innerspring mattresses bordered by modern furniture with study desks and every other amenity one might imagine. The grounds around our compound were covered with rich, green grass and flowerbeds, beautifully maintained by paid workers. Our days of weeding and policing up cigarette butts were, thankfully, left behind.

Locals referred to our new post as Sequoia Field, but its official designation was Eighth Army Air Forces Flight Training Detachment. Visalia is located in the heart of the San Joaquin Valley, a large, lush landscape of small towns and very rich farmland. It is that part of California's Central Valley situated south of the Sacramento-San Joaquin Delta. Due to its climate and terrain, it was literally stuffed with flight-training and fully operational military airfields, and there also were a number of auxiliary fields used for landing and takeoff practice, so the skies over the valley were alive with training planes and other military air traffic. Sadly, midair collisions were not uncommon. One of our first and most important lessons was to "keep (our) heads out of the cockpit and clear (our) immediate flight before attempting any maneuvers." It was life or death advice.

The PT-22 aircraft we would be flying in Primary School was developed from a family of light, sport trainer (ST) aircraft built by Ryan Aeronautical Company of San Diego, California. The first model, a sleek, aluminum-clad low-wing monoplane was first flown in June 1934. It was the brainchild of T. Claude Ryan who had previously participated in the design and production of Lindbergh's famous *Spirit of St. Louis*.

As a kid, I had built models of the Ryan ST and considered it to be one of the most beautiful small aircraft I had ever seen. The Ryan ST had a sleek, inverted, inline Menasco engine that gave it the look of a classy racer. To me, it was the Cadillac convertible of small airplanes. However, the inverted engine had proved troublesome in early models, and our PT-22s sported a Kinner radial engine that was more reliable but less beautiful than the inline engine of the Ryan ST. Although I loved our PT-22s, the Kinner radial was equipped with a short exhaust stack on each of its five cylinders. Underway, it emitted a clatter of explosions that quite literally destroyed the romance and raciness of our little machines. The Kinner was described as a "rough running engine."[59] That was a masterpiece of understatement.

PT-22 Ryan. (*Primary Flying Students' Manual* prepared by the Army Air Forces Training Command.)

The cockpit was amply large to allow ingress and egress while wearing a parachute that was absolutely required on all flights. It was the kind of airplane that you could put on, like a well-worn sweater, and feel comfortable. The controls were standard and well arranged, and there was a strong rollover bar that would protect a pilot in case of a nose-over accident.

Communication between the front-seat student and the rear-seat instructor was accomplished by an ancient gosport; a flexible speaking tube that stretched between the front and rear cockpits. One end was attached to the student's helmet, while the other was fitted with a small megaphone. The megaphone allowed the instructor to scream instructions and profanity through the hose and into the student's ears. At times, I feared the fury of the instructor's anger would actually melt the entire system. At other times, I prayed that it would.

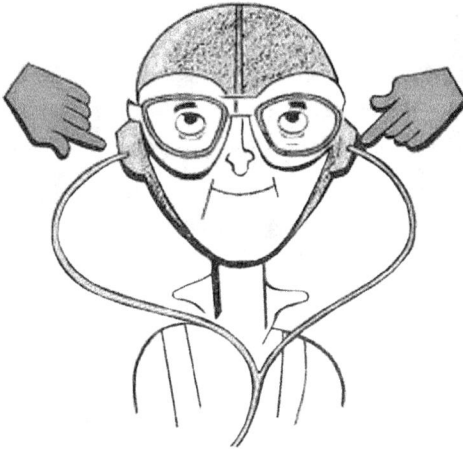

Gosport illustration. (*Primary Flying Students' Manual* prepared by the Army Air Forces Training Command.)

We began flying the day we arrived, and it was a tremendous experience for each of us. Success in the venture had become a part of our makeup, and the tenor of each day was established by how well we had done in our latest flight session. The little Ryan Recruit (as it was named) was a bit tricky, particularly on takeoffs and landings, but surely not as tippy as its counterpart, the Stearman PT-17, which had narrow landing gear and a tendency to ground loop. The nose of the Ryan projected above the pilot's line of vision when the aircraft was in a landing or three-point position, thus, partially obscuring the ground in front of the aircraft. To determine the precise distance above the ground when landing, it was necessary to look out the sides of the plane—not a major flaw, but it took some getting used to.

PT-13D Stearman. (Photo by Adrian Pingstone. Released to public domain.)

I quickly accrued nine hours flying time. I was adept at spins, stalls, and other maneuvers but still not up to snuff in my landings. I voiced my concern in letters home as well as to my instructor, Ted Acheson, who told me, "Shut up! You *worry* too much!"

I decided to follow his advice...despite the fact that some candidates were already washing out due to their apparent inabilities or discontent with a task they had so long pursued.

TWENTY-SEVEN

The weather had turned rather cold by Tuesday, 19 October 1943. We were still flying in light, summer coveralls, but I had given up wearing my heavy GI boots in favor of old-style tennis shoes. I thought the change would give me a lighter touch, particularly on takeoffs and landings. That morning, we flew out of a small, dusty auxiliary field. After landing, my instructor shouted in the gosport, "You got it."

We taxied to the edge of the runway. Acheson crawled out of the rear seat and leaned over to latch the seat belt together to prevent it from snarling the rear seat controls. Over the infamous popping of the engine he hollered, "Take her around a couple of times but come in after one landing if I wave my arms at you!" With that, he jumped down off the wing and walked to a grassy area where he sat down.

I was on my own.

Unless you have experienced a first-time solo flight, it's hard to describe it—feelings of doubt, confidence, faith, excitement, and total self-reliance blend as your mind races ahead to cope with each step: taxiing, takeoff, passes, turns, approach, and landing. The intensity is breathtaking—too profound for words. In exchange for the commitment, you are forever set apart, save for a unique few; and after completing your first solo flight, you possess a special affiliation with the sky.

Feeling never more alone than at this moment, I taxied in the familiar S pattern to the downwind end of the runway. Turning slightly into the wind, I held the brakes and went through the CIGFTPR checklist: Controls, Instruments, Gas, Flaps, Trim tabs, Pitch, Run up. I revved the engine up to 1,700 rpm and checked the magnetos: first left then both, followed by right then both. The mag drop was negligible…all OK. I advanced the throttle to full rpm, and then dropped back to a fast idle. When I released the brakes, the airplane moved slightly forward, and a touch of rudder pointed her down the runway.

There was a momentary squirm to settle myself more squarely on the chute seat pack—a movement that became an ingrained habit on every takeoff and landing in every aircraft I ever flew—then I pushed the throttle to the end of the quadrant, and the Kinner instantly broke out in that rough and ready roar that was at once ugly and reassuring. There was that bit of veering born of the engine's torque, which I cured with a slight touch of rudder pressure.

As the plane reached 60 mph, I pressed the stick forward to bring up the tail and then added some backpressure. Suddenly, the wheels cleared, and we were climbing. With only one pilot aboard, she quickly picked up speed and altitude. It was as if she'd been released from an earth-bound tether to taste the heavens that were rightfully hers. I continued to climb out to 600 feet, rolled left into a 90-degree turn, and maintained the rate of climb. At 800 feet, I executed another 90-degree left turn, decreased power to cruising rpm, and rolled the elevator trim forward for level flight. I was now on a downwind leg parallel to the runway and could look down and see that Acheson was still sitting in the grassy spot he'd chosen. By the time I was in the middle of the downwind leg, I knew I had become the master of this wonderful little airplane and the air through which we flew.

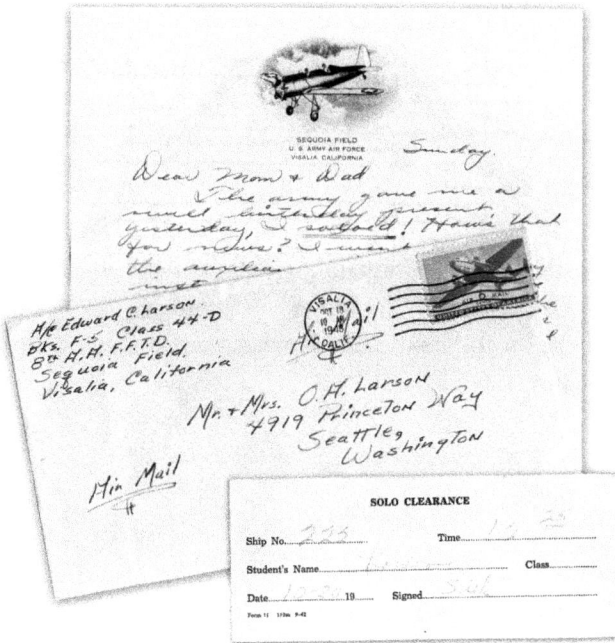

Letter home after my first solo flight. (From the author's collection.)

I had stretched the downwind leg out a bit, so I cut back the power, pulled out the carburetor heat, and then executed a 90-degree left turn onto the base leg of the traffic pattern.

After checking the glide angle and airspeed, I turned left again and lined up with the runway for final approach. Checking airspeed and glide angle yet again, I saw I was a bit short and added a squirt of power as I continued the glide angle. The ground rose to meet us as we crossed the threshold with ease and landed with a delicate bounce on the first third of the runway.

Truthfully, I don't even remember looking at Acheson to see if he waved me off. I pushed the carburetor heat control off, pushed the throttle full forward, and climbed out for a second pass. This time, I cut the downwind leg short and turned on to the base leg pretty high. I put down full flaps, and we came down like an elevator to a good landing, again in the first third of the strip. When I taxied over to Acheson, he gave me the thumbs up. Then he took the controls and flew us home.

Needless to say, I was euphoric. No longer classed a dodo, I didn't have to wear my goggles around my neck; I could put them on my helmet like any self-respecting pilot. God, what a day it had been!

The war was raging outside the periphery of our sheltered flight training detachment. Joint Allied Forces were slogging northward through heavy rains in a struggle for Rome, and it was tough going on other fronts as well.

On 14 October, the US Eighth Army Air Forces had mounted a major airstrike against the ferociously defended German ball bearing factories at Schweinfurt.

Aerial view of B-24 Liberator hit by flak over Italy. (US Army Heritage and Education Center. US Signal Corps photo AC 57043.)

Early on, losses of B-17s and their crews were so catastrophic and unsustainable that raids were abandoned until fighter cover could be provided to the bombers to and from targets. (US Air Force photo.)

In the tragic raid, a staggering 77 B-17s were completely destroyed, with another 121 aircraft damaged. The losses were so catastrophic and unsustainable that such raids were abandoned until fighter cover could be provided to the bombers all the way to and from targets. The protective angels would come in the form of P-51 Mustangs with drop tanks. But on that fateful "Black Thursday," the angels were not yet available to stop the carnage. Moreover, there was a heavier, more tragic cost than lost and damaged aircraft: In this single raid, 590 airmen were killed, and 65 were taken as prisoners of war—a sure sign that we were badly needed.

Morning flights in late October were tough. The cockpit of the Ryan was pretty much a deep freeze, and frozen hands don't contribute much to excellence in flying. Lo and behold, within the week, we were issued heavy, fleece-lined flying suits, and things looked better for us fledgling pilots. We were becoming rather proficient in the small trainers, with plenty of confidence and a longing to fly "more airplane." Flights were now experimental in nature, and we were trying more to prove we were hot stuff. I was never out front in courage or aggressiveness, but I loved the aerobatics and occasionally stretching the airplane a bit.

One particular morning, I was attempting to gain proficiency in executing the Immelmann Turn, a maneuver that combines a half loop with a half roll at the top to simultaneously achieve altitude and change in flight direction. The maneuver was rather widely used in dogfights during World War I and was named for German fighter pilot Max Immelmann, whom I assure you was a far better pilot than I was.

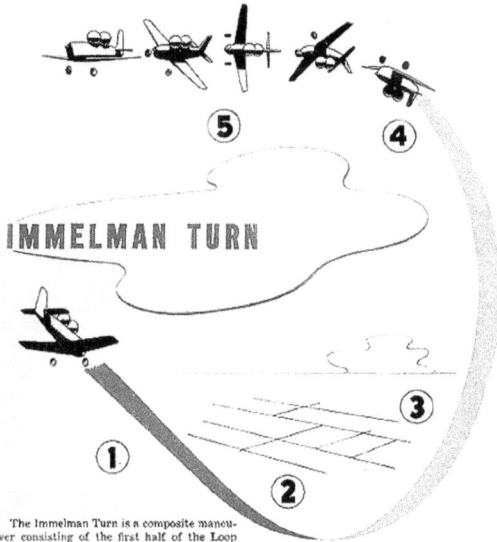

IMMELMAN TURN

The Immelman Turn is a composite maneuver consisting of the first half of the Loop and the last half of the Slow Roll. The airplane reverses direction 180 deg.

PROCEDURE

1. Place the airplane in a dive to obtain speed approximately 50 mph above cruising.
2. Use the throttle the same as in a loop.
3. Begin the maneuver the same as a loop.
4. On the top of the loop, when the nose is approximately 20 deg. above the horizon, ease the stick diagonally forward, which will stop the loop and start the roll. At the same

time, apply rudder pressure in the opposite direction from aileron pressure.
5. Continue aileron, stick, and rudder action as in the last half of the Slow Roll.

YOUR INSTRUCTOR WILL BE WATCHING FOR THESE ERRORS: Failure to co-ordinate controls, use of abrupt rather than smooth control movements, failure to gain sufficient initial airspeed, pulling up too abruptly in first half of loop pulling up too slowly, loss of orientation.

115

Immelman (sic) Turn instructions. (*Primary Flying Students' Manual* prepared by the Army Air Forces Training Command.)

On my first attempt, I dove to pick up airspeed, which is essential to completing the maneuver, and pulled the Ryan into a tight loop. As I continued the loop with the aircraft vertical to the ground, I reasoned that increased backpressure on the stick might speed up the loop portion of the maneuver and leave a bit more airspeed to roll out at the maximum height of the half loop. At maximum height, the aircraft would, of course, be upside down.

Things were going well, and the ground was rolling over my head as I increased the stick pressure even more, but just as this great pilot was about to accomplish the perfect Immelmann Turn, the little Ryan, having suffered enough, began violently shaking and buffeting. I suddenly found myself in an inverted, high-speed stall in which the airplane was no longer flying, but simply flopping around like a dead duck. In such moments of discovery, the movements of man and machine become confusing and unpredictable, and I still cannot describe the aircraft's gyrations. I only know that moments later, we had degraded to a rather vigorous left tailspin, and I was headed for someone's rice field about 2,500 feet below. With the airplane in a left tailspin, I was in familiar territory, and it was a simple thing to affect recovery as I had done a hundred times before. It had been an intriguing experiment conducted at sufficient altitude to insure my survival.

I never did learn to perform the operation properly in the little Ryan and finally just quit trying.

About two weeks before we completed our program at Visalia, I was flying southeast of the field on a cold morning when suddenly, a flashing Aldis lamp called me in for an emergency. I entered the approach pattern following several other aircraft and landed without incident. We parked our airplanes and congregated to learn the nature of the problem. We were advised that there had been two fatal

PT-22 crashes at other Primary fields in the previous two days. All our aircraft were grounded until further notice.

Later that afternoon, we were notified that the cause of the crashes had been identified: A heavy aluminum tube that formed the leading-edge structure of the horizontal stabilizer had fractured at the site of a rivet hole. This fracture had allowed the stabilizer to fall off one of the aircraft while in flight and had caused the horizontal stabilizer to fold upward against the vertical stabilizer and rudder on the second downed plane. The result in both cases had been catastrophic; the pilots were killed.

Two airplanes on our flight line exhibited the fatal flaw. When I examined the beginnings of the telltale fractures on our aircraft, I thought about all the loops, snap rolls, and tailspins we had practiced in the skies over Visalia. We had been very fortunate indeed. A flurry of activity on the flight line followed as mechanics installed small transparent plastic windows over the section of riveted tubing where the failures had occurred. In two days, we were flying again. Needless to say, a close visual inspection of the horizontal stabilizer's leading edge became part of our preflight check on each and every airplane we flew. Being a natural coward, I thought often about the incident and handled the aircraft a bit more delicately than I had done before.

Two days before we left Visalia, Instructor Acheson and his wife invited his five students over for a picnic dinner. We chipped in to buy him a very nice little cocker spaniel as a family pet. Ted, his wife, and their little boy were delighted with our gift, and we enjoyed a wonderful evening with hot dogs, potato salad, and the new family member. As we were leaving, Ted called me aside. In a quiet voice, he confided to me that the two check pilots who had evaluated me in the air had both advised him that my flying skills were "near perfect." Self-serving as it seems, I have never forgotten that praise.

Instructor and Primary Class 44-D flight students at Visalia. (PROPWASH Class 44-D Graduation Book. From the author's collection.)

Primary Flight Training was over. All the worry and concern had faded into the often-cloudy skies over Visalia. I left with exactly the required sixty-five hours and the knowledge that I'd cleared another hurdle in the most difficult challenge I'd faced in all my nineteen years.

It would be fifty years before I climbed into another Ryan PT-22 cockpit and cranked up the Kinner with its raucous and ragged sound. The thrill was still there...just as it had been the day of my first solo flight.

Such feelings never fade.

TWENTY-EIGHT

W e were transported to Air Force Basic Flight School in Chico, California, on 7 December. In my first letter home following transfer, I described the place as "damn near as cold as Nebraska." The small university town where our base was located lies at the north end of the Sacramento Valley, close to the foothills of the Sierra Nevada and Cascade mountain ranges. It is one of the most fertile agricultural areas in the world; and for a time, it seemed one of the coldest. We were back to living conditions that could only be described as strictly GI. The barracks smacked of Lincoln, absent only Sergeant Maddox, our old drill instructor. There was, however, some excitement in the air. We would be flying new, bigger, and faster airplanes. Our new steed was the Vultee BT-13 Valiant; and it would prove to be a handful.

The BT-13 was first delivered to the US Air Forces in 1940 and became the basic trainer for fledgling Army and Navy aviators. Weighing more than three times the little PT-22, the BT was a big plane for a just-beginning pilot, and it looked and felt like it. The aircraft, vastly more complex than our primary trainers, was equipped with a radio;

a two-speed propeller; and a nine-cylinder, 450 hp Pratt & Whitney radial engine—a far cry from the 160 hp Kinners we had flown in Primary. The first time I looked in the cockpit, I wondered if I could ever get the plane off the ground; it seemed as though there were bells and whistles all over the thing.

Vultee BT-13 Valiant. (US Air Force photo.)

A couple of days after we arrived at Chico, we began flying. It was getting very close to mid-December; and although we were in California, the next few months' weather would not be all that great for budding pilots. With the schedule we had to keep, the transition to these new planes was a bit worrisome, and I indicated some feelings of intimidation in my early letters home. The BT was described as an unforgiving airplane. There was no viciousness about it, but it took some handling, and our instructors were regular Air Force pilots—tough and demanding; so there was no gentleness in the cockpit. There was no time for it.

The minimum time to solo the BT was five hours of dual instruction. Slow learner that I was, I think I soloed at seven and a half hours during the second week of flying and ground school. It wasn't a good situation. The weather fluctuated between so-so and bad and was getting worse. The change to the more complex and demanding airplanes was a big step, and the lack of continuity in flying each day was a definite handicap to everyone involved. The stress level was building, and that is always counterproductive in the learning process.

A couple of days after my solo flight, I took off and headed north to practice some air work. Out of the open canopy on my right, the Sierras rose from the valley in a litany of massive snow-covered peaks. To my left, the coastal range lay warmly lit by the morning sun. There were no other airplanes in sight, and the blue above was filled with cumulus clouds resembling huge, fluffy marshmallows— white for sure, but shot through with golden sunlight, giving the whole of them the aura of some sort of cloud castle—like a Maxfield Parrish painting at its best.

As I looked about, in that moment, I experienced a sudden transformation, a true out-of-body euphoria, a sense of unity with all that was happening around me...a feeling so profound, so intense, that I remember it completely as if it just happened minutes ago. Truly spiritual, it left me stunned by the peacefulness and sense of belonging I felt— an epiphany that rendered me forever different somehow from what I had been before I left the ground that day. Such an experience would be badly needed in days ahead.

Airplane crashes seldom result from one catastrophic mistake or mechanical failure. Rather, they are the culmination of a series of insidious incidents or errors that, when linked together, form a synergistic trail to disaster. An unflipped switch, a valve turned slightly short of its proper detent, inattention to an oil pressure gauge, a missing cotter pin or bolt...all these things taken individually may pose no threat whatsoever. Together, they may join to form that single event that terminates the future of a pilot and his crew.

Several days following that transformative flight, I was again flying solo and some distance from the field. It was a decent day, and the morning was enhanced by an unusual bit of sunshine. An urgent message suddenly came over the radio to all aircraft in flight: The field was closed due to an emergency.

I climbed safely above the traffic pattern—to an altitude of about 4,000 feet—and immediately noticed a plume of black smoke rising from the south end of the field. As I got closer, I could make out fire trucks and ambulances a slight distance from what I recognized immediately as a crashed and burning BT-13. Someone's luck had run out.

After circling for perhaps an hour and a half, all flying aircraft were finally cleared to land. The crash site was still a welter of trucks and emergency personnel as we parked our planes in a somber procession and quietly gathered in small groups at the edge of the field. Soon after, I got word that the crash had been a fatal one. We had lost a fellow cadet, and I had lost a good friend.

The young man who died that morning was a handsome, totally likeable kid with a host of friends and a beautiful young wife. She had traveled to Chico from her hometown to be with her young and energetic husband. The time they shared together would be woefully short. Their dreams of a future ended tragically in the blazing wreckage at the south end of the Chico runway. That morning, she was working at the Post Exchange, only a quarter of a mile away.

An examination of the wreckage indicated that the airplane had begun its takeoff run with the elevator trim control rolled completely back, forcing the airplane into an unsustainable nose up position as soon as it left the ground. In this case, the aircraft climbed vertically for perhaps two hundred feet, stalled, fell off on one wing, and hurtled, nose first, into the ground, probably under full power.

The elevator trim control on the BT-13 was a wheel about ten inches in diameter located on the left side of the cockpit in plain view of the pilot. Its purpose was to trim up the aircraft and establish a level flight attitude without the necessity of applying constant forward or rear pressure on the stick. Its neutral position for takeoff was essential, and the *T* for trim tabs was part of the CIGFTPR checklist we voiced before every takeoff.

It is impossible to imagine how or why the trim tabs were rolled back to such an unusual position. There would be no rationale for completing such an action. Perhaps a cadet getting cockpit time sought to familiarize himself with the control and experimented to see the amount of trim tab produced by an extreme nose-up setting, then neglected to return the control to a centered position. But why wasn't the trim tab setting noticed and corrected during the pilot's preflight checklist? With more experience flying the BT, the pilot might have recognized what was happening and forced the stick fully forward while returning the trim tab wheel to the centered position. But that would require near-instantaneous action on the part of the pilot; and at this point in time, we were simply not that accomplished in handling the new planes.

The loss of this young friend was a blow to all who knew him; and as the dark and stormy weather hung on through December, precluding any type of flying, a deep melancholy set in. In search of better flying conditions, our commanding officers decided to move us south.

On 11 January 1944, we arrived at sunny Victorville Army Air Field, about seventy-five miles northeast of Los Angeles. Our prospects brightened, and we resumed flying right away. Soon, we were completing our Basic Flight School requirements according to plan.

Our scheduled graduation seemed pretty well assured.

TWENTY-NINE

I started feeling pretty bad on the thirteenth of January. It was tough to fly, and it got worse. Two days later, I had a raging fever and checked in with the medics. I was immediately admitted to the hospital for a severe respiratory infection. It couldn't have happened at a worse time. Our class was scheduled for flying and ground school completion at the end of the month; at which time, we were moving on to Advanced Flight Training. We still had a whole regimen of flying and ground school to complete before then. If I didn't complete all phases, I'd be held over till the next class; or worse yet, I could wash out.

Flight training was no bed of roses, and the rotten weather we'd endured at Chico coupled with the fatal crash had affected everyone's outlook. The threat of failing to keep up or washing-out was with us night and day. The chance of being held back to the next class was equally devastating. I had shared a virtual lifetime of experiences with a bunch of guys who'd become my brothers. The thought of being left behind was a crushing blow, and I'd be damned if I was going to let it happen.

The first couple of days in the hospital, I was too sick to be very aggressive. On the third day, I awoke somewhat better but mindful that I was falling behind in air work, instruments, nighttime and formation flying, Link Trainer time, ground school, and everything else. I had to get the hell out of there. On the morning of 20 January, I finally badgered them into putting me back on flying status. The situation was pretty grim but not impossible. I had only eleven days to complete the equivalent of a whole month's flying and ground school.

There was another problem. My instructor advised me that although I'd done well before getting sick, he was concerned that I'd missed too much time to sufficiently build up my flight skills. He was wholly reluctant to go ahead, saying, "I don't want to be responsible for pushing you ahead and having something bad happen."

I begged him to let me have a check ride with the chief instructor. Finally, he agreed.

It was a pretty dicey maneuver, but I didn't realize how risky it was until I met the chief instructor on the flight line the next morning. He was a captain who obviously didn't like his job. Tall and heavy set, he was surly, overbearing, and threatening. He used a minimum of words to direct me into the cockpit. It would be a long morning in the air with this sonofabitch.

It was a warm day, and the airplane handled beautifully. Although I was not at the top of my game, we did every maneuver known to the mind of man, and I flew well. Never was there a hint from the instructor about the quality of my performance, only surly orders on what to do next. After more than an hour, we returned to the field. I entered the pattern and executed a very decent landing...not perfect, but very nice.

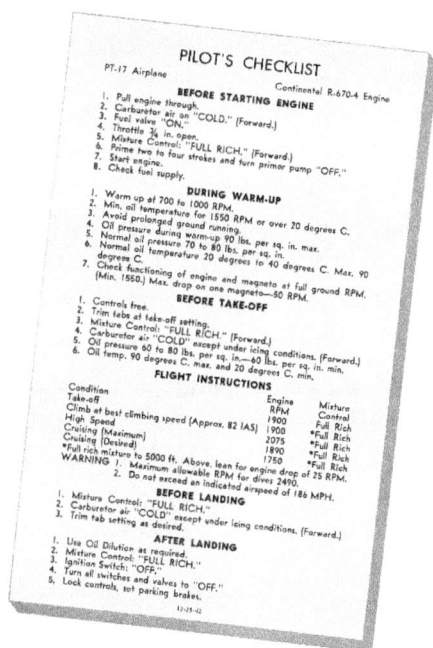

PILOT'S CHECKLIST
PT-17 Airplane
Continental R-670-4 Engine

BEFORE STARTING ENGINE
1. Pull engine through.
2. Carburetor air on "COLD." (Forward.)
3. Fuel valve "ON."
4. Throttle ¾ in. open.
5. Mixture Control: "FULL RICH." (Forward.)
6. Prime two to four strokes and turn primer pump "OFF."
7. Start engine.
8. Check fuel supply.

DURING WARM-UP
1. Warm up at 700 to 1000 RPM.
2. Min. oil temperature for 1550 RPM or over 20 degrees C.
3. Avoid prolonged ground running.
4. Oil pressure during warm-up 90 lbs. per sq. in. max.
5. Normal oil pressure 70 to 80 lbs. per sq. in.
6. Normal oil temperature 20 degrees to 40 degrees C. Max. 90 degrees C.
7. Check functioning of engine and magneto at full ground RPM. (Min. 1560.) Max. drop on one magneto—50 RPM.

BEFORE TAKE-OFF
1. Controls free.
2. Trim tabs at take-off setting.
3. Mixture Control: "FULL RICH." (Forward.)
4. Carburetor air "COLD" except under icing conditions. (Forward.)
5. Oil pressure 60 to 80 lbs. per sq. in.—40 lbs. per sq. in. min.
6. Oil temp. 90 degrees C. max. and 20 degrees C. min.

FLIGHT INSTRUCTIONS

Condition	Engine RPM	Mixture Control
Take-off		
Climb at best climbing speed (Approx. 82 IAS)	1900	Full Rich
High Speed	1900	*Full Rich
Cruising (Maximum)	2075	*Full Rich
Cruising (Desired)	1890	*Full Rich
*Full rich mixture to 5000 ft. Above, lean for engine drop of 25 RPM.	1750	*Full Rich

WARNING 1. Maximum allowable RPM for dives 2490.
2. Do not exceed an indicated airspeed of 186 MPH.

BEFORE LANDING
1. Mixture Control: "FULL RICH."
2. Carburetor air "COLD" except under icing conditions. (Forward.)
3. Trim tab setting as desired.

AFTER LANDING
1. Use Oil Dilution as required.
2. Mixture Control: "FULL RICH."
3. Ignition Switch: "OFF."
4. Turn all switches and valves to "OFF."
5. Lock controls, set parking brakes.

12-25-42

Pilot's Checklist, 1942. (Primary *Flying Students' Manual* prepared by the Army Air Forces Training Command.)

He directed me to the ramp and ordered me to taxi down a line of parked, tied down planes. Ahead was a vacant spot close to the line shack, and he gruffly ordered me to park in that location. When I reached the point where I should begin a turn to the right into the space, I pushed on the right rudder. NO RIGHT BRAKE! Fortunately, I was taxiing very slowly, so I cut the throttle and was able to stop the BT holding only the left brake.

Through the intercom, he shouted, "What the *hell* are you doing stopping *here*?!"

I picked up the microphone and responded, "Sir, the right brake isn't working."

He exploded, "Bullshit, you're in trouble because you can't follow a simple order! *I've got it!*" With that, he jammed his feet onto the rudder pedals, grabbed the stick, and rammed the throttle forward. With the sudden burst of power, the airplane rotated viciously on the left brake; in a second, we had executed a breathtaking 180-degree change in direction with our right wing narrowly missing the vertical fin and rudder of the aircraft adjacent to us.

Several line crewmen stood by with amazed looks on their faces, wondering what the hell had just happened. Meanwhile, still holding the left brake, the chief instructor shut down the engine, hopped out of the cockpit, and directed me to red X Form 1A, indicating the aircraft was not flyable because of an inoperative right brake. That was certainly no news to me.

As he started walking away, I followed. "Sir," I persisted, "can you tell me how I did?"

He continued walking. Without turning around he muttered, "Your flight check was OK."

HUA! I'd just taken one of the biggest gambles in my brief flying career, and I'd won! I was moving ahead with my brothers.

CHAPTER TWENTY-NINE

North American B-25 Mitchell. (US Air Force photo.)

Lockheed P-38J Lightning. (US Air Force photo.)

Our numbers were dwindling.

Sadly, during the last days of Basic Flight School, my class—Squadron 44-D—suffered a second fatal crash. In addition, there was an increase in the number of cadets who washed-out or requested voluntary transfers from the pilot training program. There is little doubt in my mind that the acceleration of our training and the accompanying pressures brought to bear accounted for the increase in number of those dropping out.

I was flying up to six tough hours a day, working on landings, stages, air work, night flying, and instruments; on the ground, I was in Link Trainer. On 24 January, we were scheduled to restate our preferences for the aircraft we would most like to fly in active duty. Both of my instructors advised me to pursue single-engine fighter training, probably at Luke Field in Arizona. In one of the biggest mistakes I ever made, I continued to opt for B-25s or P-38s. I would truly rue that decision in the months to come.

Our last day of actual flying and ground school was 31 January 1944. We learned the majority of us would be sent to Twin-Engine Advanced School at Stockton Field, about fifty miles southeast of Sacramento. Stockton was a quiet, rather staid little town tucked into the huge farming region of California's Central Valley. The US Army Air Forces Western Flying Training Command operated our twin-engine training facility there. It was standard GI, and I suspected it was a sort of benign place where nothing much ever happened.

I was right.

THIRTY

We arrived at Stockton on 9 February 1944. After seeing the airplanes that we'd be flying, I cursed myself for throwing away the chance at Advanced Single-Engine School. If Stockton could be described as benign, its planes were downright boring.

The Cessna AT-17 Bobcat, also designated the UC-78, was named for a small but terribly ferocious beast; however, "Pussycat" would have been a more appropriate title for this aircraft. First designed as a personal twin-engine light transport, it was pressed into military service as a cheap trainer for twin-engine neophytes—and it was exactly that. Fabric-covered, tubular-steeled, and boxy framed, it looked more like a carton used to ship an airplane rather than a plane itself. Two seven-cylinder, 245 hp Jacobs engines powered the wooden, fixed pitch props. Top speed (on a powered dive and a perfect day) was 195 mph, cruising was about 175 mph. If it sounds presumptive of me to badmouth the Bobcat, I apologize. I realize I still had plenty to learn. It's only because a fixed-pitch prop plane is like a car with a one-gear transmission—there is little adventure in it, and the Bobcat was about as far as one might get from a P-40 or P-51. But it was all we had, so we flew it.

With the advent of twin-engine training, most of the "feel" left our flying. We were learning to fly by procedures with extensive checklists covering the flight of the aircraft. This new way of piloting was different from our primary and basic training instruction. There would be no half rolls, snap rolls, or aerobatics with the Bobcat. No more weaving through cloud castles or looping the plane, canopy open, with the sky above one moment, then the earth above the next.

Cessna AT-17 Bobcat. (US Air Force photo.)

There was still plenty to learn. Radio and navigation procedures became more complex and demanding. Engine failure in a multiengine aircraft wasn't funny. Such an emergency demanded quick and precise procedures that would allow the airplane to maintain flight on one engine. Should that engine failure occur on takeoff, a pilot's skill in handling the emergency and feathering the dead engine would constitute the difference between life and death.

I soloed pretty early on the AT-17 and will say that I did not feel the same satisfaction that I had from soloing the Ryan or the BT-13. It took a little getting used to flying with someone sitting next to you all the time; although, it was clearly understood that the guy in the left seat was the guy in charge, and to the best of my knowledge, no one ever had a problem with that. We usually flew four to six hours per session, splitting the time between flying as pilot and copilot. Each position had its specific duties and responsibilities to master, and there wasn't any clowning around in the cabin. But despite the lack of excitement generated by the Bobcat, we still looked forward to becoming absolutely proficient, and we never lost sight of the fact that the "Bamboo Bomber" could kill us if we got too big for our britches.

I wrote home in mid-March that we were doing a lot of rather demanding flying, including some cross-country trips, night and day formation, constant single-engine simulation, low-frequency beam orientation, and letdowns; in fact, all the techniques that would be required in medium or heavy bomber aircraft. In addition, we frequently shot stages. These were exercises in which we were scored on how close to a designated mark on the runway we could land the airplane. In a letter home, I reported that I had scored second highest in our squadron. It really didn't make that much difference; the next time, it would be someone else. The skills learned in the AT-17 would shelter me in the months ahead on patchwork fields and in airplanes much faster, heavier, more lethal, and demanding.

Overseas, the Rome-Berlin Axis was beginning to collapse like the proverbial house of cards. Choking on their own evil, our enemies' last gasps would still maim and kill a lot of guys I held dear. There was an overwhelming desire within Squadron 44-D to raise our own small brand of hell in Europe or the Pacific. We all longed for the chance to hasten the bastards to their final, well-deserved fate. The disaster that was Pearl Harbor had aroused a sleeping giant whose terrible resolve would eventually crush the Axis powers with stunning finality. This is what we were working toward, and it was all we desired to accomplish. In late March, I advised my family that I would probably be overseas flying copilot on a medium or heavy bomber by mid-June or the first of July. It was more than a status report; in fact, it was a fervent wish.

Graduation Day for Squadron 44-D was scheduled for 15 April 1944, and it was fast approaching. Training and flying remained intense and on schedule, but each of us silently acknowledged that our goals of becoming pilots was within grasp. So much had happened; we had accomplished so much since leaving Oakland more than a year before. We had developed mentally and physically, morphing from kids into men capable of wrecking havoc on an enemy that we truly despised. I would ask the reader to understand and empathize with this terrible anger. It was born of three years' grief and suffering visited upon each of our families and the communities from which we'd come. Bodies of young men and women we had known and loved now hallowed the ground in every corner of the earth. To expect compassion from us in those years was to expect too much.

Hell-raisers over Europe: *Memphis Belle* crew, ca 1940s; one of the first B-17 bomber crews to complete twenty-five combat missions with its crew intact. (National Museum of the United States Air Force.)

Martin B-26B-55-MA Marauder (s/n 42-96142), 1944. (US Air Force photo.)

Assigned to the 596th Bomb Squadron, 397th Bomb Group, 98th Bomb Wing, 9th Bomber Command, 9th Air Force in Europe, this "X2-A" was named Dee-Feater. Note the numerous mission insignia and D-Day invasion stripes painted on the aircraft.

Signs indicated that we were closing in on graduation. On 24 March, we assembled on a grassy area adjacent to the hangers to receive orders for our next duty stations as qualified pilots of the United States Army Air Forces. It was intensely stressful knowing that our appointments would affect our entire future military careers. Where we went would establish what we would become. Most would be assigned to various bases in the country to receive transition training in B-17 and B-24 heavy bombers. Some would be sent to fields designed for training in medium bombers such as the B-25 Mitchells or B-26 Marauders. Few, if any, would be assigned to single-engine fighter transition. That had been my dream, but it was no longer within reach because of my selection of twin-engine advanced training. When my name came up, I got the best assignment I could hope for: Single-Engine Instructors' School in Taft, California. Perhaps the opportunity to fly fighters wasn't beyond my reach. Best of all, my buddy Pete Mignin was going to Taft, too.

Local haberdashers soon began delivering new officers' uniforms to the various barracks. These were all carefully hung in clothes closets in anticipation of the big day. It would have been an invitation to bad luck should they be tried on before graduation. Meanwhile, cadets' relatives were coming in for the ceremonies, and my mother arrived from Seattle to join the festivities. At 39, she was beautiful and mingled easily with my friends, instructors, and the rest of the party.

Graduation Day arrived sunny and full of promise of the rewards we had so long pursued. A morning flyover was followed by a coffee gathering during which a million military training half-truths were related with great pride, if not total candor, by long-suffering cadets. These tales of terrible trouble and travail were freely rendered to enthralled and attentive relatives and friends at a gathering that took up much of the morning. Following these activities, all cadets were then assembled on the parade grounds where we received our coveted silver wings and commissions as Second Lieutenants, Army of the United States (Air Forces). We were entitled to have our wings pinned on by whomever we chose, and I selected Mom to pin on my wings. Of course, it was a special moment for both of us. I'm sure she was very proud; and for me, earning my wings will forever remain my fifteen minutes of fame.

US Army Air Forces Pilot Silver Wings.

The ceremony was closed by a single order: "Dismissed!" By tradition at that moment, we cadets mouthed a great roar, took off our new officers' visor hats, removed the metal grommets from the crowns, and threw the grommets high into the air.

Grommets now littering the parade area would never be replaced, and the crowns of our hats would assume a crushed appearance caused by wearing earphones while in flight Thus, our hats would adopt the "fifty mission crush" appearance that would become a hallmark of every AAF pilot.

Two more Washington State men soon will be on active duty as full-fledged pilots of the Army Air Forces.

E. V. GODFREY, E. C. LARSON

They are Edward C. Larson, son of Mr. and Mrs. O. A. Larson, 4919 Princeton Way, Seattle, and Edward V. Godfrey, son of Mr. and Mrs. Grover Godfrey, Route 1, Box 1589, Kent.

The coveted silver wings go to them as members of a class of student officers and aviation cadets graduating from the Army Forces Pilot School (advanced two engine) at Stockton Field, Calif.

Before entering the final and advanced course at Stockton Field, Cadet Larson completed 18 weeks of primary and basic training at Visalia and Chico, Calif., and Cadet Godfrey at Twentynine Palms and Merced, Calif.

* * *

Newspaper clipping with graduation announcement. (From the author's collection.)

As we departed the parade area, there was yet another tradition to follow. A group of enlisted men stood by waiting to salute the new lieutenants as we passed. In return, we handed each of them a paper dollar bill. Those dollars bought a lot of beer at the Stockton Soldiers' Club that night.

In retrospect, the whole of that day seems a bit like the culmination of a run up a very long, steep hill. When you reach the top, the fatigue is so compelling that for some little time it overshadows the victory of accomplishment. Bent over, hands on knees, your lungs heave as you struggle to catch your breath and reclaim the strength the climb has stolen. After that, you look back at the starting point, knowing beyond any shadow of doubt that you will be forever better than you were before you started.

THIRTY-ONE

ollowing graduation, I received a two-week leave, and my mother and I returned to Seattle. There were fond greetings from friends and family, dinner parties, luncheons, and a few dances with girls I'd dated in high school and college. One morning, I chose to go to my old high school to visit some of my former teachers. While I was away at training, I had written to my English and history teachers, each of whom I was particularly fond, and they had answered my letters. Our brief meetings were poignant and meaningful; they talked to me as if I was their own son. I was deeply grateful for that.

I was feeling a bit ill at ease—after all, I had friends spread out all over the world fighting a war—and after about a week into my leave, I was impatient to return to my buddies and start my new assignment. Don't get me wrong. I deeply loved my family, but changes I'd experienced since enlisting had indelibly marked me with a seeming necessity to be back where I belonged. I made some excuses to Mom, Pop, and Gram and cut my leave short by a few days, making my way on my own to my new assignment.

The trip to Taft was a joke. I started out on the train from Seattle, switched to a bus in California, and then hitchhiked the last forty miles to Gardner Army Airfield. What a hell of a way for a pilot to travel! But if my modes of transportation were less than glamorous, Gardner more than made up for it. It was a wonderful place—a world away from any military situation I had ever encountered.

I arrived at the entrance on 2 May 1944, packing a B-4 bag, sweating profusely, and whistling the recent Judy Garland hit, "A Journey to a Star."[60] It has been seventy years since I stood there that early May morning; and yet, the musical score, lyrics, and the gate at Gardner Airfield remain indelible memories. I cannot explain the strange connection between music and place; no mention of it appears in my letters. I only know the steel-bond connection between that place and that song remain inexplicably vivid and still fresh. If I hum but a few bars of that tune, I'm transported to that dusty field entrance and the incomparable time I spent there.

The airfield itself lay shimmering at the southern end of the San Joaquin Valley, forty miles west of Bakersfield and nine miles to the east of the small town of Taft. Incredibly, the little town had first been named Siding Station II. Then, about 1900, at the request of the local populace, the town's name was changed to Moron. This unfortunate selection was made in an attempt to relate the hamlet to Morro Bay, a pleasant coastal town situated to the west. Thankfully, that name was later abandoned, and Taft was adopted as the town's name to honor President William Howard Taft.

Only three or four miles to the east of the airfield lay a large, shallow body of rank water that had seeped up from the earth's bowels in some prehistoric era. It was

Undated World War II photo of Gardner Army Airfield showing flying cadets. (US Air Force photo.)

Aerial view of Gardner Army Airfield. (US Army Air Forces photo.)

euphemistically named Buena Vista Lake. The trilogy of Taft, Buena Vista Lake, and Gardner Airfield were the only punctuation marks in a porcupine landscape of heat and oil derricks. The area lacked grace and featured summer temperatures ranging between 91 and 97 degrees Fahrenheit.

A bit of intriguing history about Gardner: A year and a half before my arrival, a skinny kid who was subject to airsickness had taken his basic training there. He went on to become one of the greatest fighter and test pilots of the United States Air Force. Interestingly, Chuck Yeager had likewise been stationed at Victorville as an airplane mechanic before entering flight training.

Chuck Yeager next to experimental aircraft Bell X-1, #1 *Glamorous Glennis*.
(US Air Force photo.)

On October 14, 1947, Chuck Yeager, flying a Bell X-1 aircraft, became the first man to break the sound barrier. The plane he flew was named for his wife.

The fact that General Chuck Yeager and I had served at the same air force installations abruptly halts any other career comparison between the two of us.

I obtained a room at the bachelor officers' quarters (BOQ), which if not plush was certainly quite adequate. It became immediately apparent that, as a commissioned officer, I had entered a different world. My pay had risen to the lofty sum of $285.00 per month, a princely amount for a nineteen-year-old kid. I had access to membership in the officers' club and officers' mess and any and all other privileges the base had to offer. As new officers, we were all a bit mesmerized by our change in status, but I detected no overt arrogance or sense of entitlement among the guys I knew and had trained with, and I believe I handled all these new privileges as well as most.

There were twenty-five of us in the instructors' class, which was scheduled to last for five weeks. The last two weeks we would be instructing training students who had already soloed. The instruction would utilize the BT-13 and the North American Aviation T-6 Texan. The AT-6 was somewhat similar to the BT-13, but with a 600 hp Pratt & Whitney R-1340 Wasp engine and retractable landing gear. Although I had become genuinely enamored with the BT during my basic training, the AT-6 was simply the loveliest military plane I ever flew. The Texan was a mere half step behind the early fighters of World War II, and I am eternally proud that I learned to fly it well.

The ratio of students to instructors at Gardner was three or four to one, an almost ideal situation, and from the first, the course could be regarded as excellent. We flew incessantly from morning to night, mostly in BTs. Quite naturally, our proficiency, confidence, and abilities improved with each passing day; and in the course of the instruction, we were able to investigate every aspect of the airplane and the techniques and nuances of control that would make it perform precisely as we intended.

For me, flying single engine again was a rebirth, and I treasured every moment of this assignment since it could possibly lead to a transition to fighter planes—a chance for which I longed. Soon I was so familiar with the BT-13 that it seemed almost an extension of my body. I could go through any procedure with my eyes closed and touch each control or switch appropriate to that procedure. This kind of familiarity was common to all of us and boosted our capabilities immensely. My interest in aerobatics continued at a high level, and my proficiency became a source of personal pride. Every one of us rose to the top of our game, and it was hard to remember that we were actually being paid to have this much fun.

Our instructions in instrument flying were particularly demanding. We had undergone rather intensive instrument training in basic and advanced schools, but this was different. The instructors at Taft required near-perfect precision in nonvisual flight. All-instrument flying was conducted "under the hood." The student flew in the backseat with a qualified instructor sitting in the front cockpit. A heavy canvas hood was then pulled over the rear cockpit, which precluded all visual references to the outside world. I always thought a sign reading "abandon hope all ye who enter here" should be hung on the shrouded rear cockpit.

US Army Air Forces Vultee BT-13A (s/n 42-1453) at Minter Field, 1 March 1943. (US Air Force photo 41047 A.C., AFHRA 080129-f-3927s-246.)

The United States Army Air Corps and, later, the US Army Air Forces used the BT-13 as a basic trainer. The Army replaced it with the AT-6 before the end of the war.

North American AT-6, National Museum of the United States Air Force. (US Air Force photo 100609-F-1234S-035.)

When the hood first covers your world and earth, horizon, and sky are literally taken from you, one more unsettling fact still rears its ugly head. Be advised: There is no such thing as flying by the seat of your pants! Absolutely no attention or credence can be paid to the human body's sense of movement or direction, and any dependency on inner-ear messages is always wrong and usually fatal. In the darkness, you must understand that the instruments alone will provide the only pathway to your mortal salvation. And in the world of nonvisual flight, not all instruments are equal. Some will speak in a constantly straightforward manner, delivering clear and concise messages to your mind. Others will speak in tongues, and their messages must be translated to comprehend. At 200 mph, you must learn quickly to interpret these small creatures and respond appropriately to survive.

Some few years ago, I was privileged to ride in the copilot's seat of a magnificent Cessna twin-engine jet. At the outset, I was stunned by the appearance of the instrument panel before me. It was, for all purposes, totally alien and totally unintelligible. The new generation of instrumentation, now termed avionics, amazed me with its versatility, the totality of its messages, and its capability to communicate. While staring at its wonders, I could only calculate its value in terms of lives that could have been saved in my time had this technology been available sooner. The aircraft and instrumentation of my era predates by seventy years the staggering advances in science and electronics that form the heart and soul of our contemporary airplanes.

Our training planes were equipped with virtually the same flight instrument package as our operational aircraft. By the term "flight instruments," I refer to those instruments that allowed us to actually fly the airplane. This designation excludes engine gauges and the like. Most important among our flight instruments were those three that depended on gyroscopes to deliver their vital information. In the parlance of our time, they were, in order of importance, the artificial horizon (altitude indicator), the directional gyro or DG (heading indicator), and the turn and bank (needle-ball) indicator.

Artificial horizon indicating left bank procedure. (*Instrument Flying: Basic and Advanced, Special Edition, 1944*, Army Air Forces.)

The artificial horizon was a miraculous instrument that did exactly what its name implies. In a world of potential confusion, its lovely face projected a small dependable line that always remained parallel to the world's real horizon line. A small airplane was superimposed on the indicator line so that a quick glance at the sacred object would tell the pilot if he were climbing, diving, turning, or level.

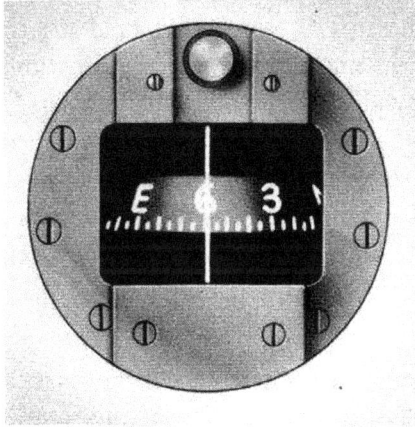

Magnetic compass. (*Instrument Flying: Basic and Advanced, Special Edition, 1944,* Army Air Forces.)

Directional gyro. (*Instrument Flying: Basic and Advanced, Special Edition, 1944,* Army Air Forces.)

The magnetic compass, though accurate when properly calibrated, was a wonderful direction indicator when the aircraft was sitting on the ground. In flight, it was subject to twisting and tumbling in its fluid bath, thus driving the pilot nuts. The directional gyro could hold a stable reference point in space, and when it was aligned with the accurate direction provided by the magnetic compass, that heading could then be set on the DG's rotating compass card providing a stable and reliable reading of the aircraft when in motion. These two instruments were a godsend to a pilot when reference to the outside world was eliminated by darkness, weather, or the infamous hood that was used to confound us.

Vacuum or electric current spun the small, heavy wheels inside the gyro instruments. They rotated at speeds up to an amazing 18,000 rpm, providing a stable position or point in a world of disorientation. The two instruments "held hands" to present their blessed message to the pilot, a virtual indication of the attitude and direction of his aircraft.

One might ask, "What happens if the vacuum line breaks or the electrical system fails and the little gyros stop spinning?" The answer is the party's over. Then the pilot must turn to Plan B.

The turn and bank (needle-ball) indicator was the third in my listing of gyroscopic instruments. Not pretty and a bit inarticulate, she was a wallflower to be danced with only through courtesy. But if the other two gyros left the party, the needle ball would be easy to love if she took you home. The instrument was fitted with a gyro-controlled vertical pointer. This pointer would display a deflection to either side if the aircraft began turning. Below the needle, a ball, free to roll from side to side, was encased in a curved glass tube. If the aircraft's bank was too steep for its rate of turn, the ball would fall to the end of the tube adjacent to the inside of the turn, thus indicating the airplane was slipping. If the ball were forced to the outside of the turn, it would indicate the aircraft was skidding with a bank too shallow for its rate of turn. In a perfectly coordinated turn, the needle would indicate a turn in progress while the ball would remain poised exactly in the middle of the tube. Flight in a straight direction with wings level was indicated by a centered needle and ball.

Turn and bank indicator showing coordinated turn. (*Instrument Flying: Basic and Advanced, Special Edition, 1944*, Army Air Forces.)

If you asked the needle ball if you were climbing or diving, it was tongue-tied and unable to answer that life-or-death question. In the absence of the artificial horizon, only the airspeed indicator (altimeter) could give you a straight answer. Quite simply, if you were gaining speed, the plane was losing altitude, which meant the nose of the aircraft was pointed down and you were diving. If you were losing speed, the plane was gaining altitude, which meant the nose of the aircraft was pointed up and you were climbing.

A competent pilot could keep the ball centered by rudder movement, the needle centered by aileron movement, and the airspeed constant by careful elevator control. All three things accomplished, your airplane would miraculously fly straight and level in the worst of storms. The technique was called, logically enough, needle-ball airspeed. It demanded total concentration and total vigilance since the eyes had to constantly sweep across four instruments, mouthing four varied concepts, which must be monitored, collated, and acted upon with speed and precision.

We all found it difficult, but we learned to do it and blessed the moment when we could pull back the hood and see our earth and sky once again. There would be more instrument flying after Taft, with no instructor and no hood over the rear cockpit. The views of earth and sky would be taken from us many times by vicious weather, a hell of a lot of violent turbulence, and the sweaty hands of fear that groped beneath our dirty oxygen masks, robbing us of breath and threatening to choke our composure.

It was the end of May, and the heat at Taft was becoming oppressive. Gardner Airfield was in a slight depression surrounded by low, desert-like hills, a virtual sand trap for the clinging heat. Temperatures on the actual runways were so high that our BTs became sluggish and reluctant to leave the ground.

We now had students of our own in addition to our daily sessions of instructors' school. Surprisingly, I found myself yelling at my kids—most of them older than I was. Teaching was a tough job requiring constant vigilance of the student and his actions in the airplane, and we were instructing our students in a plane that reacted like a rank rodeo horse. A soft voice was ineffective when a student was riding heavy bottom rudder on the last turn into the field while a plane was whispering *stall, stall, stall* in your ear. Coupled with these conditions, the afternoon turbulence was becoming extreme. The only area of still air was over Lake Buena Vista, and airplanes flocked like flies over that area of smoother air. After much thought, I avoided the lake and the possibility of a midair collision in favor of a rougher ride.

On the afternoon of 31 May, my instructor received orders to report for B-17 transition. I hated to see him go. He was a fine pilot and a great teacher. We rang hell out of the airplanes we flew together and laughed about it when it was over.

I regret that I never saw him again.

THIRTY-TWO

E arly June simmered in the San Joaquin heat, and it seemed to get hotter with each passing day. Tuesday, 6 June, I awoke with the certainty that flying that morning would be another wild ride of thermals and just plain industrial-size turbulence, but we got the news early that this was not to be an ordinary day. This was D-Day, and forces of the free world were manning a gigantic armada, signaling the long-awaited attack on Fortress Europe by the Allies. Our flying went on, but it was fueled by hope and constant reports from the beaches of Normandy.

*YOU ARE ABOUT TO EMBARK UPON
THE GREAT CRUSADE TOWARD WHICH WE HAVE
STRIVEN THESE MANY MONTHS.
THE EYES OF THE WORLD ARE UPON YOU...
I HAVE FULL CONFIDENCE IN YOUR COURAGE,
DEVOTION TO DUTY, AND SKILL IN BATTLE.*

~ GENERAL DWIGHT D. EISENHOWER
ORDER OF THE DAY: 6 JUNE 1944
SUPREME HEADQUARTERS, ALLIED EXPEDITIONARY FORCE[61]

D-Day Invasion, 6 June 1944. (Photographer: Chief Photographer's Mate [CPHoM] Robert F. Sargent, USCG. National Archives, Collection FDR-PHOCO: Franklin D. Roosevelt Library Public Domain Photographs, 1882–1962. National Archives Identifier: 195515.)

Dodging Nazi firepower, troops wade through surf to secure a beachhead during the Allied invasion.

The scope of the invasion attack was so immense it defied imagination. Churches and chapels everywhere were filled with every style of communicant; it was as if the faith of free people everywhere was shoring up our troops with prayer as they battled their way across the beaches and stormed the walls of France. I felt humbled and hopeful with a tinge of regret that I was not directly involved. I'm sure nearly every man, woman, and child on the base visited Chapel that day at least once. It was a day to be on your knees.

No one remarked about the heat or turbulence. We were all keenly aware of the significance of what we were doing and where we might fit in this desperate struggle of good against evil. I knew very well on that day many of my deployed friends were close to harm's way, and it weighed heavily on my mind. Paul Ostrander would be finishing transition in P-47s before joining the Seventy-Eighth Fighter Group at Duxford, England. Johnny Condon's submarine would be running on the surface, charging batteries just north of Kwajalein in the Marshall Islands. Bobby Dornblaser would be taking a Japanese machine gun round in the lower back, just starting his pain, but ending his war. Bill Wetzel would be flying his B-17 on a low-level raid over railroad marshalling yards in support of the invasion. Don Spangle would be flying a C-47 loaded with airborne troops bound for a drop zone five miles east of Omaha Beach. My buddy Pete was flying an F6F out of Vero Beach preparing to join a carrier night-fighter squadron. Sure, we were all young in years, but we were mature in experience; and on one of the longest days of our lives and this war, we did what we'd been taught to do.

As far as I knew, my colleague Van was a pretty good pilot and instructor, but everybody screws up at one time or another.

One nice, bright morning, Van and his student flew to an auxiliary field to practice landings and takeoffs. They were just entering the traffic pattern at the isolated field when the engine suddenly stopped dead without warning or even a cough. Van took over and made a dead-stick landing that would have earned him an A for accomplishment. While sitting quietly in the middle of the dirt runway, he then decided to check the forms on the BT that had just quit on them.

Each airplane carried two forms: 1 and 1A. These critical documents were found in a heavy aluminum case on the left of the cockpit. Forms 1 and 1A provided status reports for that particular aircraft, and the documents were as much a part of the airplane as the rudder. Any mechanical problems, no matter how small, were to be entered on the forms at the end of each flight. A plane not flightworthy should have a large red X marked on one of these forms. The pilot's responsibility was to check the forms before each flight to establish the status of the aircraft he was about to fly. This action was mandated by the preflight checklist. To Van's great relief, on examining the documents, he noted a huge red X indicating the BT had bad magnetos. Van and his student had grabbed the wrong airplane!

Wanting to clear the runway, Van tried starting the BT. The engine powered up with no trouble, so he ran it up to full power without a hiccup—it ran beautifully. Knowing he'd be in big trouble for flying a grounded aircraft, Van reasoned that since the engine was running so well, maybe they could take the plane back to Gardner, park it, and take the correct plane without anyone knowing the difference. It was a brilliant scheme. Van cranked up the BT again and checked the magnetos. They were functioning perfectly, so he and his student taxied to the end of the runway, lined up, and took off flawlessly. The day would be saved after all.

At about 600 feet, the engine quit cold. This time, the area ahead was filled with fences and outbuildings. Nowhere to land!

It is a huge mistake for a pilot with a dead engine to try turning back to the airfield from which he has just departed.

The loss of altitude in the 180-degree turn necessary to retrace the takeoff simply will not allow the aircraft to reach the landing area. After completing the turn, Van tried the impossible task of stretching a glide. Trying to do this by flattening out the glide angle to get more distance doesn't work and invites the inevitable stall. Several hundred yards short of the runway and at extremely low altitude, the BT quit flying and dropped like a rock, hitting the dusty desert with such force that the impact drove the landing gear struts up into the wing roots. It also jarred the hell out of the airplane's dynamic duo. Even the radio was knocked into permanent silence.

The disconsolate instructor and his student sat by the compressed BT until someone noticed their plight and contacted the Gardner tower. An aircrew was flown out to the field. Their assessment? The aircraft was a dead bird. The two pilots had been blessed by an overload of good luck.

The cadet who had been scared witless by the crash was totally innocent but did not fly for a few days. After an official proceeding, Van was confined to quarters for a week and taken off flight status for a month. A lot of laughter and jokes followed the incident, but fortunately, no funerals.

About the middle of June, I received a letter from my birth father indicating he was working as an inspector for Lockheed in Phoenix. He wrote that he intended to fly to Taft to see me. I hadn't seen him in seven years, which was about par for the course, and I viewed his plan as impossible. All general aviation was shut down in areas along the coast, and California was a nest of restricted areas where only military aircraft were allowed. I took his intention as so much blue smoke; although, one never knew what that man might do.

A week later, Gardner received a visitor in the form of a new Navy pilot who had come to see a friend, one of our instructors. He was flying a Grumman F4F Wildcat; and of course, both pilot and plane were of intense interest to all of us who were slogging around in BTs and AT-6s. A group of us surrounded him in the officers' club that night, bombarding him with questions about Navy flying and his first-line fighter.

The next morning, I flew early—a short, cross-country instruction flight. My student and I returned in late afternoon. Immediately, it became apparent that something had happened that would cast a pall of sorrow across the base for weeks to come. Within the hour, I learned what had happened.

The Navy pilot had enjoyed breakfast with some of our instructor crew. After offering goodbyes, a small group of our pilots had walked him out to the flight line and his Wildcat. This airplane had a cartridge starter that required a special blank shotgun shell, which when fired, produced a blast of pressurized air and turned over the engine. The Navy pilot made numerous attempts to get the engine started and in the process used all the starting shells he had in the airplane.

Two of our pilots had flown to a neighboring Navy field and returned with a box of shells to continue attempts at starting the engine. Finally, it started, and the group moved away as the pilot taxied to the end of the runway and ran through his preflight checklist.

Receiving permission for takeoff from the tower, he departed. To the joy of his onlookers, he circled the field and then dropped down for a low pass over the runway. Only fifty feet above the ground, he flashed by the waving group, then at the far end of the runway, he pulled up and began a slow roll to the left. All appeared normal until he became inverted. Onlookers watched with horror as the aircraft's nose dropped; and with full power on, the F4F dove into the mesquite a mile from the end of the Gardner Airfield runway. The pilot of course died instantly.

There seemed to be no apparent reason for the tragic accident, but a subsequent investigation revealed the fatal mistake that had so quickly taken the life of this young pilot. It was determined that in the confusion of starting the engine and saying goodbye, he had neglected to fasten his seat belt. When he took off and buzzed the field, he never noticed he was unsecured; and as he pulled up for his slow-roll salute and the aircraft became inverted, gravity took over, and he literally fell away from the controls. It was impossible for him to reach the throttle, stick, or rudder pedals, and the still inverted airplane simply nosed down at full speed, slamming into the desert floor.

The accident took a toll on everyone, especially those of us who had met this engaging young man. The absolute irony was that a goddamn unfastened seat belt had stolen a life full of promise.

It was hard to accept.

THIRTY-THREE

I flew early on 30 June and was back in my room writing letters when the phone rang. It was my father. He and his wife Mamie had just landed at the Taft Airport, a little strip on the other side of town. They wanted me to come and pick them up.

I borrowed a car; and all the way to the tiny airport, I wondered how the hell they had managed to get from Phoenix to Taft. The whole area was closed to civilian flying with restrictions everywhere.

When I got to the unused strip, Dad and his wife were surrounded by a group of locals who were chatting them up about their trip. Parked in the afternoon sun was the yellow Piper Cub in which they had made the five-hundred-mile journey. Though stunned by their arrival, I was cordial and joined the welcoming committee. There was some curiosity expressed by the locals about how they had gotten permission to fly the little Cub through restricted air space; and one of them, apparently a pilot, was especially interested in their responses since he hadn't seen a civilian plane around for years. My dad mumbled something about his employment as a Lockheed engineer and started jabbering about P-38s and investigating small airfields, and the double talk—at which my dad excelled—seemed to satisfy the crowd.

The strip was enhanced by an empty unlocked wooden hanger, and we pushed the Piper into its shaded interior, closed the door, and got the hell out of there, leaving the locals scratching their heads in wonder about what was actually going on.

I took them to town where they got a room in what might be described as a primitive motel; then we spent an hour surveying the little place once called Moron. It was typically hot and typically dusty; and Mamie, a really lovely woman, was very quiet, while my dad and I chatted about airplanes and flying. He now held a civilian instructor's license and had recently received an aircraft and engines license, which allowed him to serve as an aircraft mechanic. An examination of their lifestyle indicated there was a bit of the Will-o'-the-wisp surrounding them—my dad was pretty much always on the move, while all Mamie wanted in her life was a small garden that she could care for.

I expected to spend Saturday with them, but Dad had friends in Bakersfield that he wanted to see; so instead, we planned on me treating them to dinner that evening at the officers' club, and I arranged to pick them up at the motel at 1800.

Saturday night, I waited for them for more than two hours. When they didn't show up, I returned to Gardner, had a couple of drinks and dinner, and went back to the BOQ. I finally got a call at about 2300…with Dad explaining they had missed the bus and had just gotten back to Taft.

Since they had to leave early the next morning, I offered to take them to the airport. It had been one hell of a short visit.

When we arrived at the airport early the next morning, the place was deserted. A large padlock had been installed on the rickety hanger door, indicating the edifice was not to be entered. We looked through the cracks and could see the little Cub sitting tranquilly on the dirt floor. My dad searched around and found a rusty length of pipe that he used to pry off the lock, hasp and all. From that point, it was an easy task to roll out the plane. They didn't waste time. Mamie held the brakes while my dad propped the Cub. There was a short goodbye, and the last I saw of them was as the little yellow plane cleared the end of the strip and headed east toward Phoenix. I'm sure they stopped somewhere close for gas, but God knows where. As for the lock and the scofflaw break-in, I called them a couple of days later, and the subject never came up.

There was one poignant highlight to their visit when my dad voiced the question, "When's your birthday?" I wasn't a bit surprised. I hadn't received a birthday card from him in all my nineteen years.

June melted into the dog days of July. By now, we were deeply involved with our students and the daily routine of flying. The heat continued unabated, but we were beginning to accept it as an unpleasant fact of life. We were gathering a lot of flying time, some in my beloved AT-6. With more than 150 horsepower over the BT, it was simply a dream to fly. I volunteered to take over the aerobatic instruction for two of our classes and did well. In the process, I had two young

Women's Auxiliary Service Pilots (WASPs) as students. They were both diligent and apt, and I'm sure they became fine pilots.

On 18 July, we flew early. I took my first student to an auxiliary field to practice takeoffs and landings. Meanwhile, my other students had been bussed out to the field; and when we landed, they surrounded us, which was pretty typical. I got out of the back cockpit and started toward the stage shack before realizing I'd left my grade book on my chute in the rear cockpit. These small grade books were strapped to our legs during flight to allow us to grade students while in the air. Grades were private, so I trotted back to the airplane to retrieve the errant book. As I jumped up on the wing root, my foot slid off, and I came down hard on the concrete ramp. The pain was very intense. It was clear I'd done some damage somewhere.

An ambulance was always present at each auxiliary field; but if one were used to transport me back to Gardner, all flying would cease until the ambulance returned, and a whole morning of flying would be lost, so I suggested a student fly me back. I struggled into the rear cockpit on a leg that was looking much worse, and we took off. After a short flight, we entered the landing pattern at Gardner. My best student was flying, but we landed like a rubber ball bouncing down the runway. Worse yet, we garnered a bit of unwanted attention from onlookers who were expecting a ground loop. I royally chewed out the kid. I've been sorry about that ever since.

A quick trip to the hospital for x-rays revealed a broken ankle. It would be awhile before I could fly again. Being taken off flight status was a huge concern to me, particularly after my "incarceration" at Victorville. But there was nothing I could do about it. I couldn't even use crutches for a few days.

The base hospital had a great staff, cute nurses and all, and the flight surgeon and I got along famously. I indicated early on that I was thinking about a career in medicine, and that seemed to intrigue him. Some eyebrows were raised when I was allowed to observe a hernia operation up close and personal. I think Doc did it to see if I'd faint.

I didn't. There wasn't even a drop of sweat on my brow after everything had been buttoned up.

By 24 August, I was healed up and returned to flight status. My hiatus had been a drag, and it felt great getting back into an airplane again. Although I was rusty, after a few check rides, everything came back. We were flying AT-6s more often, and that was like icing on a cake.

As we moved toward September, the war was bearing down hard on the Germans and the Japanese. The Axis was falling back everywhere and being decimated in their retreat. The last days of August saw the liberation of Paris and Florence in Europe and Guam in the Pacific. There was handwriting on the wall, but it was still too faint to decipher.

Before my sojourn in the hospital, I had teamed up with two other pilots to fly after hours. As flight instructors, we were permitted to check out airplanes for cross-country flights; and on several occasions, I'd flown to Stockton to see a young lady I'd met during advanced training. I found these flights totally relaxing and so fulfilling; they added a new dimension to the joy of flying.

My friends, "Charlie" and "Dave" (not their real names), had become, like me, extremely familiar with BTs and AT-6s. We had flown together enough that we knew each other's characteristics and habits, and that interdependence allowed us do some rather dicey stuff. Our casual attitudes could have pointed toward trouble, but we really knew how to fly; and no kid could be expected to handle his own 600-horsepower hot rod without screeching the wheels once in a while.

We three flew vee formation incredibly close and never suffered an accident or a bent wing tip. If you're flying lead, you can watch the scenery and fly your airplane bearing in mind there are two guys hanging out there just scant feet from your wingtips following every twitch of your ailerons or rudder. If you're a wingman and flying in tight, it means your eyes never leave the lead plane. You shouldn't even know when you're landing until your throttle's pulled way back and your wheels start to turn.

Our favorite playground was naturally a discreet distance from the home field. Located in what we reckoned was part of the Cuyama Valley, it was totally devoid of structures and residents, inhabited only by jackrabbits and the occasional sidewinder and coyote. Our main notion of fun was to assemble in an echelon formation several thousand feet above and several miles north of the valley. Our target, usually imagined as a Japanese cruiser, was in truth a group of scrubby trees on the valley floor. The battle plan provided that the lead aircraft would execute a Hollywood-style peel off by abruptly pulling back and sideways on the stick and rolling the plane into a turn-and-inverted position. Then we would execute a Split S or steep dive down toward the target at the best speed we could wring out of our trainers. After we had "bombed" our target, we would drop our planes right down on the deck and roar across the valley just feet above the scrubby brush that pockmarked the ground. This may not sound like much, but to us it was the greatest ride in the world—and it was free. It was also exactly what one *should* do with an airplane once in awhile—as long as you didn't get caught!

Our routine of instruction moved into September with cooler days and nights. It was getting so you could fly just about anywhere around Gardner without your teeth rattling from turbulence. The war was going on full blast, but we had lots of afternoons to float in the pool and drink beer. It didn't feel quite right, but we were as far from danger as if we were playing a pick-up game of half court on one of our neighborhood streets back home. Even so, the faintest of hearts can sometimes stumble into harm's way.

One afternoon, my formation buddy Charlie and I decided to fly for fun. We checked out a BT-13 and figured to do a few aerobatics and just horse around for a while. We'd been up a little more than an hour when we noticed it was nearly cocktail hour, so we thought we'd better head back. I was flying front seat, and Charlie was in the rear just looking around. I hollered at him that I was going to do a short spin before we quit for the day, and he gave me an affirmative over the intercom, so I cleared the area, pulled the power back, and raised the nose up pretty steeply. As expected, within a few seconds, the airplane began to shudder and shake. I held the stick back; and a moment later, we fell off on the left wing and began a tailspin towards some oil derricks several thousand feet below.

The spin felt normal, and after about three turns, I applied strong right rudder, then forward stick; but there was no stopping the rotation…in fact, it seemed to increase speed slightly. I went through the standard recovery procedure again but with similar results. The airplane simply would not stop rotating. By now, Charlie was wide-awake and extremely interested, and he had initiated a recovery effort from the back cockpit—but to no avail. Thankfully, we had begun the spin at a fairly high altitude…but the handwriting was on the wall: It was throw-back-the-canopies-and-try-once-more-before-bailing-out time!

I tried the recovery again, and after applying right rudder, this time, I jammed the stick forward as hard as I could. There was one more half rotation; and then suddenly, it stopped, and we were in a dive almost straight down. We still had altitude, so I leveled out very gently to avoid another stall.

I don't know about Charlie, but I was trembling like a willow leaf, and I suspect he was doing the same. With some very adequate cussing, we discussed the situation over the intercom. The standard spin recovery, so automatic to both of us, had never failed us before. After parking the BT, we contacted a line crew chief, explained what had happened, and of course, put a large red X on Form 1. The drinks tasted pretty good that night with the ice in our glasses jingling merrily in our still shaking hands.

A few days later, we contacted the maintenance chief regarding the incident. He informed us that one of the wings had been washed out; in other words, it had been twisted so that the angle of incidence where the wing met the fuselage had changed. It was his opinion that the wing damage had occurred in a very hard landing.

The aircraft was removed from service, which was good enough for us. Neither Charlie nor I want to fly that thing again.

THIRTY-FOUR

Change was in the wind. Germany was falling back everywhere under pressure from the Allies; lights over all of Britain were winking on again; and the engines of Spitfires, Hurricanes, and Mustangs were ticking down to silence. These fighter planes had written a thrilling page in the history of air warfare, and the pilots who flew them had inscribed one word—VICTORY—in the skies over England.

> *JAPAN HAS BEEN LISTENING TO THE OMINOUS SOUND OF THUNDER IN THE WEST. ONE DAY OUR LIGHTENING WILL STRIKE IN THE EAST.*
>
> ~ *TARGET: GERMANY—THE US ARMY AIR FORCES' OFFICIAL STORY OF THE VIII BOMBER COMMAND'S FIRST YEAR OVER EUROPE*

The war in the Pacific was on the verge of becoming a horror for Japan and its residents. With the capture of the Marianas Islands, the United States would create a monumental bombing platform close to Japan. In the months to come, bombers flying out of Tinian would literally and figuratively flatten the Emperor's delusional dreams of grandeur.

We were feeling the change as well. In the last week of September, many of us received orders to report to Albuquerque, New Mexico, for transition training in B-24s. This war was winding down; within months, the pilot training program would be almost totally curtailed. There would be no fighters in my future.

My last day of flying at Gardner was 30 September. My log shows a solo flight of exactly one hour. It was a goodbye flight to the best assignment I would ever have. The concern over midair collisions was pretty well gone; and on this day, only a handful of planes cruised the skies. I climbed up to altitude, did some snap and slow rolls, a few lazy eights, and engaged in some plain and simple airplane daydreaming. It had been a long road from where I had started. The planes I was now flying had become a part of me, and I felt intense fulfillment from my days at Gardner. That would be enough.

I landed and taxied to the apron. With a head full of memories, I parked the Vultee Vibrator and pulled the mixture control back to idle cutoff one last time. For a moment, the engine sort of clanked and slapped; then there was silence. I climbed out and walked away without looking back. I would never fly a BT-13 again.

Our orders called for us to leave Gardner on 10 October and report to Kirtland Army Air Field in Albuquerque five days later. Gordon, a fellow instructor (and obviously from a family of means), suggested I travel with him to our next post. He was driving a lovely 1942 Chevrolet convertible, a gift from his family. I was totally impressed with the car.

Because of the war, only 110 were built that year, and his was a beautiful rich green. She looked brand new.

Green 1942 Chevrolet Deluxe.

We started out on 11 October in high spirits, looking forward to four days of pleasant sightseeing in the American Southwest. The driving distance, figured off a free gas station roadmap, was about nine hundred miles and pretty much due east. Our course was heavily dictated by the faded centerline of Route 66. It would become one of the most celebrated interstates in our country's history after singer Nat King Cole did his bit to make the road immortal.

The landscape was new to us, mostly arid and desert-like, but Gordon had plenty of gas stamps. (Where they all came from, I didn't know and didn't ask.) As the miles rolled by, I found him to be congenial but a bit strange and not given to easing the miles of tumbleweed and sand with useless conversation.

Image: Route 66 highway sign. (*Manual on Uniform Traffic Control Devices*, 1926. Public domain.)

When we neared the California-Arizona border, Gordon voiced his desire to cut through a section of what then constituted Navajo Indian Reservation. The weather had become a bit wet and windy, but the new convertible was, as the proverbial saying goes, "as snug as a bug in a rug." We stopped at several lookout areas and small, unremembered towns along the way. Both of us were impressed by the almost nonexistent interstate traffic. The war and gasoline rationing had stopped all that.

We finally pulled in at a marginal auto court and gas station for the night. The accommodations made even Lincoln look like the Hilton. The place was dirty and featured a bare, overhead light bulb that was deemed sufficient for any wayfarers that might stumble in. Its rays were the color and strength of weak lemonade, barely lighting two shabby iron cots with linen that had apparently remained unchanged since Pearl Harbor. Partial darkness was probably a blessing.

Illustration of gas stamps, ca 1944.

The proprietor was grizzled and as dirty as his room, with fat bib overalls and his hand out for an undeserved stipend. After we registered, Gordon asked about road conditions ahead, particularly through the reservation. The "innkeeper" responded with a condescending soliloquy by telling us that the road through the reservation was in terrible shape since no maintenance had been undertaken since at least 1941. Then, with an unmasked sneer, he queried, "Don't you know there's a war on?"

That stupid remark, voiced a million times during the war years, served as an ill-disguised cliché and often an excuse for bad food, bad lodging, and bad everything. Since Gordon and I were both in uniform, it was particularly insulting.

Our "host" followed up with some elaboration about the route we should follow to Albuquerque "if we had any sense." With thumbs hooked into his gravy-stained coveralls, he ended his speech with, "What the hell would you want to see 'injuns' for, anyhow?"

As we sat on our iron cots, I remarked that as dirty and repulsive as the guy was, I still placed some credence in what he had to say. Gordon, however, was intent on going through the reservation for a look at history and culture. The deciding fact was that it was his car, and he was going to see some real Indians. Never unprepared, I had stashed a bottle of bourbon in my B-4 bag, so we had a couple of drinks and went to bed. Something was biting me all night long, but whatever it was, the red welts went away after a couple of days.

We got underway early the next morning and made good time under a series of line squalls that periodically drummed rain on our canvas top. Our passage across western Arizona was marked pretty much by miles of silence, broken only by Gordon's periodic mutterings about "where the damn turnoff to the reservation" was. We finally reached the crucial juncture, and perhaps as a harbinger of things to come, the rain increased to a mild cloudburst. No matter, Gordon chose "the road less traveled."

We had gone only the equivalent of about five miles when the rude cautions offered by our innkeeper of the previous night proved to be precisely correct. This was a homemade road, at times, so rough we barely made headway, and it would remain nearly impassable until we broke out of the reservation and got back on the highway. In the next multitude of hours, we slogged through ruts and swelling creek beds that threatened at times to set us afloat. There were countless Tinkertoy bridges with rotted decks to be crossed, and perhaps a million potholes that nearly brought the little Chevy to its knees. It was easy to imagine each jarring shock loosening the car's nuts and bolts until it finally disintegrated into a pile of parts. It was our good fortune that we never got stuck. We had no shovels or tools for digging and probably wouldn't have been found till the following spring.

Scenery along Navaho Nation "highway." (From the author's collection.)

We passed a number of small villages with facades of worn-out cars, broken wagon wheels, and tilted outhouses, but there was no one to be seen. All of the Native Americans were staying inside their hogans and out of the rain. The reservation crossing finally ended after dark with registration in another dumpy auto court.

The years have stripped me of any verifiable times en route or details about when or where we finally turned back on to the blessed highway. I do recall looking back on Gordon's car that night, sitting forlornly beneath the auto court's VACANCY sign. It was a mess, covered with mud and tumbleweed scratches. We had scored one damaged front fender after hitting a bridge railing and a tear in the convertible top from an encounter with a large mesquite brush. Strangely, Gordon didn't seem too distressed by the damage. His assessment of the experience was summed up with a laconic admission, "I guess we shouldn't have gone that way."

We hauled our bags into the room and just sat in silence for a few minutes. Recognizing a cause for celebration, I finally opened my bag. I could have finished the bourbon cache by myself, but displaying a sense of fairness, I shared it with Gordon, my tour director. I dropped off to sleep that night mulling over an important fact: Since leaving Gardner Airfield, I couldn't recall seeing even a single Indian.

THIRTY-FIVE

We rolled into Kirtland Air Field at about 0100 on 15 October. I wrote only a few letters while there. I was neither thrilled at the assignment in store for us, nor was I enchanted by the place. A trip to the flight line failed to produce any feeling of belonging.

The Consolidated B-24 was a huge airplane for the time, and the inside of it was roomy—like three-bedrooms-'n-two-baths roomy. The bomber version of the aircraft carried eleven crewmembers in a boxy fuselage that was 68 feet long, 18 feet high, and had a wingspan of 110 feet. The Liberator's empty weight was 36,500 pounds, and its proposed gross takeoff weight was set at 65,000 pounds. She was powered by four Pratt & Whitney R-1830 turbocharged engines producing a gross 4,800 horsepower for takeoff. It was a far cry from the 30 hp four-banger in my 1928 Chevy sedan.

Consolidated B-24D Liberator, National Museum of the United States Air Force. (US Air Force photo.)

There were three basic versions of the B-24: The garden-variety bomber configuration came complete with bomb bays, turrets, and waist gun stations; the C-87 cargo version featured a cavernous fuselage for bulk hauling; and the C-109 or tanker version was fitted with eight flexible fuel cells capable of carrying 2,900 gallons of high-octane aviation fuel, making it a darling of the skies. The C-109 variant was often referred to as the C1-zero-BOOM due to its penchant for exploding without warning—and a lost engine on takeoff was inevitably catastrophic. All models were slow climbers, and when loaded, they were hard to fly. If a right outboard engine was lost in flight, it took the full pressure of both feet on the left rudder pedal to even maintain directional stability, and a fully loaded C-109 was difficult to land. With serious liabilities on takeoff, during flight, and on landing, it wasn't an airplane to love.

Consolidated B-24D Liberator, National Museum of the United States Air Force. (US Air Force photo.)

For all its power and size, the B-24 left me cold. On the flight apron at Kirtland, these aircraft sat sullenly, like three-legged pterodactyls. Many had been modified by removing the nose turrets. That surgical procedure had resulted in gaping holes that were closed over by drafty sheet-metal hoods lacking any finesse. Many of the training planes were war wearies; a very few were later models.

It's one thing to dislike a specific airplane and another to remain stupid about its operational characteristics, and we worked very hard to learn as much about the B-24 as possible. Although our stint as instructors in single-engine airplanes made the transition to the Liberator more difficult, it was obvious to everyone that the more we could learn about the aircraft, the better we would fare in combat.

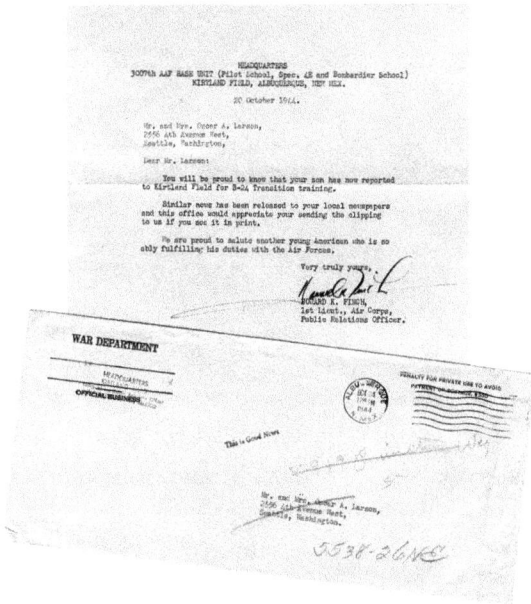

Letter from Kirtland Command to my parents. (From the author's collection.)

The ground school at Kirtland was very intensive. There were one hundred fifty students in our group. The school was committed to producing seventy-five pilots and seventy-five copilots, and most of those involved in the program did their best to comply with expectations, despite the flight instruction being very mediocre. Overall, the flight instructors seemed a bit lackluster in their jobs, and the results showed it. I could understand the frustration they felt with their assignment, but their attitude didn't contribute much to building up student flying proficiency.

Link Trainer (early flight simulator) at Freeman Field, Seymour, Indiana. TSgt James R. Schneid is shown at the controls. (Public domain.)

We did receive a lot of Link Trainer time that honed our instrument and radio procedures proficiencies. It was imperative for us to become fully acquainted with low-beam letdown procedures allowing us to land the B-24 in minimum weather conditions. In addition to ground school, we received twenty hours of flight instruction, which most of us felt was totally inadequate to properly learn how to handle and command the big bomber in combat.

Even ground handling was difficult. There was a severe lag in the brake system. If the pilot pushed on the brake to turn while taking off, there would be a long hissing sound, a moment's wait, and then the brake would be applied. The neophyte pilot would always overbrake, and the airplane would zigzag down the taxiway like a drunken swan. A steerable nose wheel on the B-24 would have been a godsend.

Cockpit, Consolidated B-24D Liberator, National Museum of the United States Air Force. (US Air Force photo.)

I recall one particularly dramatic afternoon closer to the end of our flight instruction. I was in the copilot's seat and the crew chief was sitting on a small stool between the pilot and me. As we landed, I looked out and saw the number three inboard engine had died after landing. I reported it to the instructor-pilot. There was no great problem here, we were on the ground and didn't need the right inboard engine anyway...or so we thought.

The pilot and I were conversing casually with the crew chief as we approached the apron filled with fueled B-24s. We were headed directly for the middle of the flock. Suddenly the pilot screamed, "NO BRAKES!"

While talking, we three had completely overlooked the fact that the number three engine, which had died after our landing, was responsible for maintaining proper pressure in the braking system. While taxiing in, the brakes could still operate because of an accumulator tank that stored a small amount of hydraulic pressure for emergency use. As we used the brakes while taxiing in, we had emptied the pressure in the accumulator, and in this moment of crisis, we had nothing left.

At the same instant the pilot shouted out the warning, the crew chief leaped to the rear of the flight deck and threw on the emergency hydraulic pump. Our brakeless B-24 was still headed for a catastrophic ground collision when barely fifteen feet from the nearest parked B-24, we finally came to a bobbing halt.

We never neglected the right inboard engine again.

During our stay at Kirtland, I believe I bombed the city of El Paso, Texas, at least five times. Fortunately, the citizens of that fair metropolis were totally unaware that their town had been completely destroyed by an unknown pilot who could barely fly the plane. We flew a lot of practice bombing runs at night, many times under a "bomber's moon" bright enough to help light up a ground target. There was a haunting beauty to these trips. Starlight haloed the plane, and the flames from the engine stacks painted the sky outside our wings an ethereal blue, while the countryside below seemed at rest in a silvered light that carried with it serenity and peace. The whole of this beautiful nocturnal landscape was in sharp contrast to the spirit of destruction that rode shotgun with a B-24 and its crew.

THIRTY-SIX

As we rolled into November, the weather deteriorated to an offering of almost constant rain. This month would witness President Roosevelt's victorious campaign for an unprecedented fourth term in office. It would also witness the first raid of Marianas-based B-29s on the homeland of Japan, an event that would eventually lead to the total devastation of an enemy whose criminal behavior had been steeped in cruelty from the onset of this terrible war.

Fifteen flight instructors from Gardner Airfield had transferred to Albuquerque. Our experiences at Gardner had made single-engine pilots out of us, and we were regarded as some kind of miscreant group as far as the other B-24 pilots were concerned.

On 12 November late in the afternoon, one of the pilots from our Gardner bunch came into my room waving a sheaf of orders. He was highly excited and informed me that within the week, a bunch of us would be sent to the Overseas Replacement Depot at Greensboro, North Carolina. From there, we would be transferred overseas—perhaps as soon as the end of the year!

I looked at the list. My name wasn't on it. They would be going on without me. I was stunned. I'd been with some of these guys, like my buddy, Pete Mignin, since we studied together at the College Training Detachment in Des Moines. This news was incredibly disappointing.

I searched the list again. My friend, "Ron" (not his real name), was included on the transfer orders. Ron was a quiet and capable guy, someone liked by everyone. He had married his hometown sweetheart while we were still instructing at Gardner; and his young wife, a sweet girl, had left her home in Kansas to be with him as long as she could. News of Ron's transfer would be devastating to her; and though unvoiced, it would be difficult for Ron, too. When I saw his name on the list, I called him and asked him to meet me right away at the officers' club.

After we'd had a drink, I told Ron that I wanted to take his place on the transfer list to Greensboro, explaining that all my buddies were being shipped out, and I wanted to go with them.

He absolutely refused.

I then reminded him that he now had a responsibility to his new wife. "What in the hell is she going to do without you?" I asked.

This obviously pulled at his coattails. We talked for an hour, and he finally agreed to check with Command in the morning.

We didn't have much time.

The next morning, Ron went to the adjutant's office and stated our case. The sergeant in charge informed him that the orders had already been cut, and there would be no changes. When Ron called me with this news, I told him to stay put, and I would meet him at the adjutant's office in a half hour.

When I got there, we met with the sergeant. I asked him to please reconsider our request. I knew Ron was reticent to push too hard because of the nature of the situation, so I did most of the talking. I enumerated my reasons for wanting to take Ron's place: I had a lot of time in with the guys who were being transferred; we were all frustrated, single-engine pilots; and most important, Ron had just been married, and the request for transfer change was totally my idea.

The sergeant was a nice guy who listened and seemed to appreciate the circumstances; but when I finished, he told us that time was really short to amend the transfer orders, and the final decision would come from the adjunct's office. As we prepared to leave, he added, "I'll see what I can do."

It was a stressful wait. I kept thinking that I didn't want to stay in Albuquerque sitting in the shade of a broken-down B-24D while the war went on without me. But I didn't have long to be concerned. Ron and I both received calls from the adjutant's office early that afternoon. The change in orders had been approved. I was formally transferred to Greensboro, North Carolina, to report there no later than Saturday, 18 November. The die was cast. We'd pulled it off!

We had a big party that night and got a little drunk. I vaguely recall the whole bunch of us singing "Friendship" together...probably more than a little off key. It was a happy moment; but no doubt, the two happiest people in the group were Ron's wife and me. There was no heroism or sacrifice here, only a twist of fate that turned into a win-win situation for all involved. Ron would remain at Kirtland for a few more weeks and then transfer to a B-29 transition base in eastern Washington. He never left the states for the duration of the war.

The trip to Greensboro put me back on Route 66. Joe, one of the other renegades in our group had a nifty Ford convertible sedan; and four of us piled in and headed east through Amarillo, Oklahoma City, Little Rock, Memphis, and Nashville, finally reaching Greensboro on 18 November in just the nick of time. There was one unforgettable experience on our journey. At some juncture, we decided we needed a bit of bourbon. Unable to buy reputable whiskey because of the hour, we purchased a bottle of Old Oak from a cooperative cabbie. It was vile tasting—like it may have come from a car battery; but as usual, I downed my share. I fell asleep in the back seat and awoke sometime later to the worst headache and stomachache I had ever experienced. My colleagues were in pretty much the same condition. We briefly considered returning to Little Rock and killing the cabbie, but reason prevailed, and we continued on. It seems fascinating to think it was so bad that I still remember it after all of these years. It's also amazing to recall that we drank the whole bottle.

Greensboro is located in Great Smoky Mountain Country; and as we approached, we entered a land of rain and dense deciduous forests that at once seemed the soul and spirit of the place—thick mists and wood smoke that are the same yet different from the rain forests of my native Pacific Northwest. There is a peaceful, benign quality about this wooded land.

The Overseas Replacement Depot (ORD) was completely devoid of any hint of airplanes. The base was a holding tank filled with guys waiting to be filtered out to spots where they were most needed. It was a place for arriving, staying a very short time, then moving on to places unknown and unimagined. Like its temporary occupants, the buildings were transitory shelters, similar to Lincoln, Nebraska, but at this point, the barracks situation was relatively unimportant.

Beer and boredom were the rations of the ORD. There was little else to do, so I took to extensive walking through the nearby countryside. I felt at home here. North Carolina seemed a broad-leafed parody of the forests back home, and the wet and musty thickets and brambles reminded me of Puget Sound, the place of my beginnings. When the weather soured enough that walks were no longer an option, I read. One book in particular I remember: *The Man Who Killed Lincoln*, by Phillip Van Doren Stern. I recall it vividly; it was adequate company for the constant rain on the barracks roof.

We were granted a seven-day furlough on 27 November, presumably because we were headed overseas. There wasn't enough time to get to Seattle, so I elected to head north for a solo trip to New York. I booked into a small hotel in Manhattan and walked the streets for a couple of days with a craned neck checking out all the skyscrapers. I did the Stork Club, Times Square, and other tourist stops—all places I'd read about.

By chance, I walked into the USO to see what entertainment was available for GIs. A nice lady advised me of a dance that was being held that night at the former home of J. P. Morgan; GIs were welcome, so I had dinner and sauntered into the palatial residence about 2030 that evening.

It seemed to be a rather upscale affair. The girls wore lovely evening dresses and were obviously well chaperoned. The music was Big Band and excellent. Rather early on, I exchanged glances with a very pretty brunette and asked her to dance. She was bright with a great sense of humor, the sort of girl you might take home to show off to your mother, and we danced together most of the evening. When too soon the witching hour arrived, I asked her if I might see her again. Her brow creased into a frown, and she informed me that the girls in the group were prohibited from dating GIs.

People were leaving, and she excused herself. A moment later, she returned and slipped a note into my hand as she gave me a friendly peck on the cheek. Then we said goodnight. It was a definite capper on the evening when I looked at her note and saw she'd written down her phone number. I called her the next morning. She lived rather close to my hotel, and we met for lunch and spent the day together sightseeing, laughing, and talking endlessly.

After an extended hansom cab ride through Central Park, we had dinner at the Lafayette Hotel; and later, we hit a couple of nightspots for a drinks. She was nineteen, and I'd just turned twenty, but no one questioned us, and we had a great time.

I had to report back to Greensboro the next day, but before I left, I saw her once more. As we said our goodbyes, she gave me her snapshot. We were like so many thousands of others—ships passing in the night. I can't help wondering where this friendship might have gone had there not been a war and the inevitable military orders.

We exchanged a few letters after I was deployed overseas, but I never saw her again. I hope she's had a good life, like I've had. She was a neat young lady, and I wish that I had met her in a different place and time.

That was one hell of a leave.

THIRTY-SEVEN

Our gang of renegades got orders on 5 December to be in Miami, Florida, in four days. It was becoming obvious that we were going somewhere east—but where our final destination was...well, that was anyone's guess.

When we arrived in Miami, we were billeted at the Floridian Hotel. The former luxury spa on the strip had been confiscated by the military to house transient officers bound for wherever their fates would take them. Four of us from the Gardner bunch roomed together, including my best buddy, Pete. We were now dangling from a string of uncertainty. *Where were we going? What the hell would we be flying? How long would we be gone?* And somewhere in the back of our minds, I'm sure we wondered, *would we be coming home?*

Miami was another sit-and-wait situation, with one exception: This time when we got orders to leave, we would be leaving in a hurry. Our instructions were to maintain a readiness status that would allow us to depart with a two-hour notice. We were issued musette bags for extra gear, shoulder holsters, and .45-caliber automatic pistols as side arms. Our baggage was kept just an arm's reach away, and no one started a book of over one hundred pages. There was really not much to do except lay on our bunks and kill time.

Traveling Companions. Drawing by Ed Larson, 2014.

Pete and I had both done some sailing; and one afternoon for diversion, we rented a small dinghy. While sailing across the bay, we noticed a nearby small island, which supported a huge cyprus-ringed mansion. As we approached, a minor squall came up causing us to capsize. We swam, dragging the boat behind us, to the island's shoreline. While we sat there drying out, we were more than a little surprised by a burly watchman who confronted us.

"What the *hell* are you doing on this island?"

We both thought it was obvious; we were having trouble drying out our boat. But this didn't seem like the time or place for a smart-ass answer. He was armed and advised us that the island in fact belonged to Alphonse Gabriel Capone, the notorious gangster. He also informed us that Mr. Capone and his friends would be very unhappy to see us on the property.

Under the circumstances, Pete and I departed immediately, even though the sail was still soaking wet. Needless to say, the guard didn't wave goodbye, and we didn't either. We returned to the rental dock, paid an additional fee for upending the boat, and chalked up the afternoon to another full-fledged adventure for our memory books.

As December rolled on, the promise of Christmas hung like an ornament on a brightly lit tree—a tree far away—in a home more than 3,500 miles to my west. I sent a couple of checks to provide for family gifts. It was simply too complicated to get out and buy stuff that wouldn't fit or was the wrong color. In a sense, Christmas was a contradiction. There were the usual tinsel and lights; but somehow, they had faded. The war had changed us. The tiny infant in the manger promised a peace and goodwill that seemed more unattainable than ever. I straddled two worlds now; trained to earn peace and respite for a troubled, war-weary world, I slept with a holstered .45 hanging on my bedpost.

Germany launched a surprise major offensive on 16 December 1944 in the Ardennes Forest region spanning Belgium and Luxembourg. The Ardennes had already been sanctified by the deaths of thousands of soldiers killed there during World War I. This was Hitler's last, futile, murderous attempt to retake the city of Antwerp. Casualties on both sides were agonizing, and the fighting was close up and personal.

COURAGE IS FEAR HOLDING ON
A MINUTE LONGER.
~ GENERAL GEORGE S. PATTON

Photo: US First Army tank men huddled around an open fire receive Christmas presents near Eupen, Belgium, 30 December 1944. (US Army photo.)

The battle raged on under skies filthy with rain, fog, and clouds. Our Mustang and Thunderbolt crews bit their fingernails while waiting to get off the ground; and for a time, it appeared the Germans might hold the upper hand. Then a break in the weather came on a prophetic Sabbath. The morning of Sunday 24 December dawned bright and clear, and our fighters and bombers took off with everything they could lift off the ground. The P-47s and P-51s turned the Ardennes into an American shooting gallery, strafing and destroying every German thing that wiggled.

American soldiers take defensive positions in the Ardennes. (US Army photo.)

The Battle of the Bulge lasted forty-one days. It was the largest, bloodiest battle fought by US troops in the Second World War, with more than 89,000 casualties and 19,000 mortally wounded. Frigid conditions took out thousands more.

I would lose friends there. I would know more who survived the physical scars but never overcame the mental and spiritual wounds suffered in those terrible days of conflict. On a low-level shooting spree, Roy Johnson picked up ground fire and slammed his borrowed P-47 Thunderbolt into the small ridge bordering an exquisitely beautiful Belgian valley. My buddy, Bob Morgan, traded shots with a German infantryman and won the exchange only to discover his opponent was thirteen years old. He carried that battle with him until his dying day. Nothing comes cheap.

I don't recall much of what I did on Christmas Eve. After a couple of highballs, the group of us had dinner, the entrée spiced with reveries and talk of home.

A few minutes after I returned to my room, there was a knock at the door. It was a sergeant who advised me that I should be downstairs in the lobby in an hour with all my gear. I was to await transport to the airport for an overseas flight.

"You mean *all of us*?" I asked.

"No sir," he replied. "Only Lieutenant Larson is on this order."

We were completely mystified. We had always believed our gang would be transferred as a group to wherever we were going. But time was short. This was no time to argue.

I made a quick trip to some of the other rooms to tell friends "Merry Christmas and goodbye," and then I grabbed my stuff. I was down in the Floridian's foyer with time to spare, so I used a pay phone to called a young WAVE I'd met in Miami and tell her "so long." Then I waited with Pete and a couple of the other guys for a final farewell.

Within minutes, a jeep pulled up. I tossed my stuff into the back, jumped into the front seat, and held on as we pulled away from the curb. Unfamiliar with the locations of the various Army Air Forces Base Units on the orders, I asked the sergeant driver where in the hell we were going.

"I'm dropping you off at the airfield off 36th Street; then I'm going home," he replied. "I think most of you flyboys are headed for Brazil!"

PHOTOGRAPHS

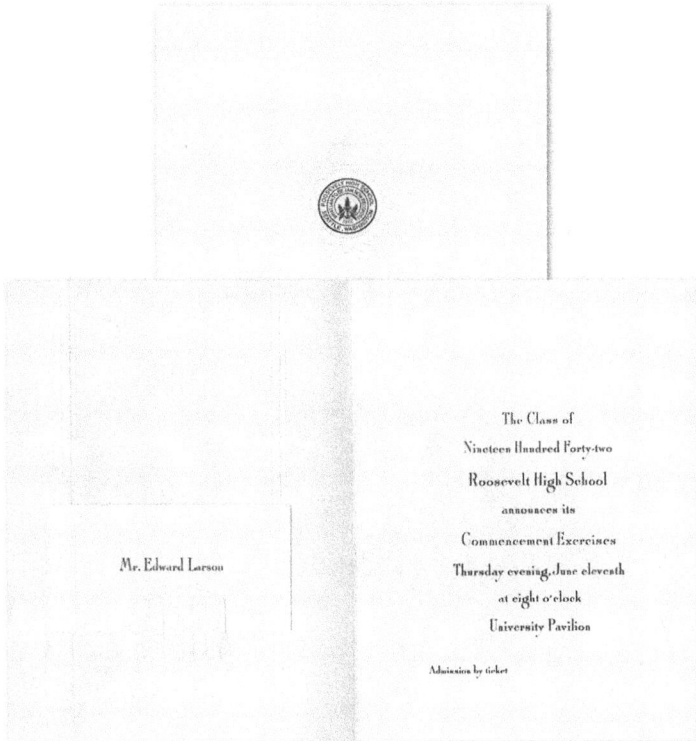

The Class of

Nineteen Hundred Forty-two

Roosevelt High School

announces its

Commencement Exercises

Thursday evening, June eleventh

at eight o'clock

University Pavilion

Admission by ticket

Mr. Edward Larson

Roosevelt High School Graduation Announcement, June 1942.

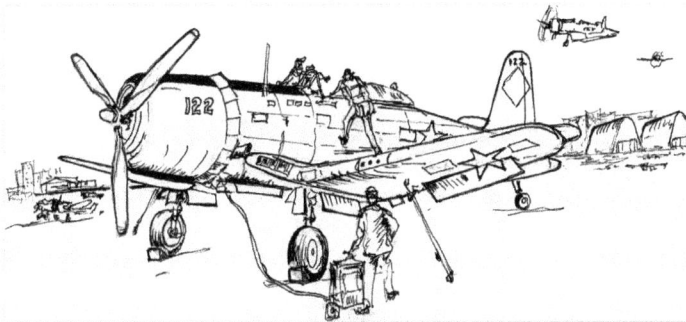

"Graduation day came and went, and my buddies and I put our futures on hold while we awaited the call for military service. I signed up for a few short art classes concentrating on aircraft illustration; but after a week or two, I dropped out. The only compass in my head pointed toward the AAF and active duty, and I vegetated on the back burner of impatience and ennui."

Lincoln - March 1943

"It's damn cold in Nebraska in winter..."
Me in front of T-917.
Lincoln Army Air Field, March 1943.

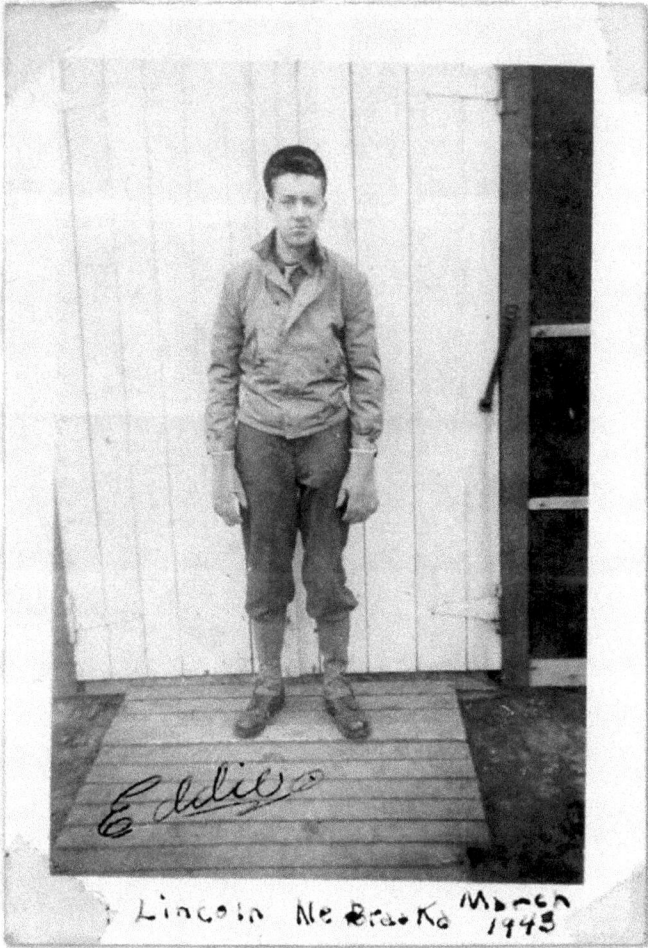

The Author as a Battle-Hardened Veteran.

"General Washington"

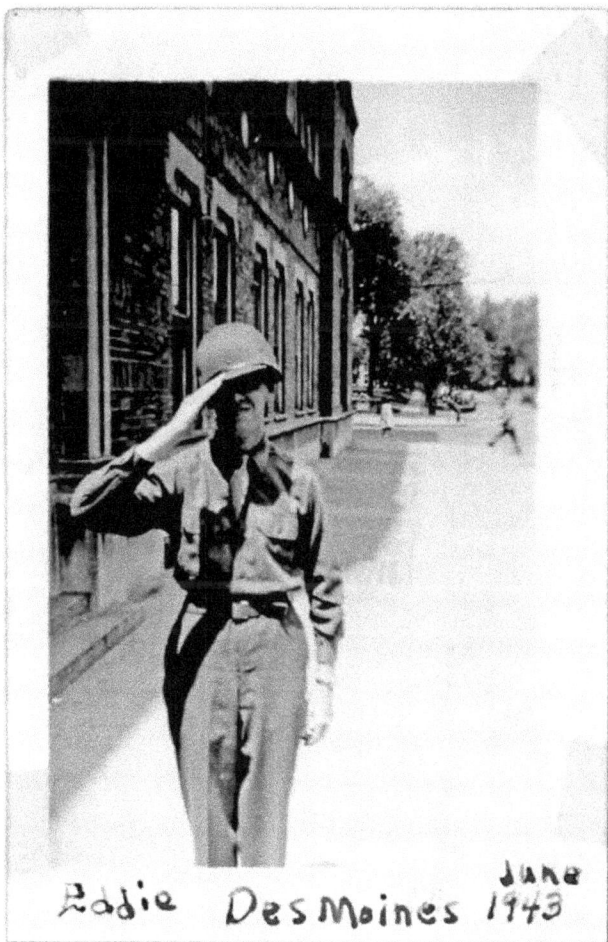

Eddie DesMoines June 1943

CTD in Des Moines, Iowa.

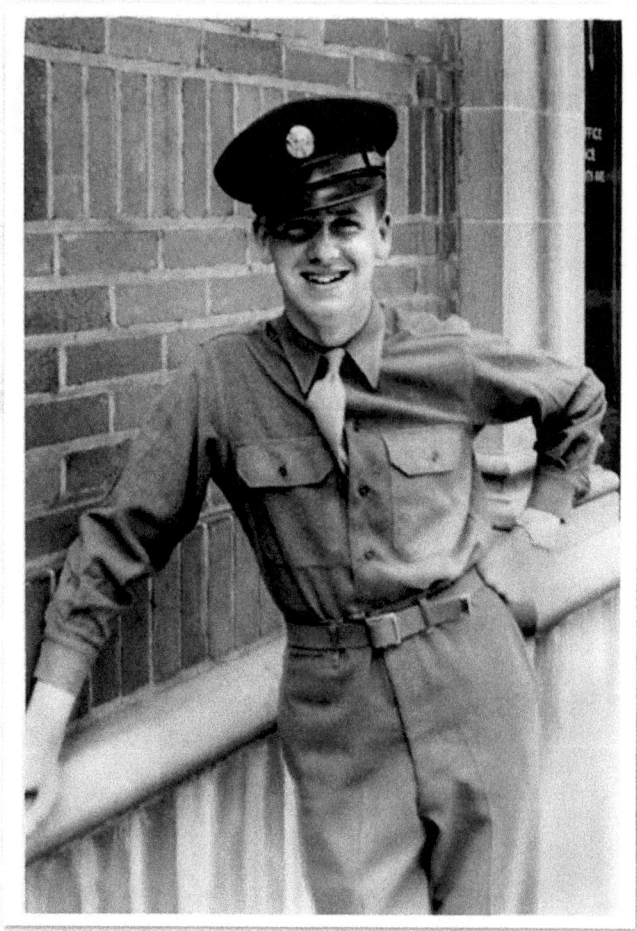

The Author at Drake University.

In need of weight therapy.

"...in addition to our educational responsibilities, we faced constant drilling and physical training. In short, it was a tall pole to climb, but at the top was a wonderful carrot: The last week of our CTD, we would receive ten hours of flight training...."

Graduation Day for Squadron 44-D was 15 April 1944.

EA Larson 2014

PART THREE

THIRTY-EIGHT

The drive to Miami Army Airfield wasn't long, but it was memorable. Along the entire route, subdued evidence of a War Christmas had sprouted like a determined poinsettia in a hostile desert. Bunting with season's greetings adorned storefronts, and trees twinkled through windows of humble homes; and once or twice, we drove past the faint sounds of carolers. On this night, children would be awaiting Santa's arrival with a breathless excitement that is the rare gift of the very young; but for me, this jeep ride and this Christmas Eve would be remembered as the loneliest, most alone I would ever know.

The sergeant driver delivered me to a terminal just off the flight line. A few military and civilian unfortunates who had picked the short straw were working, and while their dispositions were anything but merry, they couldn't have felt much worse than I did. The corporal who checked my orders advised me that I was outbound for Natal, Brazil, on a Pan American contract Douglas C-54 Skymaster and that it might be a couple of hours before takeoff. Beyond that, he didn't know anything…and obviously didn't care.

It was close to midnight when a rather surly sergeant approached, identified me, and told me to follow him. Outside, there were several guys hovering around a C-54, which was made visible by an open cabin door and lights streaming from its windows. I asked the sergeant where the rest of the passengers were, and he told me that my name and a freight load were the only items listed on the manifest.

I was dumbfounded by this news and not pleased to be the only guy at the dance. When I asked him if this solo trip was a common occurrence, he replied that it happened now and again and that it was "probably due to some screw up in the orders."

Douglas C-54 Skymaster. (US Air Force photo.)

I climbed the ladder into the spacious cabin of the plane, and the sergeant tossed up my gear and left in a silence that overrode any hint of Christmas wishes or goodbyes. The cabin had a pretty good load of freight already lashed down, including two Pratt & Whitney R-1830 radial engines that seemed to dominate the collection of stuff we'd be carrying. *Perhaps my 150 pounds had topped off the load?* Not likely.

I moved forward to the flight deck and introduced myself to the three-man crew. They were all Pan American Airways flight officers: pilot, copilot, and navigator/radio operator, and they welcomed me aboard. They seemed to be in relatively better spirits than anyone else I'd encountered in the past few hours, and I asked the first officer if I could stay on the flight deck for takeoff since I was the only passenger onboard. He invited me to take the extra seat in the cockpit and advised that we'd be leaving shortly.

I strapped myself into the seat a little to the rear of the flight deck, determined to keep my eyes open and my mouth shut. This crew had thousands of hours of overwater flights, and they whipped through their preflight procedures as if they had written each one.

A couple of minutes soon turned into a half hour...then longer, giving me some time to look around. The C-54 cockpit seemed eons beyond the B-24, although, there had actually been only two years between development of the two planes. The C-54, obviously the more recent, smacked of a newer style and more functional design—both hallmarks of a Donald Douglas aircraft, and the instrument panel was well organized with neatly clustered flight and engine instruments making for easy and fast diagnoses of flight and engine performance. The console was wide and well considered, and there was ample comfortable seating for a crew of four. I was totally impressed by this machine.

Douglas C-54 Skymaster cockpit, National Museum of the United States Air Force.
(US Air Force photo.)

Finally, the airplane was buttoned up. Within minutes, the four Pratt & Whitney R-2000 engines were purring like a contented cat. Already this airplane had redefined my concept of a four-engine trash truck like my beloved B-24. This plane was sweet and seemed to have dropped in from another planet.

Obtaining clearance, we taxied to the end of the active runway. After a brief takeoff check, the pilot looked around and flashed me a smile and a thumbs up. With throttles punched forward, the C-54 picked up speed, and after a short, velvety takeoff, the wheels came up. Power was pulled back to climbing RPM and boost, and we were on our way to British Guiana. This was a magic carpet ride.

The southeasterly course between Miami and Georgetown would take us across the eastern tip of Cuba, the western tip of Puerto Rico, and over the northeast coast of Venezuela. The route was watery save for the short distances we would fly over the Caribbean islands we crossed. The distance was about 1,960 statute miles, and we could expect about 180 mph out of the C-54. All things considered except the winds aloft, I figured we would make Georgetown about eleven hours after takeoff—around noon Ed-Larson time.

We'd been pretty chatty during my time in the cockpit, and so the feelings of loneliness I had carried aboard with my gear had been largely dispelled by the companionship I'd been given since our departure. This crew was a bunch of normal guys—just airplane drivers like me, except their skills were worlds ahead of mine. It was getting on to the wee hours of the morning when I thanked them and went back to the cabin to grab some shuteye.

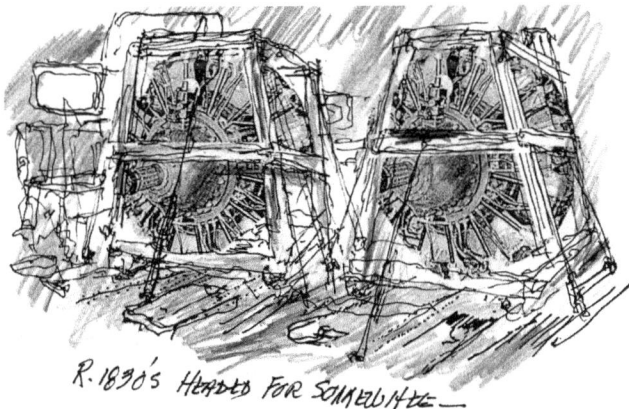

R-1830s *Headed for Somewhere*. Drawing by Ed Larson, 2014.

A couple of blankets were folded over a jump seat. They looked like they had a lot of miles on them, but I figured I couldn't catch anything too bad, so I rolled up in them between the two crated engines and propped my jacket under my head for a pillow. The steady hum of the engines was a soothing lullaby, and the light in the cabin was low and unobtrusive. Soon, I began falling asleep.

I have attempted to be completely candid in the writing of my experiences because nothing could be accomplished by enhancing the years of which I speak, but this next episode may stretch the credulity of my reader. I beg your indulgence, and I promise you, the following is true.

As I nodded off, something extraordinary happened. It came in the form of a sonata—music clearly audible and faultlessly performed. Its ethereal beauty was both tender and unnerving; and at first, I thought I was dreaming. I bolted upright, frightened and looking around for the source, but there was none. The droning of the engines would have wiped out any sound system. I was now completely awake and moving about as the music continued. After several minutes, I lay down again, listening to music that went on with such lovely clarity and content that its sound transcended the engines' droning, soothing my anxiety, and wrapping my crumby blankets and me in a feeling of well-being, utter contentment, and peace. And then, it just faded away. And I knew I'd been given a gift for which I should be deeply grateful.

I slept several hours and awoke fully rested as early morning light streamed into the cabin. After washing up, I made my way to the flight deck and joined the crew for coffee. A box of pastries, some packaged sandwiches, and fresh fruit rounded out our morning meal. All three crewmembers looked fresh after grabbing naps en route. Obviously, the autopilot hadn't slept at all.

After an invitation, I plunked down in the copilot's seat and flew the airplane for an hour or so. It was truly a beautiful aircraft to fly, light on the controls and totally stable with no tricks or surprises. I maintained heading and altitude very respectably and felt I could land this plane with no trouble; but of course, that was out of the question.

Due to tailwinds, we made Georgetown a little early. The crew greased the C-54 onto the active runway and taxied to a hardstand in the transient area for refueling and an overnight stay.

This would be my first Christmas deployment.

THIRTY-NINE

S tepping from the plane in Georgetown was like stepping into a steam bath. I had never experienced the heat and humidity of the tropics, and this was a genuine shock. The country lies about five degrees north of the equator, and it is covered in dense overgrowth. The only jungles I had ever seen were those in the Tarzan movies; these were for real. Open spaces were actually carved out of the tropical forests with machetes; and where there was vegetation, the vines, trees, and underbrush were impenetrable.

In addition to the vegetation and heat, this stopover was made most impressive by the giant buffet of fresh tropical fruits available at the transient mess. Meals were served from a long, market-like shed, and the fare was wonderful. I obtained a billet for the overnight and slept under mosquito netting for the first time in my life. There was, however, little respite from the heat—even at midnight—and this night there would be no repeat of the recital that had made my trip thus far so memorable.

Breakfast, again replete with fresh fruit, made up for my sleepless night. After gathering my gear, I caught a transport back to the plane. The crew was already onboard, checking weather and other pertinent flight information, and they greeted me warmly. I seated myself in what had apparently become my place on the flight deck as the crew completed the preflight. In a half hour, we were buttoned up. Soon we were airborne, heading again southeast, leaving steamy Georgetown behind.

Trip from Miami to Georgetown to Natal. (Map data: Google.)

The distance to Natal from Georgetown is approximately 1,800 miles—around ten hours flying time—and we would skirt the coasts of Surinam and Brazil en route. The scenery was stunning. Below and to my right was matted jungle stretching unbroken to the western horizon, while on my left, the Atlantic, windswept and dynamic, rolled forever toward the east. Between these two immensities, we sped toward our destination.

I took an early stint at flying the C-54 from the right seat. We had been told by a briefing officer that all aircraft were advised to stay close to the coastline—with very good reason. In case of engine failure or other problems, it was imperative to head for the coastline to ditch since the endless jungle forest would completely conceal a crashed aircraft, making rescue unlikely. As we droned on for hours, we could see no clearings, no rivers, no villages—nothing but solid jungle canopy obscuring everything beneath it. Of course, I was aware that we were practically replicating the route of Amelia Earhart's final circumnavigation attempt, and I found the prospect thrilling. We would fly nearly the same track except where she took a more northerly route across the Atlantic. Looking down, I wondered what she and her navigator Fred Noonan must have thought as they cruised over what I saw as a jungle of no return.

In the world of flight, lives depend totally on the integrity of the aircraft and the engines that fly them, each part whirling like a tiny galaxy with its orbit and purpose. Should there be a disruption—a fractured piston skirt, a galled wrist pin, or a blown head gasket—the results are immediate. Failure might buy the keys to the kingdom of eternal rest. Flying over these remote regions, I was keenly aware that should fate assault us, we might sleep forever in the jungle or the sea.

We arrived at our destination on 27 December, and I was relieved to discover an equatorial heat greatly tempered by sea breezes. There seemed no war here, only sun and sea…and waiting.

I was assigned a billet in the transient officers' quarters. It smacked of a beach resort with every amenity one could imagine, and the bar and mess were elaborate and supported by the required memberships of all those officers passing through.

It appeared every GI's first purchase upon arrival was a pair of Natal boots—and I soon discovered why. They were an absolute necessity. Made of soft leather, they were pull on, midcalf high, with plain toes and durable soles. I bought two pairs and loved them. When they finally wore out, I found capable cobblers to resole them with the rubber from used airplane tires. Thus repaired, the soles remained totally intact while the uppers dissolved into pieces out of constant wear.

Five days after my arrival in Natal, the rest of my Kirtland gang showed up. Nothing was ever discovered as to why I'd been booked out ahead of them, but things were getting back to normal. As usual, Pete and I roomed together, and the rest of our contingent was assigned lodging nearby in very comfortable quarters with four beds each and ample room for gear storage. Tonight, we would beer it up in the loveliness that was Natal.[62]

And Natal was idyllic—a fabulous enclave bordered by beaches so broad and beautiful they took one's breath away; and the food was excellent, the beer cold, superb tasting, and light—and the Brazilian cigars? Well, they were the icing on the cake. Just a few years earlier, I had been a punk kid from Phinney Ridge, flying model airplanes, reading *Jimmie Allen Club News*, and helping my uncle peddle magazines door to door to put food on our family's table. Now, here I was, barely twenty years old, flying real airplanes, making $285.00 a month, and sitting in a magnificent officers' club. By rights, I still should have been riding around on a one-dollar bicycle! *What had God wrought?*

But Natal was more than just a pretty face. It had a large base with a large mission. Troops, equipment, and war material funneled through it to the whole of Africa, the Middle East, and the China-Burma-India (CBI) Theater. We languished there for two weeks. The inevitable wake-up call came early in the second week of January. We would leave the beaches and beer of Natal and head east and north across the South Atlantic to Africa.

A look at the map would indicate that at least the first leg of our journey would not be a piece of cake. Our route would head almost due east for 1,437 miles[63] to our halfway point, Ascension Island, a pile of volcanic rock and rubble that was essentially a coaling and refueling stop for vessels and aircraft fighting the battle of the South Atlantic. It had become a steppingstone for those leapfrogging from Brazil to Africa, thence onward to wherever. Since the island was only about six miles wide, it would be a neat trick to find it after hours of dead reckoning and direction finder twisting. The second leg of our transatlantic flight would be easy: fly east. It's tough to miss Africa.

We were scheduled to leave Natal at 0100 so that we would arrive at Ascension during daylight hours. When I got to the flight line with my fellow travelers, I looked around. No C-54s. The only aircraft in our loading area was a beat-up C-87 sitting wearily on the apron in the darkness. It was impossible to believe that we were going to fly the Atlantic and halfway around the world in this "evil-bastard contraption."[64]

Unfortunately, it was true.

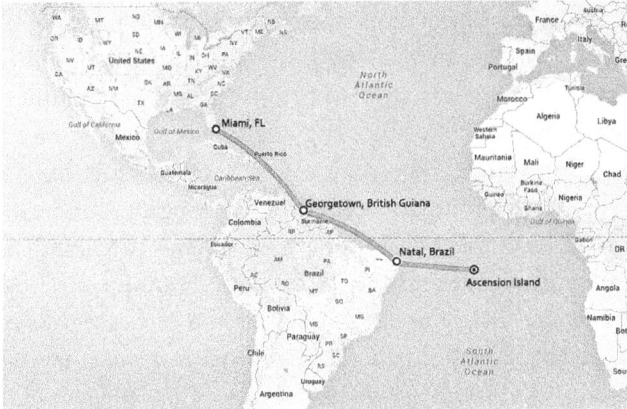

Journey from Natal to Ascension Island. (Map data: Google.)

US Army Air Forces Consolidated C-87 Liberator Express in flight, ca 1943.
(US Air Force photo.)

The Consolidated C-87 Liberator Express was a hastily designed and ill-conceived cargo version of the B-24D that we had learned to fly (and hate) at Kirtland. The airplane started from a pattern of mediocrity and morphed into one that was a poor performer and a pain to fly. It was supposed to be an answer to the USAAF's need for a high-altitude, long-range cargo plane. In short, it was an unsafe hulk that leaked fuel, had congenital engine problems, and was a bitch to keep in the air. The only bright spot was that the C-54 and the C-46 Commando would soon relegate it to the bone yard. At the height of folly, a C-87 was designed as a VIP transport aircraft for President Franklin Roosevelt. Because of its unsafe reputation, the Secret Service refused to allow him to fly in the plane. Instead, it served as a luxury transport for Mrs. Roosevelt on several of her South American goodwill trips.

Our gear had been previously loaded into the front and rear baggage areas and securely (we hoped) lashed down. We were aware that the C-87 had chronic center-of-gravity problems, and shifting cargo could be disastrous. I believe sixteen of us boarded the hulking beast with mammoth doubts and concerns. We all knew the airplane for what it was, but only a couple of guys were pulled kicking and screaming into its cruddy interior. A four-man crew—pilot, copilot, navigator, and crew chief—was already on the flight deck, and I'm sure our caustic comments about their airplane did not sit well with them.

Inside the plane, seats ran fore and aft along the sides of the cargo hold, and I grabbed one next to a dingy window. When the engines were started, I noticed the left outboard engine caught right away and seemed to run well. Not so with the left inboard. After several attempts to get it started, it finally kicked in with a tremendous backfire, a flash of light, and a cloud of gray smoke. I couldn't monitor the starting efforts on the starboard engines because I couldn't see them from my seat. Perhaps it was just as well.

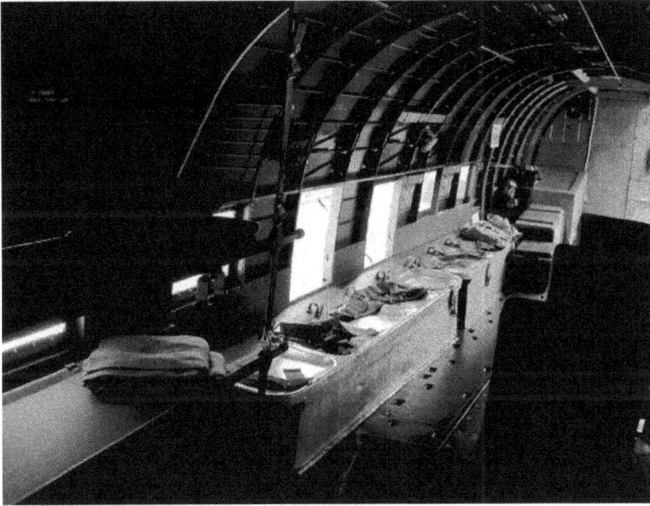

Interior seating of a troop transport. (From the author's collection.)

Our low position in the underslung cabin gave me a darkened view of the gravelly taxiway as we rolled toward takeoff position. There was also the hiss from the brakes and the ever-present up and down nose nodding that made this airplane such a delight. As the run-up began, I could mentally go through the checklist I had repeated so many times at Kirtland. One positive factor stood out in the face of this dismal journey: If the pilot and copilot died en route, there were sixteen other guys aboard who could fly this can.

As we were cleared for takeoff, all four R-1830s roared in the darkness; then the ground began rolling past faster and faster, and after what seemed like an eon, the nose came up. We were airborne...*sort of.* I peered out the window and watched the arthritic gear swing outward into the wing. It was ever so much like removing a wooden leg and placing it in a dresser drawer. We made a gentle bank away from

Natal; and on a heading of about 90 degrees or due east, we headed out over the South Atlantic toward Ascension Island and, hopefully, Africa. With the C-87's cruise speed of about 160 mph, I estimated our flight time at about nine hours to travel this leg of our journey.

It was at this juncture that our track and that of Earhart's separated for a time. She headed north from Natal to Dakar, a 1,900-mile flight that took her 13 hours and 22 minutes, a new record for the west-to-east jaunt. I reflected on this as we droned on through the darkness, the engines never skipping a beat. I'm not sure what time it was when we arrived at Ascension Island. It was black and bleak, although I considered it a wonderfully welcome haven following the long flight from Brazil.

Ascension was as wild and windy a place as can be imagined. Its single runway, aptly named Wideawake Airfield, ran on a very pronounced incline, ending quite abruptly at a cliff's edge above the inky Atlantic. There was rumor that those serving there for any length of time turned rock happy from the weather and severe isolation, and that surely would have been the case for me. It was not a pleasant environment. We overnighted and refueled and left very early the next morning. The remaining distance of 1,351 miles to Accra, Ghana, would take another eight and a half hours.

About on time, the Gold Coast of West Africa, awash with snow-white surf, appeared through our windows. Amazingly, the decrepit old C-87 had waddled across nearly 2,800 miles of the South Atlantic without missing a beat. We landed at Accra and got our first taste of Africa's equatorial climate. Although the temperatures ranged in only the mid to high 90s, the heat was oppressive, and it was hot *everywhere*. After a plane sat on a tarmac for only a short time, the temperature inside became nearly intolerable.

Our trek across sub-Saharan Africa would continue in a northeasterly direction from Accra, Ghana, with stops at Kano, Nigeria, and El Fasher and Khartoum in what was then recognized as the Anglo-Egyptian Sudan. From Khartoum, our track would again generally follow Earhart's attempted circumnavigation across Saudi Arabia and Oman to Karachi in what is now Pakistan.

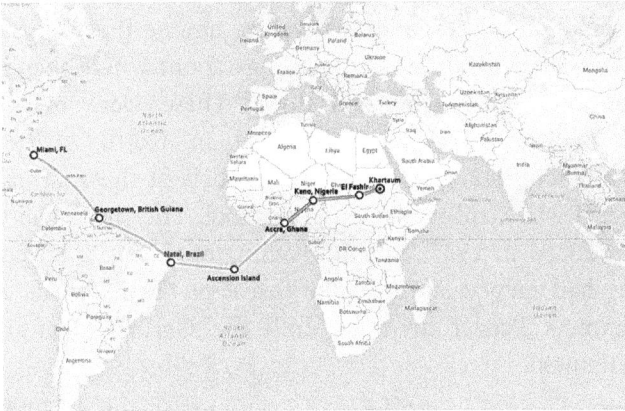

Continuing the journey: Ascension Island to Accra, Ghana; Kano, Nigeria; and then El Fasher and Khartoum in Anglo-Egyptian Sudan. (Map data: Google.)

We landed in El Fasher on a hot, windy day in a landscape that could only be described as desert hell. This was a British RAF base painted with the brush of everlasting heat, sand, and desolation, and God knows what protected the sanity of those cursed to serve here. The facilities were primitive and the desert dominant and frightening. We were billeted in miserable tents pitched in what else?

Sand—which drifted about, piling up on the windward side of even the slightest solid object.

As evening approached and the sun lowered, I took some time to walk around this place of incredible barrenness. A short distance from the hardstand occupied by our C-87 stood a group of airplanes that left me stunned by their historic implications. There were three Royal Air Force Wellington medium bombers sitting wing to wing surrounded by a randomly parked trio of old war-weary Hawker Hurricanes. I felt as though I had stumbled on some sort of aircraft natural history museum in this most miserable of places, and as I walked among these ghosts, I was assailed by all kinds of feelings about where they had been and what they had done. These were relics of the British victory over Rommel in North Africa in November 1942, and I had built models of these airplanes when I was a kid in elementary school. The Hurricane was introduced in 1937, and the Wellington in 1938. Together they had helped stave off the threat of the Luftwaffe and Rommel's Panzer divisions until the Germans' defeat at El Alamein.

Here these magnificent relics stood: silent, battle weary, covered by layers of dust and drifted sand. To me it seemed a singular honor just to be amongst them. I could almost hear the racing of the Hurricanes' engines as they roared across the desert scant feet above the endless sand to the Libyan coast. Their low-level attacks would compromise and confuse the *Deutsches Afrikakorps* soon destined to lose control of the whole of North Africa. I reached out to touch these splendid airplanes, brushing the grime from their surfaces as if to bestow upon them some kind of recognition for the legacy of victory they had bequeathed to the skies over Europe and North Africa. I am still happy I was thus affected. The memories of this interlude remain intensely vivid for me even after all these years.

We departed El Fasher early the next morning. It would be a 500-mile flight northeast to Khartoum. As we took off to the south and then turned in a northerly direction, I saw my ghost fleet of Wellingtons and Hurricanes—standing sand sculptures—awaiting the heat of another day in the hellish Sudanese desert.

The years have robbed me of memories of many of the spots where our trusty old C-87 landed to rest and refuel, but the total distance from Accra to Karachi was about 5,000 miles—about thirty hours flying time at our cruising speed. Our flight altitude was generally between six and eight thousand feet as we virtually hopped, skipped, and jumped across the African continent. I truly wish I could describe the small villages and running herds of gazelles, wildebeest, and elephants. The truth is if I saw such sights, I have totally forgotten them.

One story of the war in North Africa does bear telling. North of El Fasher stretches a forever expanse of heat and drifting sand running like fiery hell to the Mediterranean. In November 1958, the nearly intact wreckage of a B-24D named *Lady Be Good* was discovered by an oil exploration crew in the Libyan Desert. I was intrigued by the story of the discovery because the site of the crash was north of the flight track we had pursued some thirteen years earlier while flying from Kano to El Fasher.

On 4 April 1943, the *Lady Be Good* had taken off from Soluch Airfield near Benghazi, Libya, on a mission to bomb the harbor at Naples. Hampered by bad weather and low visibility due to sandstorms, the *Lady* was among the last to takeoff and never joined her bomber formation. Alone and unable to locate their target, her crew had dropped their bomb load into the sea off the coast of Italy and then picked up a southerly heading to return to base.

On the return flight, the failure of an automatic direction finder on board the aircraft forced the crew to request a steer, or suggested heading, that would allow them to return to Soluch. Because of the primitive nature of the homing device at the bomber base, radio operators were able to determine that the *Lady* was on a line of position toward the airfield but could not determine if they were inbound and approaching Benghazi, or if they had already overflown the base and were now outbound and heading deeper into the Libyan Desert. No more was heard from the plane, and it was finally assumed that it had simply run out of fuel and crashed into the Mediterranean with the loss of the entire crew.

After the discovery of the wreckage and the subsequent recovery of the aircraft and remains of eight of the nine crewmembers, another story of inexperience and tragedy emerged. Picture the stress and angst that filled the aircraft at the beginning of the mission that spring afternoon in April. The crew had arrived in Benghazi fresh from transition training only a couple of weeks prior to their first combat mission. The airplane, B-24D, AAF serial #4124301, was also new, having been assigned to the 376th Bombardment Group (Heavy) on 25 March, only nine days before the raid in which she was lost. New airplanes are always problematic, and the combination of a green crew and a new airplane, both of which were on their first combat mission, was an invitation for trouble if not total disaster.

Wreckage from the *Lady Be Good*. (US Air Force photo.)

There have been decades of conjecture about the raid and its aftermath. But the fact remains that the *Lady Be Good* overflew her intended landing location at Soluch by more than two hours and 440 miles, thus inexplicably flying on deeper and deeper into the death trap that is the Libyan Desert. Finally, in desperation and with her engines still running, her ill-fated crew bailed out. They plunged into a night so black they could not tell if they were over land or water. Eight parachuted safely, and the ninth was killed on impact when his chute failed to totally deploy. The *Lady*, trimmed for a slow descent, continued on course for sixteen miles past the bailout point and crashed, nearly intact, onto the desert floor. When she was discovered fifteen years later, there was still some water onboard in closed containers, and her radio was still completely operable.

Subsequent ground party searches found the remains of eight of the nine crewmembers who perished in the desert. A group of five was discovered together 80 miles from the crash site, and two were found over a hundred miles from the downed *Lady Be Good*. With the agony of thirst, they had struggled that far probably believing the blessed coolness of the Mediterranean coast lay just over the next gigantic sand dune. Thankfully, they never knew the seashore they sought was nearly four hundred miles beyond their halting steps.

One can leap to myriad conclusions regarding the tragedy of this accident. Was the navigator at fault for prolonging the overflight? Should they have attempted some orientation plan to better determine their location? Was it the fault of equipment failure? Lack of experience? Leadership?

In all likelihood, it was a mixture of many insignificant errors that, when linked together in a chain of happenstance, led to disaster. I would be the last to condemn anyone aboard for the tragic ending of the *Lady Be Good*. I have myself been a contributor to my own daisy chain of errors. The difference here is that I survived my personal failures, and theirs cost them their lives. As Ernest Gann so aptly put it, "Fate is the hunter."[65]

It was as true in their case as it has been in my own.

FORTY

T he landing at Khartoum was uneventful. The city lies at the confluence of the White Nile and Blue Nile, but the two rivers do little to mitigate the temperature, which hits highs of over 110 degrees Fahrenheit with amazing regularity during the summer months. After a flight of about 850 miles across trackless desert, we would head slightly southward to Aden, a seaport city strategically located between the Indian Ocean and the Red Sea. At that time still a British colony, Aden served as a hub for men and materials traveling north and east to the China-Burma-India (CBI) Theater of war.

Our whirlwind journey continued from Aden to Karachi, adding another 1,600 miles to our trek, the latter portion of which was over the Arabian Sea. By now, we had traveled over 7,000 miles in just a few days.

Next stop: Tejgaon, an airfield in what is now Bangladesh. Built by the RAF in 1941, the USAAF used this spot as a jumping-off place for men and equipment being transported over the Hump. We would be billeted here for several days of orientation and briefings.

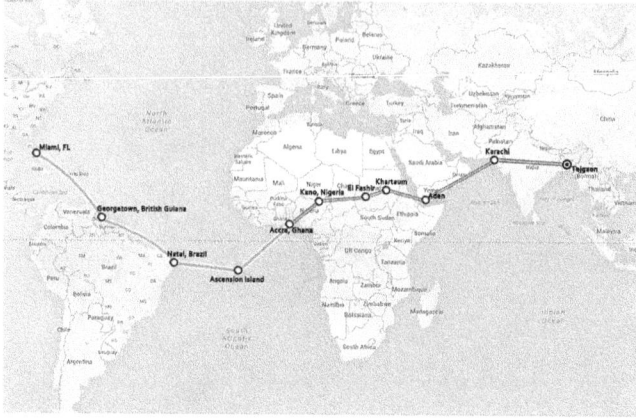

The journey continues across the Middle East to Karachi and Tejgaon.
(Map data: Google.)

Karachi, 1945. (Photos by Ed Larson. From the author's collection.)

Tejgaon was a wild place replete with threatening creatures and so jungle-like it could have served as a movie set for *An Adventure in India*. Trails to the mess hall and other structures were actually cut out of the verdant, dense jungle growth creating something of a maze, which took some getting used to.

Most feared, of course were the tigers native to the area. After sunset, there was the constant sound of nocturnal activity as they made their nightly rounds. We had received ample warning about the presence of these predators, and one standard caution remains clearly ingrained in my memory. We were advised that if a night call to the latrine was necessary, we should always carry a loaded pistol for protection. Being a natural-born coward, I always followed that instruction and spent a great deal of time looking over my shoulder in fear of attack—especially since the mess hall served as a magnet for the big cats, and it was rather close to our quarters.

As usual, Pete and I bunked together, sharing a tent in a rather large clearing surrounded by overgrowth. The weather was hot but not excessive, and our surroundings were pleasant. An Indian bearer attended to our every need, insuring that our stay was an enjoyable one.

The second day following our arrival, we received our initial operational briefing. It was in a rather large room that was equipped with maps and a slide projector. If it was designed to garner the attention of new pilots, it was singularly successful. Once the meeting began, there was not a sound to be heard other than the presenters' voices. The tension could be cut with a knife.

We were told that we would be flying much-needed tonnage of aviation gasoline, bombs, and other materials over the Hump to China and that these missions were fraught with peril and loss of crews and aircraft. We received dire warnings relative to weather, icing dangers, engine failures, and the chances of survival in the event of bailout, including elaborate warnings of hostile hill tribes who didn't suffer aviators well.

Flying over the Himalaya Mountains, 1945. (From the author's collection.)

Icing, engine failures, and miscalculations in the amount of fuel pumped off wing tanks all posed dangers for Hump pilots delivering weapons and much-needed supplies for ground operations in China.

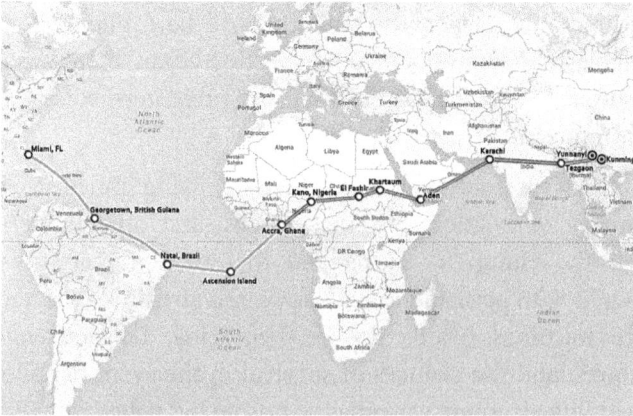

Final leg of the journey: into China. (Map data: Google.)

We had been warned early on of the problems resulting from the combination of icing and the Davis wing, which kept the B-24, C-87, and C-109 aloft. In more than moderate icing conditions, the C-87 lost lift and degraded into a flat spin from which there was no recovery. Ernest Gann, Hump pilot and author, once informed an audience "The C-87 couldn't carry enough ice to chill a highball!" Not a pleasant prospect given the flight conditions we would soon be facing.

Each of us left the briefing with a great deal more maturity than we had prior to the meeting. We shared the opinion that leadership had leveled with us, and we now knew what lay ahead. We would be flying C-109 tankers and C-87 freighters across a god-forsaken pathway of towering mountains and deep valleys. It was a rather formidable prospect.

A rather insidious practice had been in place to maximize aviation fuel deliveries to the US bases in China. On arrival at China bases, not only was the fuel shipment pumped off, but also wing tanks of the delivering aircraft were partially emptied to allow just enough fuel for the aircraft to reach home on the return flight. Since the remaining fuel allotment was based on the variables of wind and weather, it was inevitable that tragic mistakes were made. The first two weeks in January 1945 produced the worst flying weather in the history of Hump operations. The route was assailed by heavy winds, icing, and low visibility. A serious miscalculation in headwinds to be encountered on the return trip to India set the stage for tragedy. On one particular night because of wing tank draining practices, several aircraft simply ran out of fuel on the return trip. The planes and crews were lost; however, the practice of drawing off fuel from wing tanks continued.

Consolidated C-109, dedicated fuel tanker version of the C-87 Liberator Express with gasoline being offloaded. (USAAF photo.)

My first trip over the Hump was on 27 January 1945. I flew as copilot on a C-109 hauling aviation gasoline to either Kunming or Yunnanyi (I can't remember which). The weather was good, the C-109 flew well, and I mentioned in a letter home that I had flown over the Salween, Mekong, and Irrawaddy Rivers. It would be my first and last Hump crossing for a while. When we returned, I discovered that several of us, including my best buddy Pete, had been transferred to Yunnanyi, China, to serve as Airdrome Officers, whatever the hell that was; and although we would remain on flight status, we would serve as Operations Officers at US bases in China. It was a body blow to all of us whose primary mission was to fly airplanes.

A map of China will show Yunnan province lies in the extreme southwest portion of the country just touching the border of what was French Indochina (Vietnam) as well as

Lieutenant Ed Larson and a C-109. (From the author's collection.)

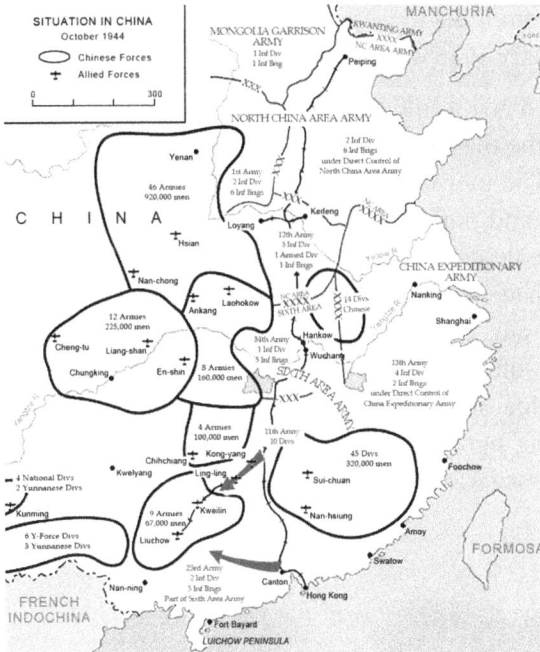

Military situation in China, October 1944. (US Army Military History Institute.)

Myanmar and Laos (not shown on the provided map). Its locale was of extreme importance in maintaining a lane of access that would enable China and the Allies to oust the Japanese from Burma and eventually coastal China. These actions were of course a preamble to the planned bombing of the Japanese homeland from bases in eastern China.

But the big planning was beyond us. Our orders had sent us to this foreign land to fly airplanes and fight the Japanese. Our understanding of the broader tactics of the war was as deep as your average mud puddle. As we saw it, our task was relatively simple: Get as much aviation fuel and ammunition and as many bombs to our Chinese allies and our own fighter groups as quickly as humanly possible. Time was of the essence. Although work was underway to complete construction on the Burma Road and allow truck traffic to flow from India to western China, the volume of such traffic in January 1945 was still only a trickle.

Yunnanyi would be a bookmark in the lives of each of us, a volume that we would read and reread for the rest of our lives. The journey there was spectacular. The ancient C-47 huffed and puffed above a Himalayan landscape that could only be described as the jaws of hell. Steep gorges lay in the deep shade of towering snow-covered peaks reaching almost up to our cruising altitude. Massive snow plumes were blown off windward sides, and snow fog trailed like pashmina shawls from the black granite peaks. It was a sobering sight and obviously a parachutist's horror, and the turbulence was violent and ceaseless.

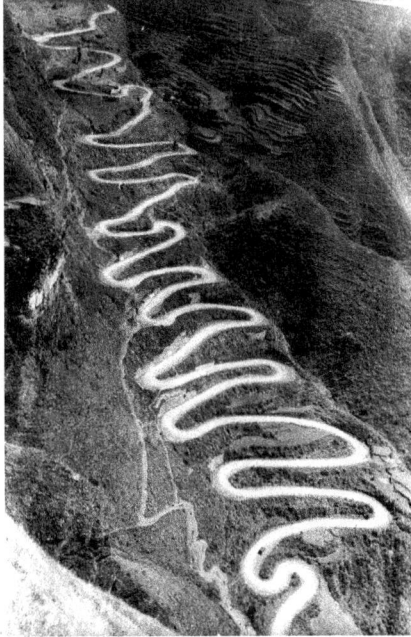

Burma Road. (US Air Force photo.)

Curtiss (C-46A-10-CU, S/N 41-12352) in flight over the Hump.
(US Air Force photo.)

The airfield at Yunnanyi apparently began as a training field for China National Aviation Corporation (CNAC) pilots. After the American Volunteer Group (AVG) was created under the command of Claire Chennault, the airfield was also used as an operational base by the Flying Tigers in their fight against Japanese aircraft in the area.

Members of the American Volunteer Group (AVG) repair a P-40 in Kunming, China. (US Air Force photo.)

When we arrived, we were billeted in whitewashed adobe-style buildings with red tile roofs. Four men occupied each room with bunk beds and closets for personal belongings. There was a small charcoal heater, which provided adequate heat, and a central generator supplied electric lights to each barrack.

Despite the amenities, Yunnanyi seemed old beyond belief. Everything about the huge valley was stamped with the chop of an ancient China. The military buildings and aircraft that rested on the valley floor were invasive—aliens from another planet. Only the native people, their villages, and their culture truly belonged here.

Primeval dwellings and shops lining the narrow streets seemed to lean inward upon themselves, relics of the centuries that had birthed this place. The whole of it was brushed with a patina of ochre dust and wear.

The people were small, wiry, and inevitably burdened by large baskets or yokes of wooden buckets worn across their narrow shoulders. Their loads could be anything—shit, bricks, or cabbages—as they scuffled along the dusty roads intent on some destination.

The women were most notable. Their faces and bodies bore the brand of constant exposure to labor under the harsh weather cycle of this high place. Facial skin resembled deeply wrinkled and creased leather, tanned to shades of darker brown by constant exposure to the outdoors and to the rice-paddy labor that sustained their austere lives. These were creatures of wind and weather, and I saw them as almost Neolithic. Their dresses were simply body wrappings: colorless, dirty, and of rough, homespun quality. Their most remarkable feature was their tightly bound feet. It seemed as though they were walking about on their ankles. From a young age, the girls' feet were snugly wrapped to deform them into small, bent, totally nonfunctional appendages in a reprehensible and cruel practice that only in recent time has come to an end.

There was no conversation with the people of this culture. They never spoke and went about with averted eyes, effectively isolating themselves from the interlopers who had so suddenly peopled their valley. One felt as though we were tolerated because we would thankfully soon be gone from their lives.

Yunnanyi Temple spear-carrier (left) and pagoda at Jizu Mountain, centerpiece of the local temple and monastery. (Photos by Ed Larson, 1945. From the author's collection.)

The Yunnanyi were a people completely onto themselves; travel between valleys of this region was unnecessary for survival. The natives had even developed their own dialects, making it difficult to communicate with others. (Photo by Ed Larson, 1945. From the author's collection.)

Had we the wisdom and maturity to study these fascinating individuals, we could have learned volumes about their ancient ways. Instead, we pretty much ignored them, treating them with scorn or indifference.

We were the losers.

The airfield at Yunnanyi was an eclectic collection of airplanes and the structures required to keep them flying. At any time, one could see C-47s, C-46s, C-87s and a motley assortment of other aircraft, parts, vehicles, and stuff randomly scattered about the landscape.

Our operations office was a moderately sized wooden building topped by what we caustically referred to as our "tower," a mealy-mouthed structure atop the operations shack standing on four-by-eight timbers seemingly too weak to support its weight. Access was by means of a wooden ladder of questionable dependability, and the entire arrangement was topped by radio antennas and homing devices also of undetermined value. The olive-drab fuselage of a long-dead C-46 fronted the office and tower, wingless and ugly, propped up to provide its last service to humanity. Painted across its side in large white letters was its name, "Hump Haven," while the field altitude of 7,040 feet appeared below. Looking forlorn and destitute, its old carcass shook a bit when buffeted by high winds and the torrential rain that swept across the valley—as if the ghost of it wanted to fly again...to rise up in anger and escape its mundane existence.

Club 46 Complete With Heat????

Men of a China ATC Base have fashioned the salvaged fuselage of a wrecked C-46 into a combination mail-room, day-room and snack bar. A partition divides the tail from the rest of the former spacious Hump flyer, and there mail is sorted and distributed. The center section is a day-room with writing tables and books, and the nose contains a snack-bar complete with stove, service counter and stools. —(ICD-ATC photo.)

This is our mail room. I've never seen the stove & stools or the snack bar!

Clipping from the ICD-ATC *Hump Express* featuring a story about the Yunnanyi Airfield. (From the author's collection.)

The Hump Haven's flight deck and main fuselage, now filled with stained coffeemakers and unwashed pots and pans, served as a transient mess hall, while the aftersection, minus rudder and elevators, doubled as our mailroom. None of it was a pretty sight...and neither was the food issued from its dank interior. Standard fare for transient flight crews was two eggs, a slab of dubious meat, and toast as tough as a buffalo hide. The whole of it could be washed down with a cup of insignificant coffee, oft times better left undrunk.

The old fuselage also featured scratchy Big Band music from a turntable that always seemed to turn at half speed, the slow rotation creating the illusion that Jo Stafford and the Modernaires sang flat and with more base than tenor.

While air traffic volume was rather high here, we were relegated to acting as overseers on all aspects of arriving and departing aircraft. Most were based at stations in the Assam Valley and were hauling gasoline, bombs, or ammunition across the Hump. From Yunnanyi, the freight was transshipped to forward bases in China.

Our CO was a youngish captain named Lynn I. Jones. He tended to be a bit curt at times, but he was a good leader, and he protected his flock. He was simply a frustrated pilot...like the rest of us.

January's bad weather continued into February, and the ever-present cold and blowing rain did nothing to make our outside jobs easier. On 11 February, we flew a C-109 loaded with aviation fuel from Kunming to Chanyi, and we logged some instrument time since the weather remained sour. As I have said before, the C-109 was not a pleasure to fly. There was the constant threat from the aviation gas cargo, and any misstep on takeoff or landing would obviously end in explosion and fire.

The next day, we test flew a C-87 that had undergone an engine change. Following major mechanical repairs, it was always necessary to slow time an aircraft's engines to allow them to run-in properly. These slow-timing flights were pretty unexciting, but the one we made with a C-109 on the fifteenth of the month became anything but routine.

Our four-man flight crew that day included CO Lynn Jones and me, radio operator Sergeant Tony Baldasare, and a crew chief. Tony was a delightful young kid with a great sense of humor and a natural exuberance that made him fun to be around. There wasn't a lot of officer/enlisted-man formality at Yunnanyi—guys did their jobs and got on well, and we'd gotten to know and enjoy Tony through our association with him on the flight line. He flew with us often.

We were flying at pretty high altitude to give us plenty of time in case of an engine failure. There were strong winds aloft that afternoon, but we had experienced only moderate turbulence; and since the weather was sunny and seemingly benign, we flew with a journeyman's attitude, keeping an eye on the instrument panel for any indications that something was wrong. The crew chief was buckled into the navigator's seat behind us, and Tony, joking as usual, hadn't latched his seat belt.

Suddenly without warning, the bottom simply fell out of our airspace, and we began a true freefall from what must have been the most remarkable downdraft ever created. It was as if we were in a total vacuum with no sustaining air. Both Jones and I grabbed for the wheels, and Jones jammed the throttles forward. The engines turned hollow as we continued to fall for what seemed forever. In the meantime, Tony had flown out of his seat and cut his scalp on an overhead switch panel. Blood was spattered all over the flight deck, and he was temporarily knocked out.

Kunming Airfield, 1945. (US Department of Defense photo.)

Slow timing a B-24. (Photo by Ed Larson, 1945. From the author's collection.)

We waited to hit bottom, and when we did, it was totally violent. Loose stuff and dirt flooded the flight deck. For a moment, I thought we would shed a wing, and had we been loaded, I'm sure that would have happened. We landed as quickly as possible while the crew chief held a towel on Tony's head to control the bleeding. He was taken by jeep to the aid station for stitches when we landed.

After things settled down, we wrote up the incident, directing the C-109 be taken off flight status and thoroughly checked for wing spar and horizontal stabilizer damage. This was far and away the most violent clear-air turbulence any of us had ever experienced. I was damn glad I never had to fly in that airplane again.

FORTY-ONE

Major events were marking nearly every day as victory in Europe and Japan seemed ever closer. German and Japanese cities were under constant assault by our bombers, and US forces entering Manila were advancing against heavy Japanese defenses. Meanwhile, US Marines had invaded Iwo Jima, our foothold for the direct bombing of Japan. On 24 February, nine thousand Allied bombers hammered German cities. It seemed the handwriting was on the wall.

Our small group of kindred souls was still trying desperately to arrange for transfers back to full-time flying status. While we had not been successful to date, we had sure as hell been persistent. Our job responsibilities were varied, but in due course, they became a daily entrée of sameness. As can be imagined, we had a great deal of time for leisure activities at Yunnanyi. We were not proud of our routine in a time of war, but the assignment was beyond our control, and it was our duty to fulfill it.

When we arrived on base, it was recognized that we had to be pretty mobile to perform our duties on the flight line.

As a result, we were assigned Willys Jeeps, which soon came to be recognized as our personal property. While other pilots were allotted their own P-51s, we had to be satisfied with overland transportation and a full tank of gas. Quickly, however, these vehicles became our own magic carpets, and we used them like toys.

On days when I was off duty, I took to searching out places for duck hunting, first checking out a shotgun from the armory before driving the small ox-cart roads that honeycombed the valley. While I was secure that there wasn't a Japanese patrol within a thousand miles, I never went unarmed. When I wasn't hunting, I usually checked out a carbine and rifle as suitable companions for my trips; and of course, it was mandatory to carry an automatic pistol at all times. The jeep made these jaunts possible. It became my ticket to solitude for which I occasionally longed, and as a byproduct of these outings, I became sensitive to the indigenous charm and quiet beauty of this ancient place.

February melted into March, and although the towering mountains surrounding us were still capped with snow, the renewed warmth had awakened ageless rice paddies and adorned meadows in the splendor of rebirth. True beauty had been laid upon this valley, and the variegated greens that painted the landscape made it breathtaking. Birds were everywhere, sometimes gathering in large flocks. Snow-white and feeding knee deep in saffron waters, they would take flight as our planes were taking off. The contrast of their chalk-white wings against the verdant green of growing rice was stunning.

On one of my trips into the foothills, I stopped to visit a small Buddhist temple near a cluster of peasant dwellings.

Rice paddies above the valley. (Photo by Frank G. Carpenter, ca 1890-1923. From the Carpenter Collection, Library of Congress Prints & Photographs Division. Number: LC-USZ62-98049 [b&w film copy negative]. Call Number: LOT 11356-8. No known restrictions on publication.)

The shrine looked as though it had stood in this place for a thousand years, and as I observed it, it beckoned me to enter.

The Kuomintang soldier guarding it only reluctantly allowed me to view the interior. It was dark inside, but a Buddhist warrior, resplendent in color and weaponry, dominated the single room. I took a couple of photographs and quickly returned to the entrance. I knew there would be many eyes peering from the dark windows of the nearby houses, and they would be watching me. A subdued suggestion of hostility flavored this stop, and I didn't stay long. Only after I had rounded a curve and left the scene behind me did my sense of comfort return.

One of my favorite stopping places was a combination dwelling and carpentry shop. Whitewashed and bearing the rich red tile roof so typically standard for the area, this building stood alone and aloof at the juncture of two small dirt roads, about five miles from the airfield. The shop portion of the structure was open in the front and covered by a shed roof for protection from the rain. The place was surrounded by rice paddies and looked as though it had sprouted from the land like the native growth around it.

The proprietor was a small, wizened man of indeterminate age. He worked with a selection of hand tools that must have been spawned in the middle ages: handmade planes, saws, adzes, bow drills, mallets, and clamps polished by the patina of years of handling, the cutting tools all unbelievably sharp. Following my first visit when I had watched him at work, I returned; and after a lengthy session of communicating with hand signals, I engaged him to build a small footlocker for my gear.

China travels. (Photos by Ed Larson, 1945. From the author's collection.)

China travels. (Photos by Ed Larson, 1945. From the author's collection.)

Using a drawing of what I "described," he began performing miracles on a supply of pine-like boards he had obviously hand planed to a delicate smoothness. When I returned several days later to pick up the locker and pay him, I was amazed at the stunning quality of the piece. All joints were skillfully dovetailed to perfection, and the whole thing was exquisitely made. It seemed impossible that such a creation could have come from the primitive tools and circumstances that surrounded this little man. The objects built with his experienced hands grew from simple materials to become things of ultimate beauty and grace. It was an awesome experience to watch him work, and I was humbled by the breadth of his artistry.

The Great Yunnan Theft occurred in mid-March. I had left my jeep parked in front of the operations building on what I recall as a pretty wet and miserable night. After my shift ended, I returned to discover the vehicle missing. Thinking perhaps someone had borrowed it, I hitched a ride to the barracks figuring I would find it with a wet steering wheel and drenched seats the next morning.

Such was not the case. The jeep I had prized so highly had vanished as if by magic. Believing it couldn't have gone far since there were few roads on which it could be driven, we scoured the surrounding countryside—but with no success. The prevailing thought was that it had been disassembled and would remain hidden until war's end, at which time it could be reassembled and sold on the black market. There was also speculation that an inventive GI might have stolen it and was shipping it home bolt by bolt to his mother. This theory lost credibility, however, when it was recognized that mailing a wrapped wheel and tire or perhaps a transmission might kindle suspicion.

The jeep was never found, and we doubled up on vehicles for the remainder of our service in Yunnanyi.

FORTY-TWO

M arch was highlighted by yet another memorable event—one we would later call "the Great P-40 Caper."

Pete and I met Herb Briggs while we were in Miami waiting to ship out. Like us, he had been stuck with the airdrome officer curse. Herb was a big, strong, strapping kid from New York with a quiet sense of humor that he dished out like ice cream, a little bit at a time. A couple of years older than I, Herb was engaged to a girl from upstate New York and talked about her a lot. We had become close buddies, and I treasured him as my friend. He was a "one of"—an original neat guy.

With time heavy on our hands, Herb and I were constantly on the lookout for activities and adventures that would enrich our lives without getting us into too much trouble. In our wanderings about the base, we had come upon a treasure beyond comprehension. Stored behind a revetment in a far-off unused portion of the field were three Curtiss P-40 fighters. Obviously war weary, they had probably served as reserve aircraft during the heydays of the AVG. We had found the Holy Grail!

Overwhelmed by this discovery, for days during our time off, we poked and prodded at the old Tomahawks, unscrewing this and prying open that. They appeared to be solid enough under the dirt and dust that covered them, and after we pulled the engines through and nothing seemed to clank or bend, I think we were both inspired by the same idea in exactly the same instant: Why couldn't we get some help to fix one up? Hell, we were both single-engine pilots with AT-6 time; we could just fly around the field, have some fun, and get some fighter time in our logbooks to tell our grandchildren about!

The scheme seemed pretty valid. At the time, the Training Command had students moving directly from AT-6s to P-40s, the P-40s serving as advanced trainers. We contacted a line chief who took a look at the relics and assured us he could get one running, agreeing to trade his time and talents in exchange for a case of booze. It was a great deal.

I remember climbing into one of the cockpits. It was a thrill just to feel an exciting airplane around me again. This was going to be the adventure of a lifetime and a vindication for Herb and me as living, breathing pilots! There was one sticky issue to overcome: We had to get a suitable new battery if we were going to get one of these planes off the ground. However, our "mechanic" had connections and assured us he could handle the issue. The next step was easy—just get our CO's permission to work on this "project" in our spare time. And since things were pretty loose around Yunnanyi,[66] we figured that wouldn't be a problem.

The Holy Grail: A P-47 behind a revetment at Yunnanyi. (Photo by Ed Larson, 1945. From the author's collection.)

This P-47 suffered the indignity of losing power on takeoff. The pilot was not injured, but the P-47 was salvaged for parts.

We drafted a letter to the Old Man, and a couple of days later, he called us both in to his office to discuss our plan.

When we entered Captain Jones's office, he put us at ease right away and then looked at what was obviously our request. I can't remember his exact words, but this is the gist of what he said: "I want you both to know that I'm really pleased to command officers with initiative and the guts to get stuff done. It gives me a sense that what we're doing here is truly worthwhile and that the officers under my command are reflecting credit on themselves, on our base unit, and on the entire Air Transport Command."

He paused for a minute, and Herb and I smiled at each other with just a touch of pride. Then Captain Jones went on, "Then there are you two goddamn idiots who come up with as crazy a scheme as I've ever heard of! You bug me with transfer requests and then top it all off with this totally idiotic idea. Have you forgotten that there's a war on? Do you think this is some kind of kiddies' playground? I'm not sending you home in a box, and if I see either of you within a hundred yards of those old wrecks, so help me God, I'll ground you until the war's over....*Do you both understand me*?!"

We both nodded in the affirmative.

"Now, Gentlemen, ATTENTION!" We both snapped into a brace. "*Get the hell out of my office*, and *don't bother me anymore!*"

Herb and I were both pretty deflated with our CO's reaction to our plan, but he'd made himself abundantly clear. In our wanderings, we had also discovered an old L5 reconnaissance plane—sort of a Piper Cub on steroids— and I had planned to ask about flying it, too; but after our meeting with the captain, both Herb and I thought better of it, and the subject never came up again.

There is a footnote to this story: Shortly after our meeting with the CO, some pilots from across the field took the planes up. They all crashed. Fortunately, no one was hurt.

About a week after Captain Jones chewed us out, I was on night duty in operations. Near 2300, we received a communication from a C-46 that was inbound from Kunming. The pilot sounded pretty tense and reported a mayday, explaining he'd experienced a tremendous explosion in his left wing. He suggested it might be a leaking wing tank, but a gasoline explosion would have destroyed the airplane in an instant, so we scratched our heads and kept him on the RT. He was about a half hour out. Since the aircraft was flying normally with no sign of engine problems and the weather was good, we cleared him for a straight-in approach and arranged for several emergency vehicles to stand by.

Five miles out, he reported that he was unable to lower the landing gear. He had tried the manual lowering procedure to no avail. Everything was jammed.

After checking his fuel load and flight control status, we cleared the runway for a wheels-up landing, shining two mobile floodlights across the runway to identify an acceptable touchdown point. Then we waited. Finally, we could see the landing lights; his approach looked fine. In the moonlight, we could pick out the plane with full flaps down, sinking lower...lower...then she was over the runway. I watched it all as if it were in slow motion. The big props hit first; and in a nanosecond, the engines were stopped forever as the propeller blades bent back over the nacelles like wet noodles. Then the belly hit the crushed granite runway with a great, ear-splitting shriek. A low cloud of dirt and granite dust streamed astern as she skidded perhaps fifty yards. Finally, the worst was over. For a moment, all was eerily quiet; then we heard shouts from the three-man crew as they bailed out of the cabin door and dashed like hell from what was left of the big whale. There was a lot of cussing and backslapping from the three guys who were sure they'd been goners.

When things settled down, we walked around the fuselage. It didn't take long to see what had happened. While taking off from Kunming in darkness, they had apparently hit some runway debris with the immense left tire of the Commando. After the gear was retracted, the giant tire had a blowout inside the engine nacelle. The explosion was terrific and had destroyed the entire hydraulic and manual gear retraction system in the left engine.

The crew was transported to the base hospital for debriefing and medical checkups that I'm sure included the administration of bourbon "tranquilizers." My operations crew was eligible for a hot cup of coffee and an initial planning session on how to remove the aluminum carcass from our runway. Since we already had one C-46 converted into a restaurant, we didn't need another. It was eventually decided that the wreckage should be hauled to a far corner of the field, behind the old revetment—its final resting place not far from our beloved P-40s.

Through March, we continued to pick up a little flight time, mostly short local runs and slow timing twin-engine transports following mechanical repairs.

It was becoming plain to see that further flying in China would be in C-46s. These airplanes were big and heavy duty, resembling nothing so much as winged orcas with massive, rather ugly landing gear. First flown in 1940, the C-46 was at the time the largest and heaviest twin-engine aircraft in the world with a maximum gross takeoff weight (MGTOW) of 45,000 pounds and a transport capacity of 40 troops, 30 stretcher patients, or 15,000 pounds of cargo. With two loveable R-2800 engines each producing 2,000 hp to power it and a service ceiling of over 24,000 feet, the C-46 could cruise at 160 to 170 mph. It was, in short, a workhorse, and its attributes made it a good choice for Hump flying.

Despite its immense size, I found the C-46 easy to fly. Sure, there were some fuel-leakage problems that made it a bit scary—but they didn't surface in any of our aircraft—and yes, there was also concern over the dependability of the Curtiss electric props, which evidenced a tendency to run away or lose pitch. Should this happen on takeoff, the results could be disastrous. But while the C-46 was not an airplane that endeared itself to everyone's heart, if you needed a heavy lifter that could fly high, this plane was a pretty sure bet.

Assailed from all sides, Germany was on the edge of total collapse. By 20 March, the Red Army had reached the outskirts of Berlin; soon after, General Dwight Eisenhower issued a demand for the Germans' unconditional surrender. The damned Nazis heard the message amid the rubble of their nation, but they did not surrender quite soon enough.

I met Paul Ostrander at Roosevelt High School. While neither of us was a great student, we were young and had fun; and soon, we were fast friends.

A C-46 Commando aircraft flying over the Himalaya Mountains. (US Army photo.)

Cockpit of a C-46 Commando aircraft, 1944. (US Air Force photo.)

Through a series of circumstances, Paul and I went through primary and basic flight training together. Paul was a fine pilot and the first in our squadron to solo in primary flying school. Our paths separated when I went on to Twin-Engine Advanced Training at Stockton, California, and Paul moved on to Advanced Single-Engine Training at Luke Field in Arizona. His was the path I wished I had followed.

Soon after his transition to fighters, Paul joined the Seventy-Eighth Fighter Group (84th Fighter Squadron) flying P-47 Thunderbolts out of Duxford. Later, the squadron switched to P-51 Mustangs, an airplane he loved.

On the last day of March 1945, Flight Leader Ostrander led a group of Mustangs across the Channel on a strafing raid over a small town in north-central Germany. When they encountered heavy ground fire, they pulled back up into the clouds. Sensing something amiss, Paul asked his wingman to check the bottom of his plane. The wingman detected a hole in the horizontal stabilizer but saw no further damage, and the two decided to return to England. Picking up a westerly heading, they crossed the Dutch coast.

Above the North Sea and about fifty miles from The Hague, First Lieutenant Paul Ostrander's Mustang caught fire, and he bailed out. His wingman, watching the situation intently, saw Paul's chute open; and as he descended, the wingman then saw the tether from Ostrander's single-man life raft come loose from his chute harness and fall away from him. Paul landed in a very rough sea and freed himself from his chute. The wingman continued circling but was soon unable to see Paul in the high waves and swell. Later, search parties returned to look for Paul, but the extreme conditions of cold and merciless sea had made it impossible for him to survive.

Allied bombing raid over Nazi targets. (Franklin D. Roosevelt Library, Public Domain Photographs, 1882–1962. National Archives Item number: 197269. Unrestricted use.)

Today, I remain burdened by a weighty grief that even time has not erased. It troubles me that Paul lost his life while he was so very young...just three short years removed from our high school days. A long life full of adventure should have awaited him.

Each day we attended Roosevelt High, we passed by a plaque in the school lobby. Its inscription reminded us "What we are to be, we are now becoming."

In view of what we lost, that seems ironic as hell.

FORTY-THREE

As March rolled into April, events were moving forward at an incredible pace. Germany was in collapse on every front, and Berlin would fall in a period of weeks. Off Okinawa in the Pacific, the Japanese were mounting a last-ditch stand with kamikaze attacks against our US Navy. It was as though we had been dropped into a vortex of activity that would change the path of history forever. But while the end of this catastrophic war grew nearer and Allied victory became more certain, before the last shot was fired, a harvest of sadness yet to be endured was waiting in the wings.

On 12 April 1945, our deeply revered President Franklin Delano Roosevelt suddenly died of a cerebral hemorrhage. A truly monumental leader and statesman, he had led an entire nation through the Great Depression and the greatest conflict the world had ever known. There was a deep and abiding regret across our country that he had not lived to see the final victory, and mourning manifested itself in a universal grief that was expressed openly in every hamlet and city across the free world. As his funeral train moved solemnly across the land, countless thousands of men and women from every walk of life honored him with the shedding of their honest tears. As was Lincoln, FDR was a man for the ages.

Franklin Delano Roosevelt's funeral procession on Pennsylvania Avenue, Washington, DC, April 14, 1945. (Library of Congress Prints & Photographs Division; Reproduction Number: LC-USZ62-67439. No known restrictions on publication.)

WE HAVE FAITH THAT FUTURE GENERATIONS WILL KNOW HERE, IN THE MIDDLE OF THE TWENTIETH CENTURY, THERE CAME A TIME WHEN MEN OF GOOD WILL FOUND A WAY TO UNITE, AND PRODUCE, AND FIGHT TO DESTROY THE FORCES OF IGNORANCE, AND INTOLERANCE AND SLAVERY, AND WAR.

~ PRESIDENT FRANKLIN D. ROOSEVELT
FEBRUARY 12, 1943

In the limited world of Yunnanyi, word was out that we would be transferred within a month or so. To my ultimate amazement, I was offered the position of Operations Officer in charge of all transient traffic. After catching hell about the P-40 caper, I *never* expected *that* to happen. Accepting the assignment would mean I would have to forego the expected transfer. However, it would also mean a promotion, and I could fly when I wanted to and enjoy other perks. I gave it some serious thought, but in the end, I turned down the offer. It was time for a change.

Several weeks before our transfer, we organized a trip to a Tibetan fair that was held annually about eighty miles from our airfield in the small town of Tali. It proved to be a fascinating experience. The native Tibetans that we saw there were tall in stature and seemed immensely hardy and strong. They were dressed in wrapped leggings and layers of gaudily colored clothing that was apparently never washed. Their wares were mostly medicinal herbs and potions with claims to cure everything. I shunned the medicine but did buy a four-stringed instrument that was beautifully made from native woods. It was totally reminiscent of the wooden locker created by my Yunnanyi craftsman.

Tali was as interesting as the natives who lived there. Like Yunnanyi, it breathed of ancient times and ancient ways. The town was nestled between high ridges and deep gorges, and the whole of it lay on the western flank of Mount Tali, the highest peak on our southern Hump route. Views from the narrow streets stretched across an immense valley that seemed without end; and the buildings, roads, and pathways, all constructed of slab and crushed marble that had been quarried high on the nearby mountainsides, were as old and as rugged as the earth itself.

Tibetan peasant and our operations crew at the fair in Tali, 1945. (Photo by Ed Larson. From the author's collection.)

It was easy to imagine the howling winds that would chill this place and its people. I would place the altitude of the village at about 11,000 feet, or 4,000 feet above the floor of the surrounding valley. I would also estimate winter habitation in this small enclave as being close to intolerable. There would be snow and plenty of it, but the demons would be the frigid downdrafts that even now in April seemed cold hearted and eternally chilling. An old Chinese proverb states, "The gem cannot be polished without friction, nor man perfected without trials." I would accept this as being totally true of this place. It seemed that these resourceful people and the buildings that rested here had been polished by winds from the beginning of time.

A feeling of euphoria was growing amongst us. The prospect of a transfer and reassignment to full-time flying status had created a sense of optimism that had improved everyone's outlook. In view of all this, I was taken aback when I entered our billet and found Pete lying on the top bunk with his hand lightly curled around the handle of his .45 automatic. I didn't really think suicide, but there was a question in my mind. "What the hell is going on with the gun?"

"I've lain here for months," he replied, "watching these goddamn rats run across the rafters. I'm going to blast the next one I see!"

I challenged the wisdom of his plan, but he was adamant, so I let it go and left to go to the latrine.

A few minutes later, I heard a loud shot from the interior of our room. When I entered, Pete was sitting upright on his bunk with the smoking pistol in his right hand. The room was filled with the smell of cordite—and the unexpected brilliance of the afternoon sun. Looking up, I saw a huge hole at least two feet in diameter in the ceramic tiles covering our roof. Several guys had rushed to the scene, and there was a rather high level of excitement and laughter issuing from the crowd.

A subsequent talk with Pete revealed what happened. Completely underestimating the damage that might be done to the tile roof overhead, he had shot at a rat and missed. Chards of tile now covered the floor, and an unsmiling Chinese houseboy spent the next hour or so cleaning things up. Fortunately, it didn't rain that night, and roof repairs were undertaken by two Chinese "roofers" the next morning. They jabbered constantly as they worked, and one could only imagine what was said. One thing was abundantly clear—they remained unsmiling during the entire task of restoration.

The end of April brought with it welcome news. Benito Mussolini, the Italian leader and Hitler's lackey, together with his mistress Claretta Petacci, had been shot and hanged by partisans in Milan. However, the best news was yet to come: We got word on 30 April that Adolph Hitler and his new wife, Eva Braun, had committed suicide in their underground bunker in Berlin. While we reveled at the news of his death, we nevertheless remained appalled at the monstrous evil he and his Nazis had visited upon our world. Following Nuremberg, most would find their justice in prison or at the end of a hangman's rope, but in the *Führer's* final days, filled with so much chaos and condemnation, they would be incessantly subjected to the ranting of a lunatic who issued commands and countermands directing phantom units of German armed forces that no longer existed.

The eighth of May, V-E Day, would signal the formal end of the cataclysm in Europe. As American fighting men, we hated our Axis enemies and welcomed their demise. For those of us who fought this war, angers have cooled over the intervening decades. I'm glad about that. My letters written at the time reflect a casehardened hatred of all things German and Japanese. The Holocaust, Bataan Death March, and bitter loss of so many lives at their hands became too large to be overlooked.

Stars and Stripes headline, Issue No 285, May 8, 1945, Paris Edition, V-E Day. (Public domain.)

Flying at Yunnanyi continued sporadically, and food at Hump Haven continued to be bad. On 18 May, we received orders to transfer to the airfield at Luliang in northeast Yunnan Province. When we loaded our gear and ourselves into the C-47 Troop Carrier, I left three things behind: my stolen jeep, the locker made for me by my local carpenter friend, and the scenery of this verdant valley so rich with rice paddies and the graceful white egrets that fed on them.

Luliang was a different ball game, a dynamic and brazen place that brought us back to war. The place was humming with airplanes and freight that had to be moved, and I was flying the day after we arrived there.

We were now operating from a 6,000-foot concrete runway, built obviously for the use of heavy bombers; and we correctly surmised it would serve as a B-29 base for a major bombing campaign against the Japanese homeland (and it would have—had it not been for the ace in the hole held by the United States and played just a few short months later). Across the field from our billets, the Twenty-Third Fighter Group was well established with P-51s and P-47s. They were flying low-level search and destroy missions to the east, and they took off with drop tanks, bombs, rockets, and whatever other hardware they could bolt on their aircraft.

There was some ground fighting going on at a small fighter strip called Chih Chiang (anglicized spelling Chihkiang or Chikiang)[67] in Hunan Province. On 10 April, Japanese ground troops had launched an offensive to capture the airfield, and fighter planes flown by Chinese and American pilots from the Chinese American Composite Wing had defended it. At one point, the Japanese ground forces were so close that fighter planes were strafing them almost before their wheels were up.

We were flying nearly every other day now—mostly C-46s and C-47s, and I felt comfortable with both aircraft. Our schedule worked out so that I made many trips to

CHAPTER FORTY-THREE

Locations of airfields in western China. (Map data: Google.)

P-51s and P-47s, April 1945. (US Air Force photo.)

Chihkiang, flying bombs, ammunition, and barreled aviation gasoline to the fighter units there. I was still flying copilot, but I made a lot of takeoffs and landings from the right seat. The copilot bit didn't bother me; the important thing was that I was flying again, and that meant everything.

Curtiss (C-46A-45-CU S/N 42- 96688), November 1944. (US Air Force photo.)

Our group had transferred from Yunnanyi as a unit; consequently, the personnel remained the same. I made several trips with Tony Baldasare as radio operator; and after the incident in the falling C-109 when he cracked his skull, I never failed to remind him to fasten his seat belt.

There weren't enough permanent barracks to house us at Luliang, so we were billeted four men to a tent. Not the fanciest of lodgings, but we were able to stay dry.

Be it ever so humble, there's no place like home. (Photo by Ed Larson. From the author's collection.)

At 6,500 feet above sea level, the original state of these living arrangements left something to be desired. Our renovations made a big difference.

I had three tent mates—all great guys: Pete Mignin, who had been with me since Des Moines; Jack "Tarz" Taylor, a flashy, funny chap from LA who was about 25 years old; and Ervin Ovick, who at 35 was the oldest of our group. He had barnstormed as an air show pilot prior to Pearl Harbor. Close by was my P-40 pal and cohort Herb Briggs, who shared an adjoining tent with three other members of our original group. Together, we were a neat bunch; and together, we were all pretty displeased with the tent situation.

To remedy our circumstances, we scrounged up some boards and built a floor surrounded by four-foot-high walls covered on the outside with bamboo matting. We then requisitioned a tent pole long enough to raise the tent edges to the height of the new wooden walls. We vented a coal stove through the ceiling of the tent and thus had a room with central heat, a warm wooden floor, and seven-foot headroom at the walls. It wasn't pretty; but to us, it was a showplace.

Next came the mattress project. We had been supplied with GI bunks and mattresses no thicker than a thin-crust pizza. Laid across a configuration of horizontal springs and wires, these mattresses provided less comfort than a Hindu bed of nails. Following the lead of those who had lived here before us, we made a scavenger trip to the "elephant's graveyard," a depot of cast-aside components of crashed or trashed airplanes. From our collection of recovered goods, we removed the inner tubes of used C-46 tires and cut them into two-inch strips. We then wove the strips across frames made of scrounged two-by-fours. After removing the old bedsprings that had made attempts at sleep so tortuous, we installed our homemade "posturepedic" mattresses. The improvement was remarkable and so was our slumber.

There would be more on the home improvement front; but first, we had some flying to do.

FORTY-FOUR

F lying big airplanes was quickly becoming second nature to us; and during the month of June, I picked up forty hours—all in C-46s. There was a lot of action in Chihkiang, and judging from the amount of stuff we were hauling in, the fighter group there was throwing around a lot of lead.

Our loads were exclusively gasoline, bombs, and ammunition, and the unloading process would have scared the average bystander out of his skin. The distance to the ground from the cargo door was about eight feet. We handled the barreled aviation fuel with some care, rolling the barrels to the edge of the door and onto pallets for lowering. The boxes of ammo were handled pretty much the same way. The 500-pound bombs we were hauling were simply rolled to the edge of the doorway and pushed out so they would (hopefully) land on a large tire left on the ground to cushion their blows. The bombs were of course not fused, but even with that, I used to duck a little if they missed the tire and hit the dirt headfirst. I saw newcomers turn pale when that happened.

Situation in China, April to June 1945. (US Army Military History Institute.)

The P-51s and P-47s at Chihkiang had some miles on them. The fighter strips were always dusty and dirty, and the airplanes were always on the move.

We had to get really low on approach at Chihkiang. (Photo by Ed Larson, 1945. From the author's collection.)

The field at Chihkiang was like a wallflower: short and skinny. There were plenty of mountains around, and we always came in really low over a bunch of trees, plunking down in the weeds before stopping as close as we could to the end of the runway. I often wondered if there might be an enemy sniper hiding out there, waiting to shoot at us; and one night, a Japanese soldier actually did infiltrate the field. When the flight crew turned on the cabin lights for the takeoff checklist, the sniper shot the pilot through the knees. After that, we left the cabin lights off.

We were now picking up a lot of nighttime and instrument hours, flying that was always a bit dicey due to the primitive nature of our radio aids. We had received several new C-46s outfitted with strange black boxes in the radio compartments. Called LORAN, these were **LO**ng **RA**nge **N**avigation devices. There was only one problem: We didn't know how to use them. I shudder to think of the number of lives they could have saved had we understood the equipment. Instead, they sat in the new planes, never turned on, while guys got lost and died.

The R-2800 engines we had on the C-46s were sweet. These were the same engines used in the P-47 Thunderbolt and Grumman F6F fighters, and you could always depend on them. Pushing both throttles to the wall turned on 4,000 horsepower, plenty of thrust to clear the ever-present hill at the end of the Chihkiang runway. If the R-2800 had a failing, it was fuel consumption. They sucked up gasoline at a phenomenal rate. I found the R-2800 to be a wonderful friend, but she was a heavy drinker.

Friendships formed on the flight deck were strong and appeared to be long lasting, probably annealed by the heat of stress and the commitment to teamwork required in time of war. I liked most of the guys I copiloted for and never felt inferior in any way because I was flying from the right seat. The pilots I liked best were team players, recognizing their copilots performed an important job and that together we bore responsibility for the safe return of airplane and crew. The copilot's duty was to understand that the guy in the left seat was boss—no matter what insignia was sewn on his own shoulder.

Flying copilot was not a sedentary job. Copilots kept busy during the entire flight. There was constant need of attention to engine performance, altitude, aircraft speed, and attitude. Fuel consumption and reserves, fuel tank selection, valve positions, and trim had to be watched. Location, current course, and course changes were paramount concerns on the minds of both pilots, and an ongoing observation of surrounding airspace was as important as any other single consideration crossing one's mind. Ignorance or lack of attention was costly and sometimes fatal.

We didn't crew up much at Luliang. Guys flew constantly with different crewmembers, and schedules were decided by the names posted on the flight roster; although, pilots could request certain copilots as regulars—and I'm proud to say two very good pilots asked me to be their regular copilot— but that didn't happen much. In my mind, it was a singular honor, and I've never forgotten it. I worked hard at learning the aircraft we flew and the territory we flew over, figuring that knowledge was the cheapest insurance I could buy.

The action increased in July. We were flying nearly every other day now—mostly into Chihkiang—with the usual loads of gas, bombs, and ammunition. The weather was not always cooperative, which added a measure of adventure to our flights.

There was a growing suspicion that the epic struggle with Japan was nearing its end, and the air was rife with rumors. It had become clear we would crush our Japanese enemy. Some believed we would soon be flying out of the east coast of China to bomb them into submission. Not one of us ever imagined the form that final blow would take.

And after that, *what*? Go home, go back to school, settle down and raise a family? All that was counter to what the past few years and experiences had made of us. It was true that war was hell, *but what about the adventure?* Flying alone at night to some remote fighter strip in a land you didn't know, battling weather across mountains that seemed to touch the sky, getting drunk with buddies...the romance of our private wars wasn't lost on us. *What the hell would we do when this was over?*

We continued to fly out of Luliang, but our group was now designated 1366th AAFBU (Mobile), which meant we could be transferred from field to field as a unit with our own aircraft. As we began picking up time in C-47 Troop Carriers, we became acclimated to the increased ground fighting in the area. We still flew C-46s more often, but we were gaining proficiency in both aircraft.

During July, I drew a Hump flight to India. It was a dream to leave the privation of China and walk into the PXs in Barrackpore, Chabua, and Assam. Their glass shelves held the world's goodies, and beer and booze were available for purchase day and night. The trip over and back was spectacular—ceiling and visibility were unlimited (CAVU), and the Himalayas appeared as I had never seen them before—colossal and snow covered, they were like icing on the cake of the world. The trip was absolutely unforgettable.

The first of August greeted us with heavy rain and dismal weather. I copiloted a load of gasoline to Nanning with Martin Hurd in the left seat. It was rain all the way and back, and the trip was difficult.

Martin was one of my favorite pilots. We worked well as a flying team, and on the ground, we enjoyed each other's company. Martin was from Arkansas and talked like a hillbilly banjo. He laughed three-quarters of the time and got on well with everyone.

When we returned to Luliang, I discovered I'd been pulled off flight status for a week to work as Operations Officer. Needless to say, I wasn't pleased now that we were flying nearly every day. I had enjoyed the responsibilities of the operations office at Yunnanyi and had performed my duties well, and that may have been a mistake since I liked flying better. There was some compensation, though. I was advised that I had been promoted to the rank of First Lieutenant, which was nice for me and news that would thrill my mother.

The weather continued to cause problems with air traffic, routings, and turnarounds, so the paperwork at my new desk job got rather involved.

I worked the flight line on 7 August. Typical of the weather we'd been experiencing, it rained. Late that morning, a sergeant from operations came running out of the office yelling, "We've dropped a bomb called 'Little Boy' equal to 20,000 tons of TNT on a town called Hiroshima!"

I looked at him as if he was crazy, thinking he'd added a couple of zeros to the story. We walked back to the office, and everyone was talking at once about a B-29 called *Enola Gay* and the damage the new bomb had done. Even then, we couldn't comprehend the extent of the devastation that had been visited on that city.

Two days later, a bomb called "Fat Man" was dropped over the city of Nagasaki, creating another towering cloud of devastation and death. Prior to the two cataclysmic bombings, the Japanese Empire had been warned on 26 July 1945 to surrender or face "prompt and utter destruction" through actions undertaken by the United States, the United Kingdom, and the Republic of China. The Japanese ignored the warning.

> *THE ENEMY NOW POSSESSES A NEW AND TERRIBLE WEAPON...*
>
> ~ EMPEROR HIROHITO
> IMPERIAL RESCRIPT ENDING THE WAR
> TRANSLATED BY WILLIAM WETHERALL, YOSHA RESEARCH

Following the bombings and faced with the threat of annihilation, on 15 August 1945, the Japanese formally announced their surrender to the Allies.

Crew from the *Enola Gay*. (Public domain.)

Most captions of this image identify those shown as Colonel Paul Tibbets Jr. (center), Commander of the 509th Composite Group, with flight crewmember, Theodore Van Kirk, third from the left. The other five men in the photo were ground crew personnel for the fateful flight.

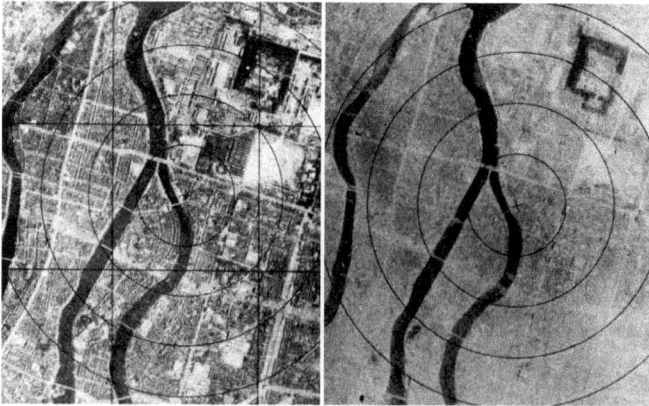

Aerial view of Hiroshima, Japan, before and after the bombing. (US Military photo. Public domain.)

CHAPTER FORTY-FOUR

Major Charles W. Sweeney and the *Bockscar* crew. (Public domain.)

Due to an inoperative fuel transfer pump and dwindling fuel reserves, Bockscar was forced to make a hard, uncleared landing in Okinawa following the bombing mission to Nagasaki. During the final approach, the number two engine quit from fuel starvation, and the B-29's reversible propellers were insufficient to adequately slow the aircraft, forcing Sweeney and his copilot to stand on the brakes and make a swerving 90-degree turn to avoid running off the runway. A second engine died from fuel exhaustion during landing. By the time the plane came to a stop, less than five minutes of fuel remained in the tanks.

*I REALIZE THE TRAGIC SIGNIFICANCE
OF THE ATOMIC BOMB....
IT IS AN AWFUL RESPONSIBILITY
WHICH HAS COME TO US.
WE THANK GOD THAT IT HAS COME TO US,
INSTEAD OF TO OUR ENEMIES;
AND WE PRAY THAT HE MAY GUIDE US TO USE IT
IN HIS WAYS AND FOR HIS PURPOSES.*

~ PRESIDENT HARRY S. TRUMAN
RADIO REPORT TO AMERICAN PEOPLE ON THE POTSDAM CONFERENCE
DELIVERED FROM THE WHITE HOUSE AT 10:00 P.M., AUGUST 9, 1945

We were overjoyed by the sudden cessation of hostilities. The Japanese were our enemies. They had begun a war with a treacherous sneak attack on Pearl Harbor. For nearly four years, they had fought and killed our brothers in savage battles on land and sea and in the air. We cheered when the news came through that they had accepted total defeat, and we cheered the fact that the bombings had ended it so quickly.

Seattle Post-Intelligencer headline, August 15, 1945.
(From the author's collection.)

We were the boots on the ground nearly seventy years ago. Now we are old, and the chorus of our voices becomes smaller with each passing day. When the last of us is gone and our voices are forever stilled, revisionists may condemn the morality of Hiroshima and Nagasaki, but those of us who were there in 1945 were saved the agony and cost of invading Japan. "Little Boy" and "Fat Man" saved thousands of American lives, and I remain deeply grateful that invasion of the Japanese homeland was a tragedy that never happened.

FORTY-FIVE

On 10 August, I was flying again—a round trip to Chihkiang. It was true the war was essentially over, but there were still a lot of people and stuff to move around, and we began hauling Chinese infantry from place to place for backup where they were needed. There were undoubtedly Japanese troops in the bush that had no idea their war was lost, and this was a concern. At the same time, an infiltration of guerilla-type groups who were followers of Mao Tse-tung and the Chinese Communists began making their presence known, and they would become more and more a source to be reckoned with as the days passed. The Chinese troops we were hauling were loyal to Chiang Kai-shek and the Kuomintang regime and therefore enemies of Mao and his followers.

The Kuomintang soldiers were a sorry lot. Their uniforms were scruffy, and they were ill equipped to fight a war. I never saw any raingear on them or in their bedrolls, and it rained plenty. I guess they just got wet and then dried out. They carried a hodgepodge of weapons; many were cast-off Mauser rifles and pistols from World War I. And never did they travel in any luxury on our homespun airline. If we were not carrying any freight, we could cram sixty-five to seventy Chinese GIs into the cabin. They sat on the floor, one in front of the other, lining up between each other's knees. Somebody must have told them at one time to shut up because there never was any conversation between them. These were primitive guys with no view of the outside world, and I often wondered if they realized they were flying or simply thought they were being tossed around in a big tin mixer. There were, of course, no seat belts or restraints for them, and many got sick. The cleanup responsibility was with their officers, and we made sure they did a really good job. If we'd ever crashed, there would have been a huge ball of them in the front end of the plane. Thankfully, that never happened.

Chinese 22D Division troops waiting to board C-47s of the Tenth Air Force. (US Department of Defense photo.)

I flew another night trip with Martin Hurd and Tony Baldasare to Chihkiang on the thirteenth. As usual, I cautioned Tony to wear his seat belt. We had a little prop trouble on the trip with the limit switch not working all that great, but we handled it OK. We'd been really lucky as far as engine performance was concerned. We were flying into some pretty sticky fighter strips now, and thank God, we'd learned to fly the airplane well. On one of the return trips to Luliang, some Maoist guerrillas took axes to the field's landing lights. We knew the area, so it wasn't that big a deal, but it could have caused some trouble for a first-time landing there.

P-51B and P-51C Mustang fighters of the US Army Air Forces 118th Tactical Recon Squadron at Laohwangping Airfield, Guizhou Province, China, 1945. (USAAF photo courtesy of the San Diego Air & Space Museum SDASM Archives. No known copyright restrictions.)

Despite the Japanese surrender, we continued hauling ammo, bombs, and gas. There was still a lot of ground action going on in places that hadn't long been in our hands; and we were sneaking into forward bases at Nanning,

Liuchow, Liangshan, Kweilin, and Myitkinya—locations that had been hotspots of Japanese ground operations. Nanning was a beautifully situated city and airfield in Guangxi Province, close to the French Indochina border (now Vietnam), and it served the Vietnamese air force during the Vietnam War. Myitkinya, Burma, had been a Japanese fighter base that early on posed a serious threat to Hump and trans-China flying. We were told that in addition to these assignments we would next be transporting troops and supplies to coastal cities such as Hong Kong, Canton, and Nanking.

Things were looking up.

Wednesday, 22 August, greeted the world with bad weather, but it would turn out to be a red-letter day in my checkerboard military career. Despite rain and wind, everyone I knew would have sold his soul to be on the trip our crew flew on this day. How we got picked was anyone's guess.

Early that morning, we boarded a load of American civilian passengers and took them to Kunming. The C-46 we were flying had bucket seats, so no one sat on the floor. The deluxe accommodations also included seat belts. When we dropped off our passengers at Kunming, instead of returning to Luliang, we were told to stand by. After an hour's worth of coffee and doughnuts, we were advised that we would be transporting a load of twenty-three Chinese generals to Chihkiang for a meeting with a Japanese delegation that was flying in for the signing of documents in preparation for surrender. Obviously, this would be a historic event and a plum for a couple of hometown hotshots! We couldn't get off the ground fast enough before somebody changed his or her mind. It was the shortest preflight check in history.

The Chinese generals weren't dressed much better than their enlisted men...and they hadn't done much flying, either. We had to fasten up several seat belts. Unlike our enlisted clients, however, these passengers could look out the windows while we were flying and actually see they were in the air. The trip went well, and the weather at Chihkiang cleared a bit, although, as I later mentioned in a letter home, the runway was "pretty much mud and rocks."

It rained plenty, and the runway was pretty much mud and rocks.
(Photo by Ed Larson. From the author's collection.)

When we approached Chihkiang, we circled the field slightly above pattern altitude to survey the scene. Everything appeared normal. There were several C-47

Troop Carriers parked on the flight line and the usual lineup of Mustangs and a couple of "Jugs" (our nickname for P-47s). There were quite a few people walking around getting mud on their shoes, but aside from all that, nothing much appeared to be happening.

We reported in on downwind and made a soft, gentle landing for our VIP passengers, taxiing up to the flight line before shutting her down. Our passengers debarked into what was now fairly sunny weather, and we were free to look around.

I was pretty excited about the historical significance of the day and what it would bring and a little surprised at the absence of fuss and feathers about the moment. As we watched, a group of GIs was setting up some rather plain-looking tables in a building close to the flight line. The tables were then covered with cloths that had all the appearance of somebody's bed sheets. Metal folding chairs were placed around the tables, and that was it. Now all that was left was the waiting.

As airmen, we were of course intrigued by what kind of Japanese aircraft might appear. There probably wouldn't be any fighters since their presence could be provocative, so we guessed a bomber or two might serve the losers' transportation needs. It was all a guess, but it sure was exciting. We probably waited about forty-five minutes before we heard engine sounds approaching. After a minute or so, a Mitsubishi G4 "Betty" powered over the hills from the east. She was blue-gray and looked a bit lethal, but she bore a huge cross on her fuselage indicating her fighting days were over. Her crew made an obvious check of the pattern and then turned onto a short final. They greased the landing without a jolt.

Japanese envoy's arrival in Mitsubishi G4 "Betty," August 1945. (US Naval History and Heritage Command photograph #: NH 62868.)

Chinese and American troops greet the Japanese delegation. (Scene from *Preparation for Surrender of Japanese Forces in China at Chihkiang*. US Army Air Forces Combat film #4311. National Archives identifier: 5476, Local Identifier: 18-CS-4311.)

Mitsubishi Ki-57 "Topsy." (Photo by William E. [Bill] Shemorry, 64th Signal Corps, US Army. State Historical Society of North Dakota, William E. [Bill] Shemorry Photography Collection [SHSND 10958-54-105-9].)

"There was much bowing and saluting." (Photo by William E. [Bill] Shemorry, 64th Signal Corps, US Army. State Historical Society of North Dakota, William E. [Bill] Shemorry Photography Collection [SHSND 10958-54-105-1].)

A few minutes behind the Betty and on the same inborn track, we spied another enemy aircraft. Clearing the eastern hills and following a straight-in approach, she landed with a tiny bounce and taxied to the flight line. I easily recognized her. She was a Mitsubishi Ki-57 "Topsy" transport, and *she was a beauty*! Painted a rich dark green with opposing camouflage colors of red, burnt orange, and yellow laid on in a dazzle pattern, her overall color mix was somehow reminiscent of an exotic frog, and she had been buffed out like a shiny ornament. Parked beside our drab and dirty fighters and transports, this Mitsubishi Ki-57 was the belle of the ball, and I hated to see her get her shoes dirty in the mud of the Chihkiang fighter strip.

The Topsy had flown in from Nanking, and we saw her disembark four individuals who later turned out to be Brigadier General Kiyoshi, Deputy Chief of Staff of the Japanese Imperial Army, along with two staff members and an interpreter. The scene was now ringed with observers, including more than one hundred Chinese and American officers.[68] Meanwhile, armed Chinese guards had surrounded both Japanese airplanes lest they be picked to pieces by uncouth American souvenir nuts.

After much bowing and saluting, the entourage was quickly loaded into jeeps and driven the short distance to where the tables had been set up. The Japanese contingent and the Chinese delegation, including our twenty-three generals, were seated in a prescribed fashion, and then the proceedings began.

The Japanese delegation was spotlessly turned out in fine uniforms complete with ribbons and other regalia. In sharp contrast, my fellow officers and our enlisted men were dressed in plain suntan uniforms, no ties, and of course, our

(Scenes from *Preparation for Surrender of Japanese Forces in China at Chihkiang*.
US Army Air Forces Combat film #4328. National Archives identifier: 18941.)

fifty mission caps pushed far back on our heads. Like our airplanes, we were drab, dirty, unkempt, and war-weary, but as bad as we looked, we had just beaten the hell out of these bastards, and everybody there—with the exception of the Japanese—was happier than if he had just won a case of cold beer.

As for me, I felt honored to have witnessed these monumental proceedings, and I imagined those aboard the USS *Missouri* for the signing of the instrument of surrender would soon be feeling the same way.

Later that afternoon, we discovered the reason we'd been part of this history-making event. The ceremony was originally scheduled to be held at Yushan in Kiangsi Province; however, the runway there had been hit hard, and so at the last minute, they were forced to change the meeting site to Chihkiang.

On our long flight back to Luliang, we chuckled about our good fortune. Somewhere in central China, there were several airplanes loaded with fuming generals and probably not a few admirals who had missed the big dance.

It was OK. We had done a good job of filling in for them.

FORTY-SIX

On 23 August, we flew a load of supplies to Liangshan. It was a fairly rough trip. We were on instruments at night nearly half the flight. Adding to the stress, we were now being constantly hassled by Maoist forces. The guerilla activity was mostly at night and confined almost exclusively to landing lights, which they cut or damaged. Thus far, no one in our crews had been shot, but we started an increased guard on the airplanes and as usual never went anywhere unarmed. When I was a little kid, Gram had called me a "gun nut." She was absolutely right, but now that I had to wear a heavy .45 automatic all the time, I didn't feel at all like Tom Mix, and the gun no longer seemed so romantic.

There was a new flurry of flying as we moved into September. A landslide of stuff was coming in from India and over the Burma Road. There were still cargos of gasoline, ammo, and bombs, but not so much as before. Now we were hauling general supplies and troops from Luliang to the forward bases, and the volume seemed to be increasing daily. Our C-46s were holding up well but only because guys were working on engines in the rain to keep us as safe as possible.

Preparing to land, National Museum of the United States Air Force. (US Air Force photo.)

Such contrast in cultures was common in the China-Burma-India Theatre and sometimes created dangers when landing our big planes.

I flew almost every day during the first week of September. Two of those trips were with Martin Hurd and Tony Baldasare. Chihkiang was becoming our home away from home now, and we knew the fighter strip and area around it like the backs of our hands. Even so, I was too chicken to ever get complacent in the cockpit.

The second of September, V-J Day, was a big day for us. When the Japanese formally surrendered on the Battleship USS *Missouri,* it meant for all intents and purposes the war was over. We didn't have to worry about them anymore. To mark that occasion, we flew a load of supplies to Liuchow. It was a night flight, and we had a check pilot with us, which turned out to be a good thing. About an hour after leaving Luliang, I came down with a serious bout of stomach cramps. All of a sudden, I was totally out of commission.

When we arrived at Liuchow, the radio operator walked me down to the dispensary where we woke up a medic to see if he could do anything for me. He was pretty groggy but said he'd see what he could do. I'm sure he was more asleep than awake when he gave me the shot. I was even more sure when he suddenly exclaimed, "Jesus, Lieutenant, I gave you a lot of that stuff!" It was immediately obvious he'd made a mistake on the dosage because I was quickly feeling the effects. I vaguely recall him stating that it was sodium amytal and that I was going to be doing a lot of sleeping. With the radio operator leading the way, I stumbled back to the plane, which by now was almost unloaded, and I sprawled across a row of bucket seats. That's the last thing I remember of the trip.

I was still comatose when we got back to Luliang, so they loaded me into a jeep and took me to the dispensary where a medic put me on a bunk and threw a blanket over me. I don't remember how long I was out, but when I awoke, the stomach cramps were gone...only to be replaced with a hell of a headache. Apparently, there had been a little V-J Day celebration at the officers' club when we returned. Herb Briggs and Pete Mignin filled me in on the details since I'd slept through the whole damn thing.

On 4 September, we made another delivery to Liuchow. A quick check of the flight roster following our return revealed a wonderful surprise. I'd been booked out for another dream trip—this time to Shanghai. I was scheduled to fly with Captain Lee Hassig, and we would depart early the next morning with stopovers in Kunming and Liuchow. Lee was a few years older than I was, and he was capable and mature. It was a privilege to fly with him, and I think he felt the same way about me. This was turning out to be an unforgettable week.

B-24 Liberator bomber takes off from Kunming Airfield, ca 1943. Note the P-40 Warhawks parked in the foreground. (United States National Archives photo, from Records of the Office of War Information, Photographs of Allied and Axis Personalities and Activities, compiled 1942–1945, Record Group 208; National Archives Identifier: 535780.)

Wednesday, 5 September, we hauled a load of equipment to Kunming, reloaded, and then flew on to Liuchow, this time with no onboard stomach troubles. Liuchow would be our jumping off spot for the trip to Shanghai. A few months earlier, it had been a real hotspot where a heavy-duty battle had been fought between the Japs and Chinese forces. The place had only been recaptured from Japanese control on 30 June, and there was still a lot of their stuff scattered around to remind us of the war. Unfortunately, most of the souvenirs were too big to steal.

On Thursday, we had a daybreak briefing. Our destination would be Kiangwan Airfield, just northeast of Shanghai. The weather was supposed to stay clear all the way to the coast so finding the field would not be a problem. The surrender of all Japanese forces had occurred only four days earlier; and we were told to expect a large Japanese presence at the airport, including a number of Japanese fighters and tactical aircraft. The flight distance was roughly 1,000 miles.

Liuchow Airstrip after recapture by Chinese troops. Note the large craters in the runway. (US Department of Defense photo.)

We had a right engine that was a bit sour and hard to start, but after a series of huffs and puffs and a lot of gray smoke, she brightened up, and we were cleared to go. We had a pretty good load of stuff on board and used a bit of runway, but she finally got off the ground, and as I pulled up the gear handle, I remember thinking: *This is going to be real adventure.*

CHAPTER FORTY-SIX

I was right.

We headed northeast into the rising sun in more ways than one. Coastal China was a few hours ahead of us, and beyond that, the islands of Japan. In the space of a half hour, we were flying over a China we had never before seen. The modern-day jetsetter can view an enormous expanse of pastel landscape from the cramped confines of his or her window seat. The 500 mph plus airspeed of an airliner at 30,000 feet blurs the earth into a toneless sameness, a panorama of featureless repetition that makes one yearn for arrival at the intended destination. Air travel is now an experience of boredom and ennui broken only by the passage of refreshment carts and trips to the same-sex toilet. *My God, what we have lost!*

Our radio operator was blissfully quiet as we flew into a dawn of incredible intricacy. We were poking along at a bit above a hundred and a half at an altitude that was probably illegal. Lee and I had set the props and manifold pressure to an easy cruise. Mundane items like cylinder head temperature and oil pressure were observed, but certainly not prayed over, and the autopilot, compass, and directional gyro were in total agreement as we headed for Hangkow, just south of Shanghai. From there, we figured we'd home in on Shanghai and Kiangwan.

Below us, an endless scroll slowly unrolled before our eyes. This was a land filled with convolutions of culture and people that predated our imaginations, a fragment of wonder whose valleys, towns, hills, and deltas had known the suns and moons of a thousand years. We were noisome, but we were birds. The form and color that had graced the Tang dynasty now graced our flight across its ancient dominion. It was breathtaking.

"Listening to Wind in Pines" by Ma Lin, before 1246. (Hanging Scroll, color on silk. National Palace Museum, Taibei, Taiwan. Free of known restrictions under copyright law, including all related and neighboring rights. wikidata: Q637407.)

Dominant were the green rice fields that underpainted this colossal landscape. We crossed countless small red-roofed villages and endless dun-colored roads peopled by water buffalo and their herders, some seeming to look aloft at their intruders, others simply remaining head down, intent on their daily bread. Ponds, lakes, and all the ageless fabrications of passing humankind dotted the panorama before us, while rivers, looking ever so much like the blue veining that crisscrossed the backs of work-weary Asian hands, meandered inevitably toward the south and east and eventually to the sea.

This emerging China was still virgin to its people. The Japanese invaders were too small in foresight, stature, and number to conquer a land as old as time. Indeed, the landscape flowing beneath us was too robust, too dignified, and too venerated by occasion and circumstance to be marked by the heel of a Japanese infantry boot. The forces of the Imperial Japanese Emperor were rather concentrated along the coastal areas, most populated and most vulnerable to invasion and control.

We continued our thrilling journey northeast, and as we drew closer to the coastline of China, the pastoral lands over which we had traveled slowly changed their clothes and morphed into urban clutter. Now reality stepped on our toes, and the job of locating Kiangwan became paramount over staring at the jumbled coastline below us. Already, the shining visage of the East China Sea filled the right seat windows. It was time to pull levers and push buttons, and we identified Hangkow and its environs without much trouble. Using the RDF, I picked up a nose null on the commercial radio station at Shanghai. It was actually broadcasting in English.

Even for a dumbbell, it was virtually impossible to get lost. The Yangtze River flowed into the East China Sea at Shanghai and that was a great signpost to tell you where you were. We picked up a bit of altitude and soon spotted Kiangwan Airfield north and east of the city. It was an eye opener. I counted twenty-seven Japanese fighters on the concrete apron, but the most incredible view was of thousands of people thronging the airport like a gigantic herd of multicolored grazers. They were everywhere, from old men to pretty little girls in flowered dresses, and a massive celebration was underway.

Crowds at Kiangwan Airfield greet the incoming 94th Chinese Army of Occupation on 8 September 1945. (Photo by Lieutenant Ewing, United States. Army. Signal Corps. Photograph furnished by the National Archives Still Picture Branch, Item number: 111-SC-268189. No restrictions on publication.)

When we contacted the tower, an English voice OK'd us to land and suggested a long final approach. As we neared the landing spot, it seemed no one was unnerved by our oncoming aircraft—only at the last minute did they scatter and clear the runway to avoid being eaten alive by our engines. Taxiing was also a problem because of the mass of humanity that had invaded the field. We were finally directed to a spot on the apron where we could shut down. As the props quit turning, a huge circle of Chinese men, women, and children began shouting unintelligible greetings to us. It was then that we observed some Japanese infantrymen carrying Arisaka rifles and working their way through the noisy crowd. They took up stations around our C-46, and it turned out they were actually guarding it from the overly zealous Chinese celebrants. *That was a switch!*

Later, in a letter home, I mentioned that Japanese troops were everywhere, bowing and smiling. There was even a group of Jap soldiers driving trucks around the field passing out free beer and soft drinks, and we viewed all this celebrating as being pretty bizarre. People who had shot at us just a few days earlier were now guarding our planes from those with whom we'd been aligned for nearly the past four years, meanwhile Big Band music was screaming out goodwill from a huge speaker. *What about Chihkiang, for God's sake? And for that matter, what about Iwo Jima, Tarawa, Guadalcanal?* It was almost too much for us, and we sure as hell didn't feel like embracing these bastards.

I noticed a new Japanese Kawasaki Ki-61 "Tony" fighter parked peacefully on the apron. It was the only one I would ever see. She was pretty and looked Italian, and there was also something of the shark about her shape. The Tony had been made operational in 1942 and appeared to me to be fairly lethal. Viewing this pretty thing from afar, I figured it was to our advantage that the fight was over.

Kawasaki Ki-61 "Tony" at an airfield in Fukuoka, Japan, 1945. (National Museum of Naval Aviation, Robert L. Lawson Photographic Collection. US Navy photo.)

Due to all the confusion and rush of inbound traffic, we were unloaded pretty fast. Our return orders directed us back to Chihkiang with a small load of miscellaneous supplies. Also aboard were a dozen cases of beer and ten cases of canned fruit cocktail...all personally purloined from another plane and obviously not listed on our manifest or our center-of-gravity check sheet.

We had a rather nerve-racking time taxiing back to the runway. The hordes were not thinning and seemed reluctant to move away from our two live props. Thankfully, we didn't make direct contact with any onlookers' skulls. Finally, we were cleared for takeoff. While we were climbing out, I could see the Japanese beer trucks still making their rounds. To the east, I counted three classic, big-eyed-chicken junks. Their battened sails were set, and they sailed a broad reach into a light easterly, probably bound for east Timor. This journey had been a magic carpet ride across the tapestry of China.

The right engine was still running a tad warm, but not to worry; we greased the landing at Chihkiang, had a few stolen beers, and got a few hours of shuteye. On the seventh, we checked over the starboard engine and found nothing wrong. As soon as we had finished playing mechanic, we cleared with operations, and late that afternoon, we were back at Luliang, still digesting the wonders of the trip.

What a couple of days this had been!

FORTY-SEVEN

Following the trip to Shanghai, I was dropped off the roster for a day. It was a good thing. I was pretty tired. I hung out through the afternoon and wrote a letter home covering the Shanghai trip and all the goings on; then I cleaned up around the tent a little. Being the youngest guy in our group, I was constantly badgered into cleanup detail. Admittedly, the tent could get a little cruddy after a few days, so I swept the dirt out the front door, where it could immediately be tracked in again.

After chow, Pete and I walked over to what was laughingly called the officers' club. Herb Briggs usually went with us, but he'd been booked out for an evening trip to Kunming. The club was like a two-car garage minus the car lifts. A few two-by-twelves constituted the homemade bar, which offered *bad* homemade whiskey and Jing Bao juice (*very bad* Chinese wine). A few Goodwill tables lined the edges of the dimly lit interior, and an assortment of cast-off chairs filled out the furnishings. The only available latrine was in the barracks next door and featured cold water only and usually no hand towels. We always looked first before washing our hands. Most of the time, I didn't even bother with water and towels; Luliang wasn't exactly Mrs. Hall's Kindergarten.

I was tired and quit early. Pete stayed on to swap tall tales with a couple of troop carrier pilots. The weather was getting colder, and the little heater in our tent felt good. It wasn't long before I had dropped off to a heavy sleep.

It was nearly midnight when I felt Pete shaking me awake. He informed me that a C-46 named *Patch and Pray* was a no-show at Kunming and already two hours overdue. Aboard the airplane were our friends, Martin Hurd, Herb Briggs, George Giancaterino, Edward Jasinski, and Tony Baldasare, who had swapped trips at the last minute to fly with the rest of our buddies.

Pete, Tarz, Erv, and I spent the rest of the night chain smoking and staring at the floor in the operations office. There was a bunch of other guys doing the same thing. We were all certain that a radio message would come in that *Patch and Pray* had landed, gear up, in a damn rice paddy somewhere, and that our friends hadn't even gotten their feet wet. But there was no message…only irritating static over the radio, sounding for all the world like crinkling paper.

By dawn, a couple of C-47s had boxed the area around Kunming, and a half hour later, both planes had picked up a faint smoke plume rising from an obvious crash. The site was just below a stumpy mountain. The crews buzzed the spot several times, but they detected no debris field, no sign of life, and no reason to hope for a different ending. No one had survived.

For a short while, there lingered a strong sense of denial, as if things could be rewound and all set right again, but this didn't last. Our group was like a small pool of water into which fate had dropped a heavy stone of sorrow. The ensuing ripples touched us all, leaving us with a pervasive sense of loss that darkened the rivers of our consciousness.

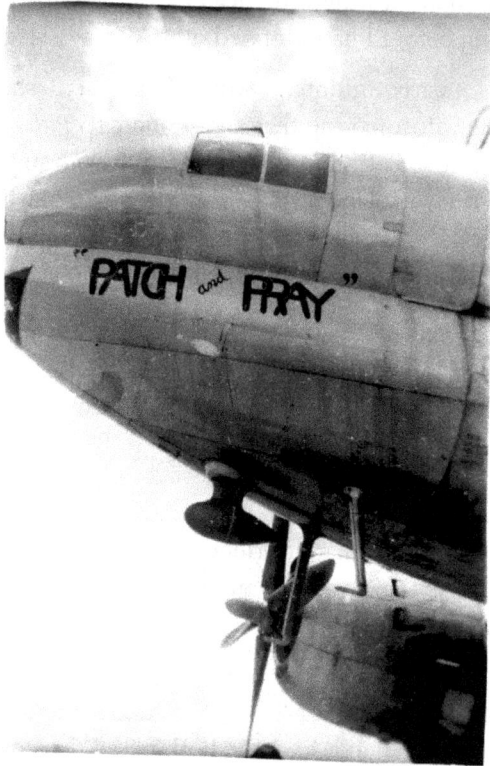

Patch and Pray, C-46 #7134. (Photo by Ed Larson. From the author's collection.)

Pete, Tarz Taylor, and I immediately met with our CO to request a few days leave to go to Kunming and attempt to expedite recovery efforts to locate, identify, and retrieve any personal effects and recoverable remains that might be returned to the involved families. We then hitched a ride to Kunming on a C-47 Troop Carrier that had a missing rear cabin door. I'm not sure why they flew it that way—it's possible the door had been misplaced or lost—but apparently, no one had fallen out of the gaping hole.

Rugged terrain surrounding Kunming crash site. (US Department of Defense photo.)

We signed up for transient officers' quarters at Hostel #1, and the next day, we were directed to the Graves Registration Office in search of details about the missing C-46 and our friends. The office staff advised us that, by all reports, the wreckage would be difficult to reach because of steep, wooded terrain. That statement was followed by the promise that Graves Registration would proceed as quickly as possible to reach the site and obtain positive identification of the aircraft and crew.

Our time in Kunming was far too limited. I was scheduled to fly on the thirteenth, which meant a "must return" to Luliang on the twelfth. It was becoming apparent that our trip to Kunming was accomplishing little, but we were trying. On Tuesday, 11 September, with time running out, we agreed that we should contact the Graves Registration Office again, advise them that we would return to Luliang the next day, and hope for more information regarding the accident as soon as possible.

Pete and Tarz went to the airport to try to arrange a return flight for the next day, while I visited Graves Registration to advise them of our plans to leave. This time, I was ushered into the office of the CO, a smallish captain behind a desk that was far too big for him.

I was not invited to sit in the available chair so I remained standing and informed the captain that we had flown in from Luliang because we were close friends of those missing in the crash. I also explained that we had to return to flight duty the next day and that we would deeply appreciate anything he might do to expedite the search for our friends. My request was made with no indication of anger or disrespect or hostility.

For a moment, he stared at me with a face that was totally impassive. Then he stood, and in a rage that was shocking, he accused me of maligning his organization and their efforts, and charged me with seeking to become involved by dictating the course of his investigation.

I was stunned by his vehemence and the violence of his words, and I suddenly realized that here was a person on the edge, an individual that was out of control and close to an emotional breakdown. Over the years, I have often thought about his tirade, and I am still unable to explain it. Perhaps his outburst was a traumatic reaction to the constant stress of dealing in loss and the recovery of remains under complex and harsh conditions.

I exited the situation as quickly as possible with the conviction he would do little or nothing to help us. If ever there was any additional information regarding the investigation of *Patch and Pray*'s fatal crash, we were never made aware of it. The Kunming effort left a legacy of unanswered questions and a lifetime of painful memories. The next morning, we hopped aboard a C-47 Troop Carrier and returned to Luliang. This trip, the airplane was outfitted with a rear cabin door.

Through a supreme bit of irony, I sit here in real time, on another September 8 and write of this life-changing event in the silence of a rather cold night. My very small dog snugs up against my slippers seeking a bit more warmth. It was on this day—and almost at this very hour nearly 70 years ago—that Martin, Herb, George, Ed, and Tony died in a nanosecond. Their lives were rubbed out in the darkness of night on a wooded hillside half a world away from the homes in which they were born, where they had loved and were cherished…and ultimately mourned. I have grown old in the constant company of this haunting memory. Why was life taken from them and given to me? I wonder if there is a more solemn question one might ask, or a heavier burden one might bear. In a lifetime of living, I haven't found the answer…nor have I laid down the burden.

> *YOU FEEL SMALL*
> *IN THE PRESENCE OF DEAD MEN,*
> *AND ASHAMED AT BEING ALIVE,*
> *AND YOU DON'T ASK SILLY QUESTIONS.*
>
> ~ ERNIE PYLE
> FROM "THE DEATH OF CAPTAIN WASKOW"

I have lived a long life under this personal siege. The enemy is homemade guilt, a noxious weed one creates in some corner of one's imagination, like a lie told often enough that becomes an insidious and destructive reality. It is triggered by the grief-filled remembrance of *Patch and Pray* and her crew, and imaginations about of the remote mountain where it all ended. First the sweat and shaking begin like a fired shot with no reason or warning. Then fear arrives like an uninvited guest, elbowing its way into my thoughts on a sunny Honolulu beach or the bridge of an Alaskan salmon seiner in a raging rain. When finally the panic subsides, there is dire need for a bottle of whiskey or anything else that can numb the pain.

Those of us afflicted must run away in an attempt to escape the specter of our own shadows. It is frightening to know this enemy will strike again, so long as we have even one more tomorrow.

When I was young, I thought this happened only to me and that it would vanish with the passing years. I am old, now; and I understand…there is no retreat from this anguish for those of us who have lost a favored soul from our beloved Band of Brothers.

On 13 September, we flew a night trip to Chihkiang and back. On the fifteenth, we flew another round-robin night trip—this time to Luhsien. The next night, in bad weather, we were again delivering supplies to Chihkiang for our little fighter-plane friends. I felt no consternation about all of this flying. I'd like to believe we were too practiced to doubt our own abilities to survive.

On 17 September, Flight Officer Max Baskett and I were scheduled to fly another load to Luhsien. It was a bright and sunny day, and I was looking forward to the trip. Max was a tall kid, a sort of down-home type, and a fine pilot, and he taught me a lot. Max and I had flown together several times; he was generous in letting me fly from the left seat and pretty much paddle my own canoe. As usual, we checked the plane over carefully, and though we had a max load on, everything seemed OK. We chatted a bit while taxiing to the runway and ran completely through the checklist. We were probably a little more particular than ordinary since I was in the pilot's seat.

Conditions were ideal, and we got clearance for takeoff and powered up. The airplane seemed to pick up speed OK, but when I raised the tail, she seemed sticky, as if she didn't want to get off the ground. Max sensed it, too, and he was watching the panel like a hawk. By this time, we were roaring down the runway. Still, the bird wouldn't fly. Everything was pushed to the wall, and we could see "Kingdom come" as we quickly ran out of runway. Finally, I felt her lift off the struts and hollered to Max to pull up the gear. We picked up some airspeed and a teacup full of altitude as the end of the runway flashed beneath us…that had been too damn close. We looked at each other, cussed, and wondered aloud what the hell had just happened. Staring at the instrument panel, we could detect absolutely nothing out of line. The airplane just seemed a little out of breath, but it was climbing OK. We talked it over, advised the tower of the aberration, and proceeded to fly on to Luhsien with sweaty palms.

Our landing there was perfectly normal and we'd burned off four and a half hours worth of gas, so things were looking up. Both Max and I looked carefully at the load and felt it might be a tad heavy, but that was just a guess. Max flew left seat on the return flight, and I sensed he felt a little better about it. The takeoff and climb out were textbook, and all the way back, he complained about my flying skills while graphically describing my ancestral pedigree. We could laugh now, but the departure from Luliang hadn't been so funny. When we got home, we checked the loading record for center-of-gravity limitations. Nothing seemed out the ordinary. But we both had a lot of hours by that time, and we knew something had been wrong that morning, so we wrote up the plane and then went down to the flight surgeon's office for our whiskey ration. It tasted better than usual after that trip.

Later that evening, Lee Hassig stopped by the tent. He had just received orders to leave for Calcutta and home. He was departing the next morning. Lee's family owned a drugstore in Kansas City, and he gave me a coupon for a free milkshake as a goodbye present. We spent a few minutes joking about the trips we'd made and the intermittent terrors we had shared, and then we shook hands and said "So long and good luck."

There would be a lot more of these kinds of goodbyes as the days wound down. Partings were always mixed with a sense of joy and a little sadness. There was the shared triumph that the war was over, and the inevitable and permanent shedding of important friendships. *What do you say to a valued friend when you know your paths will never cross again?* I still have the coupon somewhere in a drawer. I wish Lee the best.

Many of the bases were changing their primary missions or preparing to shut down, and resupply or removal of personnel and equipment was essential. We seemed to be the only game in town, and our days were filled with the sounds of revving engines and screeching tires as they hit the runway. The weather was much colder now, but our tent remained amazingly comfortable, particularly after partaking of some antifreeze at our officers' club.

It was the last day in September when I received word from home that my dad had been pretty badly injured in an airplane accident. I hadn't heard from him since he and Mamie had flown to see me at Gardner. Apparently, he had taken a job in the Midwest as a crew chief for the infant Flying Tiger Line, which had just been formed by a group of real Flying Tigers from the CBI. Dad was serving as crew chief on one of their first airplanes, a Budd Conestoga.

The Conestoga was a bizarre airplane with all the innate beauty of a two-tailed pollywog. It was constructed entirely of stainless steel and designed as a rear-loading twin-boom freighter and transport plane. Although ugly as sin, it packed a heavy cargo load for its day. If I have not made myself entirely clear, it was not a pretty airplane.

Following the accident, Ed was hospitalized for some time with back injuries. Unfortunately, Flying Tiger Lines had no medical insurance, and my dad had no money to pay the bill either, so when he was able to get about again, he simply walked out. It was my dad's way of handling things.

In a postwar meeting with my father, he explained the circumstances leading up to the crash and showed me pictures of the aircraft, which had pretty well disintegrated on impact. The details of the accident are worth repeating.

The Conestoga was hauling a load of furniture to the West Coast. In preparation for departure, the crew taxied to the head of a runway that headed directly over the city. During the run-up before takeoff, someone noticed the suction pump had failed, making the gyro instruments inoperable. There was nothing to do but return to the flight line and replace the faulty pump. During the short time required to make the repairs, the wind direction changed, and the crew was in turn directed to a different runway for departure. The new runway heading would lead them over a local golf course rather than over the city. The night takeoff seemed normal, but a few hundred feet in the air, they experienced an engine power failure, and the Conestoga crashed on one of the fairways with the crew sustaining multiple injuries. If they had not experienced the pump failure and had instead taken off from the first runway, they would have crashed in the middle of the downtown area, creating a catastrophe with probably scores of fatalities. It was simply another instance of the validity of Ernest Gann's contention that "fate is the hunter."

I did not see or hear from my dad until three years after the war was over, at which time he told me about the crash. He was always too busy to write or call; and years before, I had grown to expect this behavior.

It was vintage Ed Garrett.

I wish it had been different.

FORTY-EIGHT

T he weather had turned quite cold, and we were experiencing more rain and wind so flying conditions were not the greatest; however, most of our destinations remained above minimums so we were still airborne. Toward the end of September, a rumor broke out that Luliang would probably shut down operations as early as 20 October. That suited us to a tee, particularly with the weather deteriorating so quickly.

During the last week of September, a large number of brand new P-51s and P-47s refueled at Luliang on their way to Chinese bases on the coast. They were destined for Kuomintang forces and would supposedly serve the Chinese Nationalist Air Force in their fight against Maoist Communists in the approaching civil war. We heard later through the grapevine that most of these planes had been intentionally destroyed by the Chiang Kai-shek government when they were in danger of being captured by the Maoists. The word received went on to say a bulldozer ran down lines of these beautiful new fighters and smashed off their tail assemblies to make them forever earthbound. I am truly glad I did not witness this crime. We would have sold our souls just to fly one around the field.

Blood chit with photo of First Lieutenant Ed Larson. (From the author's collection.)

Blood chits were carried by US service personnel with a message that read, "This foreign person has come to China to help in the war effort. Soldiers and civilians, one and all, should rescue, protect, and provide him with medical care." Note the list of locations where the author served during his deployment.

Although it was scarcely newsworthy, on 2 October, Max Baskett formally checked me out as a First Pilot on the C-46. My check ride was a round trip to Luhsien, where we delivered a contingent of Chinese troops. The First Pilot designation was nice but a bit anticlimactic since I had been flying periodically from the left seat for some time. Max was great, assuring me that I was totally qualified, and it looked nice on my record, although, I had never pursued the job with much passion. I would have traded it in a heartbeat for a check ride in a P-40 or P-51. To my everlasting disappointment, that never happened.

On 3 October 1945, all flights over the Hump were officially halted. It was the end of an era. The story of flying the Hump had been penned by hundreds of guys who took their chances, win or lose. A lot of airplanes would lie in ruins to mark their route. It was particularly humbling to think of those who flew the early northern route with C-47 aircraft hampered by altitude limitations. For the early ones, it was a game of cat and mouse weaving through the world's highest peaks with one hand on the yoke and the other making the Sign of the Cross.

ATC to Carry Mail, Passengers to China

CHUNGKING— (UP) —The air transport command has made its last cargo flight over "the hump" between India and China and only mail and passenger service will be continued, it was disclosed today.

In announcing' the final cargo flight, the ATC revealed that from Dec. 1, 1942, to Nov. 1, 1945, its ships had carried 776,532 tons of war materials over the Himalayas to China from bases in India.

Losses for the period were announced at 910 crew members and 136 passengers killed or missing and 594 planes lost.

Newspaper clipping reporting the end of Hump operations. (From the author's collection.)

Note the tremendous volume of transported war materials and sustained losses of crews, passengers, and planes during the thirty-five months of service.

About this time, the China National Airways Corporation (CNAC) was looking for pilots to fly postwar routes from India to Shanghai. For some little time, I had considered signing up, but the political situation in China had become a boiling pot. The Nationalists and Maoists were at each other's throats, and we had already been subjected to the start of this dogfight. Everybody knows the outcome. The Chinese Communists ran the Kuomintang Nationalists off mainland China and into Taiwan. After the Communist victory in 1949, CNAC became a duck without feathers. By November 1949, many of its top people had defected to the mainland and the Communist cause, taking the airplanes with them. My decision not to sign a contract was a good one.

Things were really moving now, and so were we: a load of equipment to Peishi, a short haul to Yangkai; and now that the war was over, food brought over from India began to improve. We got a lot of canned goods that we hadn't seen for a year...I never dreamed I'd get teary eyed over a can of Dennison's chili.

My birthday was on 20 October; I was finally 21—an adult—and I could now legally drink and vote. All we had to celebrate with was a bottle of Portuguese brandy. It tasted great but left me with a banging headache the next morning.

I flew again on the twenty-first. When I returned, I discovered a real treat: I was scheduled to haul a load of stuff to Kunming, reload, take equipment to Chihkiang, and then head directly for Shanghai for an overnight stay. Our return trip would include a delivery of priority freight to Chihkiang and an overnight stopover in Luliang. I would be flying left seat and had become a little proud of that fact after all.

I have mentioned the increasing cold temperatures we were encountering. The flight deck on the C-46 was far more comfortable than on the B-24, but at altitude, they were both chilly and drafty; however, the C-46 had one significant advantage over the B-24: Clipped to the overhead above the pilot and copilot seats were two large heater hoses feeding hot air to the flight deck. Each was equipped with a slim, wide-mouthed plastic nozzle looking exactly like something from a vacuum cleaner. The hoses were intended to remain clipped in place and thus heat the entire cabin, although, in truth, they were highly ineffective. Somewhere along the way, some selfish genius decided to unclip a nozzle from the overhead and stick it directly down the neck of his flight suit. For us pilots, this was the most remarkable breakthrough of the war. Although everyone aboard might be freezing, the pilot and copilot, each with his own heater hose shoved down his neck, was now as warm as if beside a roaring fireplace. There was one disadvantage, though. The huge flow of warm air blew up our flight suits, giving the appearance of two balloons at the controls of the aircraft. But while we looked bizarre, our personal appearance was a small price to pay for custom comfort heating while flying.

Our trip was made in good weather all the way. The early part of the flight from Chihkiang to Shanghai was as engrossing as it had been the first time. The late fall had touched the fields and villages with the first brush of coming winter. Smoke wreathed many of the villages, and the trees had begun to lose all vestiges of the color and texture of summer. The earth of the Tang Empire was beginning to see its own breath, and its people were moving slowly indoors to warm themselves beside winter hearths and millions of village fire pits.

As we flew northeast, the night that was dropping over the East China Sea soon shrouded us with darkness. Flying on, we saw lights from the populated coastal edge delineate land from sea. Turning north, we homed in on Kiangwan Airfield. The tower was fully operational, and air traffic

Aerial view of Shanghai, China, 18 September 1945. (Photo by Lieutenant Ewing, United States Army Signal Corps. Publication of Photographs furnished by the National Archives Still Picture Branch, Item number: 111-SC-444328. No restrictions on publication.)

Over the Yangtze River, 1945. (US Navy and Marine Corps Museum, CDR Francis N. Gilreath Collection. No. 1987.096.001.138.)

control was direct and effective. After landing without any problems, we were transported to Shanghai where we billeted for the night at the Park Hotel.

At first light, we were up to check out the city sights. Our hotel had been taken over by the Red Cross to serve as a temporary hostel for allied personnel. The Park Hotel was located in the center of the downtown district and looked out over the Bund, a wide boulevard; the Racetrack, a Shanghai landmark; and the Whangpoo River.

Shanghai was unsullied by the Japanese. It was too cosmopolitan, too classy, too tough for their jackbooted legs. If indeed there had been a war here, it was only a concoction of the small people from the islands to the east, and they constituted no problem and would soon go away.

A million dramas bring a city to bristling life, and Shanghai awakened early with hordes of calm-faced people rushing to work or play as if nothing recently had happened. Streets teemed with young women of stunning beauty and promise, walking alongside those of stunning wretchedness and despair...each one living a story; most never told. I observed this vivid scene from the balcony of my hotel room—gorgeous hues of cheongsam sprinkled like jewels against the black and dirty pseudosilk of the masses, every type of vehicle imaginable clogging the narrow streets, scurrying and honking in search of some innocuous reward, the whole of it brushed with the incredibly complex, sin-filled, and seductive smell that shouts, "China!"

We had a couple of hours before returning to the airplane, and we spent it walking the streets and alleys of this storied, vibrant place. Not far from the hotel, we discovered a whole community of White Russian expatriates living in comfort and semiseclusion. The Japanese apparently ignored them. They had been there throughout the war.

It is impossible to describe the wonders we observed in the few hours we spent there. Our senses were constantly jolted by the sights and sounds and smells, making every moment a new and unique adventure. As we walked together through the city, we were assailed by countless glances and passersby's stares. We seldom spoke; each of us was overwhelmed by the enormity of what we were experiencing. We returned to Kiangwan and our airplane still astonished by the fact that, at last, we had seen the face of a China we had never witnessed before, as far from the rice paddies of Liuchow and Peishi as if they existed on another star.

It took most of the day to pick up our cargo bound for Chihkiang. While poking around, we discovered an elephant's graveyard of Japanese aircraft wreckage that had been created on a far corner of the field. It was a treasure trove impossible to ignore, a disorderly pile of aluminum trash and Holy Grail souvenirs. We walked to the site and saw firsthand the remains of the planes of our enemies.

Most of the wreckage appeared to be parts of A6M Mitsubishi Zeros. Upon examination of one smashed fuselage, the airplane more resembled a trainer than a first-line fighter plane. The cockpit was tinny and primitive, and it was easy to see why the Zeke was so maneuverable— there wasn't an ounce of extra weight incorporated into its design: no self-sealing fuel tanks, and no armor for the pilot or the engine. It was a thin-skinned, sharp-turning, and worthy adversary. If you were adverse to plate armor...and pilot safety, it would be a hell of an aerobatic airplane. I would have loved flying it; it would have been easy and fun.

Intrigued by the apparent lightness in weight of the Japanese Zero fighter, I later looked up the specification figures out of sheer curiosity. Amazingly, with a full load of guns and ammunition, the Zeke was almost three hundred pounds lighter than the AT-6 Texan—a plane in which I had instructed at Gardner Airfield. No wonder it could turn on a dime!

I stole a magneto switch and a cylinder head temperature gauge from one of the carcasses. Mysteriously, the head temperature gauge was for a twin-engine aircraft. What was it doing on this single-engine fighter? I figured there must have been some production shortage to create that seemingly errant situation.

We finally departed Shanghai in late afternoon as the setting sun brushed long shadows across the land. I set the airplane up for an easy cruise, and we continued in gathering darkness while lights of the night world winked on. At the start, the lights were numberless, defining the bustling coastal area. As we flew southwestward, the frequency of lights diminished and finally disappeared. We were now suspended above the inland reaches of an empire peopled with peasants, charcoal fires, and a lifestyle ever so close to the wheel and lever era. We were returning to the China we had grown to recognize and accept.

The landing and short stay at Chihkiang were uneventful. When we finally touched down in the rain at Luliang, it felt as if we had come home. We walked over to the dispensary for our double shots of bourbon, and while it may sound bizarre, I assure you, it was a fitting end to a five-hour night flight in inclement weather.

The day following our Shanghai trip, both Erv and Tarz got orders to head home. They left the next morning for Calcutta. Now, Pete and I were alone in the tent. The four of us had lived and flown together for nearly a year; we had shared good times and bad and in the process had become close buddies. The goodbyes were not easy. Something left our lives when we watched them climb aboard that C-47 and head west.

We were not scheduled to fly again, at least not in this war. In the course of a few days, Luliang had become a rather ghostly place of emptying tents and barracks and airplanes sitting silently in the rain as if abandoned and dejected. The spirits of guys checking flight rosters and the beguiling sounds of starting engines were gone; all that was left to us was pervasive cold, pervasive aloneness, pervasive rain. Although we had hoped to fly an airplane home, when Pete and I got our orders, they read, "Return to US by ship." It was a crushing disappointment, but apparently, the orders had already been cut. The story we had lived here was coming to an end.

On Saturday, 27 October, we were directed to deliver our airplanes to Kunming for storage and disposition. After that, we would be flightless birds, losing any and all identification to flying that we had ever known. The letter I wrote home that day said, "The weather is cold with lots of rain." There was a coldness in my heart, as well.

Our planes were weary. They had been ridden hard and bore the marks and dents of the rather coarse places they had taken us. There were no warm and sheltered hangers for these unromantic beasts of burden. They were tethered in the sun and rain, worked when needed, and quite often growled out their discontent over the sparseness of their rice bowls. Their flight decks and cargo areas were usually unkempt and worn, but their engines were cared for like precious children. Young guys with box wrenches and worn screwdrivers had kept the monstrous and complex R-2800s running for us. Our lives were constantly in their hands. A forgotten clamp or missing bolt could drastically alter all our future years. These unsung crew chiefs were our heroes, flying the airplanes as much as we were. I always remembered that—in thought and in action.

The C-46 I flew that Saturday to Kunming had a broken landing gear strut. I checked with the mechanic, and we both decided that it was flyable and would hold up for a few more landings. We took off in the late morning, and the weather cleared a bit so it was a pleasant flight. On the way, I had a hell of an idea and diverted a bit from the direct course to Kunming to pursue it because it was important to me. This was undoubtedly the last time I would fly an old tub like this, and I wanted to make the most of it.

A chandelle is an aircraft maneuver familiar to almost everyone who has taken flight lessons. It is simply a climbing, 180-degree reversal of flight direction. First employed by fighter pilots in World War I, when properly executed, invariably in a single-engine aircraft, it is a graceful, safe, statement of pilot skill. One must complete the climbing turn and level out the aircraft just before it stalls, precisely 180 degrees from the direction in which the maneuver began.

I told the copilot I had a chandelle in mind. He thought I was crazy but simply shrugged his shoulders and became instantly alert. What happened next is as clear to me today as it was nearly seventy years ago. I dropped the nose, picked up some airspeed, and lurched into a steep left bank. With a lot of backpressure on the yoke, the nose of the old beast inscribed a curving, climbing line upward across the horizon and up into the wild blue yonder. Both of us were watching the decreasing airspeed as if it was the most important thing in the world...and it was. I am no daredevil, and I had no intention of stalling the airplane when I was a few days short of heading home.

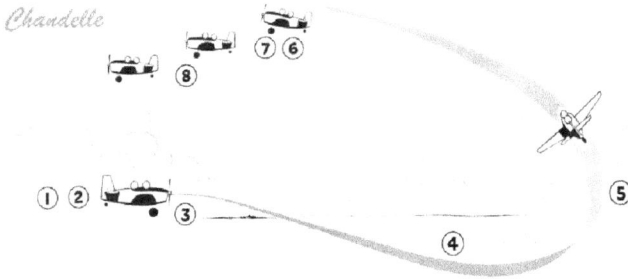

Chandelle

Illustration of a chandelle maneuver. (*Primary Flying Students' Manual* prepared by the Army Air Forces Training Command.)

The climb and turn continued as the copilot's eyes grew wider. I finally chickened out and dropped the nose close to stall speed just before we had completed the required turn. I could hear the copilot exhale as we began to pick up airspeed. My chandelle in the old C-46 Commando was *Swan Lake* on a pogo stick, pretty much a mockery and a grievous failure in flight finesse. As I expected, the old machine responded like an ancient whale, but we finished up without spinning out of control or breaking anything.

For me, it was just a way of saying goodbye to where we were and what we'd done.

We entered the pattern at Kunming, and I was really soft with the landing, holding her off ground contact until the last ounce of flight had left us. There was no drop, only a screech from the tires. The broken strut caused no problems whatsoever, but we wrote it up on Form 1 for later replacement. We would be flown back to Luliang on a staff C-47. It was cold, and I hoped it had a cabin door on it.

The spectacle of war was over. The stage lights came up as the oboes in the pit orchestra played the last measure of the score. Around the globe, billions of those still able, stood and clapped their hands knowing that peace was now the only invader. Thus, the curtain dropped on the earth's stage and on World War II. It had been the most poignant and tragic drama ever penned across the pages of mankind. Millions of heroes joined hands at stage center, bowing to an audience whose applause and gratitude rang full circle around the world. We who were the spear-carriers in the play stood, stage rear, in chorus-line fashion, smiling and knowing that our friends and families were also cheering for us, whose heroism had been limited to simply being in harm's way.

I'd like to dramatize the end of my story by saying, "I sat in the left seat on the flight deck and pulled the mixture controls to idle cut off, effectively choking the lovely R-2800 engines into the sound of nothing. I then listen in reverie as the hot engines ticked into something I could no longer hear. All that was left were my memories and the sound of falling rain against the flight deck windows."

I'd remember all that if it had really happened...but it didn't.

I'm sure we just shut her down, set the parking brake, and cut the switches. We probably looked at each other and started laughing at our chandelle, and I probably said something like, "Goddamn it, that was fun!"

When it was all over, we just picked up our flight bags and walked back through the dirty cabin. Then we climbed down the ladder and stepped out into the pouring rain...and we ran...ran to escape the downpour...ran to forget the days of pain. We ran toward home and loved ones and the promise of a new tomorrow.

MORE THAN AN END TO WAR, WE WANT AN END
TO THE BEGINNINGS OF ALL WARS.

~ FRANKLIN DELANO ROOSEVELT
FROM A SPEECH PREPARED FOR APRIL 13, 1945[69]

PHOTOGRAPHS

Primary Flight School Buddies.
(I am in the middle row on the far left.)

"Invariably, I was the youngest serviceman in any group of my peers. To keep up, I was forced to fit a mold that was older than my years and experiences. It was not an easy role to fill. Somehow, I muddled through."

Spear-Carrier and a C-109.

"We were told that we would be flying needed tonnage of aviation gasoline, bombs, and other materials over the Hump to China and that these missions were fraught with danger and loss of crews and aircraft."

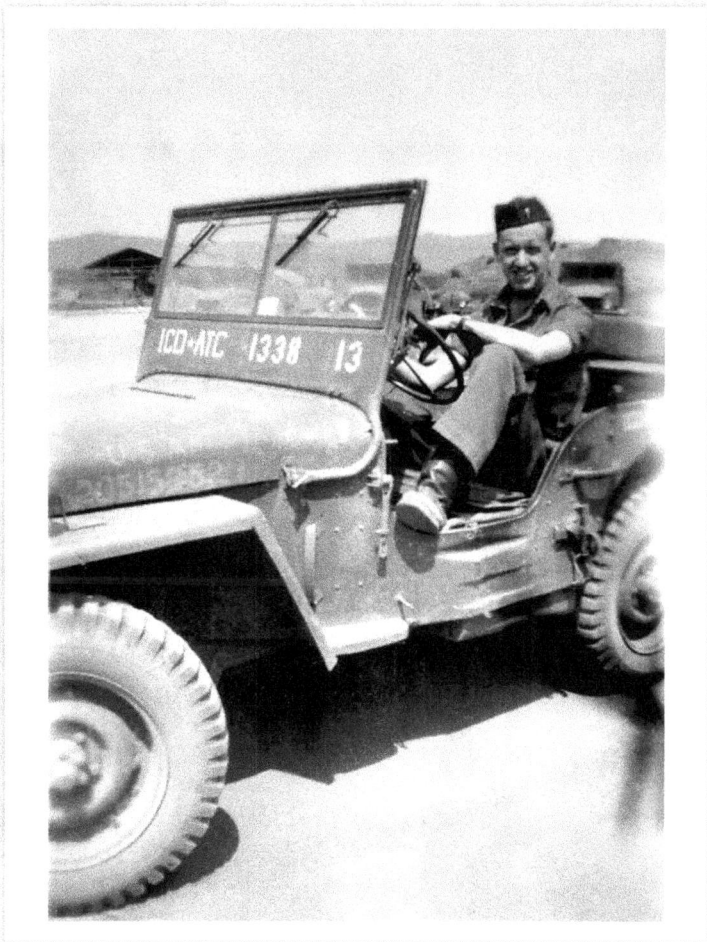

The Author and his jeep before it was stolen.

"In spite of the amenities,
Yunnanyi seemed a place of the ages,
old beyond belief."

"...we were billeted four men to a tent.
Not the fanciest of lodgings but we were able to stay dry."

In the copilot seat with the heater hose.

"We set the props and manifold pressure to an easy cruise, and the autopilot, compass, and directional gyro were in total agreement on a heading for Hangkow, just south of Shanghai."

Me and some of my buddies
(I'm standing in the back row, third from the right).

Tent Mates
(I am in the front row on the right.)

EPILOGUE

This book is mine. It is a true account of a kid who loved airplanes, learned to fly, and went to war, a basket weave of laughter and tears, passion and death, with the leavening of pervasive sorrow stirred in. Such droppings have sullied the battlefields of every armed conflict since the beginning of mankind...these are the *real* spoils of war.

In the narration of my story, I have written of the fatal crash of the C-46 Curtiss Commando we called *Patch and Pray*. It was not my intention to provide more details of the deaths of my beloved friends on the last flight of a/c 43-47134. My book was written and the story told; all should have been finished. But following the completion of the final draft, I casually asked my granddaughter to see what she could discover about the events of seventy years ago in a primitive land half a world away.

She reacted immediately to the resonating memories in the mind of her now nonagenarian grandfather who had lived through it all; and within hours, she provided me with information that I was sure had vanished in the ensuing years since that fateful day when I lost my friends.

The effect was stunning to me, a resurrection of the melancholy and self-imposed guilt that have walked beside me through all the intervening years. For want of a better term, I have always called them my close companions, and the survivor's cross that has burdened me for seven decades, has, with time, become bearable. It is part of who I am.

First Lieutenant Martin B. Hurd, first pilot on the fatal flight, was my friend. He and I flew together often, and from the time we first met, we had hit it off well. A week before the crash, Martin had asked me to be his regular copilot, and I had agreed. Had it not been for a duty roster change that night, I would have been sitting next to Martin in the cockpit of *Patch and Pray* on her final flight.

The facts of the crash are these: On 9 September 1945 at 00:04 CWT, C-46 #7134 departed Luliang, China, on a one-hour flight to Kunming. Aboard were five crewmembers and a rather small load of registered packages, mail, and six fifty-gallon drums of aviation gasoline. According to preflight documentation, the center of gravity was "ideal for the C-46."

Flying copilot that night was First Officer Herbert R. Briggs. The radio operator was Anthony "Tony" Baldasare. Crew Chief Corporal George F. Giancaterino, and Student Crew Chief PFC Edward Jasinsky were also onboard.

The weather that early morning was reported as "broken sky cover with four to five miles visibility, little wind, and stratus cloud conditions with a cloud base of 8,000 feet with tops rising to 9,000." Some thunderstorms were reported with tops to 22,000 feet, but overall, flight conditions were acceptable, posing little to no threat to airplane or crew.

The accident investigation disclosed no assigned flight altitude en route. That question is moot in view of the fact that the aircraft did not strike any surrounding mountains or hills.

About forty-five minutes after the aircraft departed Luliang, a group of Chinese farmers heard and reported a loud explosion near their sleeping village. Search planes took off at dawn and soon reported smoking wreckage in a valley 23 miles east of Kunming. Ironically, *Patch and Pray* had hurtled out of the sky to a final resting place not in one of a thousand Yunnan rice paddies, but in a field of high-standing yellow corn. Both engines lay half buried in the black soil of the field, and the airplane had completely burned save for a small section of the vertical fin, which bore the numerical identification 7134.

Unburned tail section of *Patch and Pray*, C-46 #7134 following the crash. (Aviation Archaeological Investigation & Research [AAIR].)

Several days later, a ground search of the crash scene failed to disclose a readily apparent reason for the crash. The aircraft appeared to have spun in, possibly the result of crew disorientation or involvement with violent air turbulence from the thunderstorm activity in the area. Since the remains of the aircraft were not scattered over a wider area, a midair explosion was ruled out.

The report closes with the laconic statement: "Because of the total lack of evidence as to contributing cause factors of the accident, no constructive remedial recommendations can be offered. No other official conclusions were reached."[70]

I am deeply touched as I write this. In view of the intervening years, I am struck by the fact that I am possibly the only person still alive who can remember these young men, their smiles...their jokes...the sound of their laughter. I lived with them, drank with them, and flew with them. They gave everything they had and died while I lived on.

The crash site photo shows the ragged remains of the vertical stabilizer bearing *Patch and Pray*'s tail ID 7134. Waving beside it are several stalks of yellow corn, seemingly ready to be picked. This is a picture of life and death in a land where we once walked together, worked together, and flew together...it was a place far from home, in a time long, long ago.

Requiescat in pace, my friends.

AND SO IT IS OVER. THE CATASTROPHE ON ONE SIDE OF THE WORLD HAS RUN ITS COURSE. THE DAY THAT IT HAD SO LONG SEEMED WOULD NEVER COME HAS COME AT LAST.

~ ERNIE PYLE
UNPUBLISHED

Ed and Fiona. Photo by Patricia D. Richards, 2014.

≈ ✪ ≈

"Lead them straight and true; give strength to their arms, stoutness to their hearts, steadfastness in their faith. They will need Thy blessings. Their road will be long and hard....Success may not come with rushing speed, but...by Thy grace, and by the righteousness of our cause, our sons will triumph....The darkness will be rent by noise and flame. Men's souls will be shaken with the violences of war. These men are lately drawn from the ways of peace. They fight not for the lust of conquest. They fight to end conquest. They fight to liberate. They fight to let justice arise, and tolerance and good will among all Thy people. They yearn but for the end of battle, for their return to the haven of home."

~ Franklin D. Roosevelt
Address to the Nation, D-Day, 6 June 1944

ACKNOWLEDGMENTS

There is much plodding in the process of writing a book. Viewed realistically, it is the simple act of putting one foot or word in front of the other and thus lurching slowly toward an intended goal. In the course of each, one might require a walking stick, Band-Aids, a good pair of boots, and a mental compass to point the way. I needed all of these and more.

I began the journey of this writing as an old man and arrived at my destination much older. Along the way, I received incomparable help, direction, encouragement, and counsel from a virtual army of friends, strangers, and family. I am humbly grateful to all of them and am wholly sensitive to the fact that without their selfless participation, this book would simply not exist. To each of you, my most profound thanks.

To Marilyn, my wife, friend, and lover. Laughing, she ran on ahead of me a bit ago, looking along the bank for a shady spot where we can sit and share the basket and the wine.

To Sheila Setter, my "sainted" editor. For months, she has labored over this manuscript. In so doing, it has become her creation as well as mine. Editing, proofing, crediting, authenticating, she never messed with my words but turned them into something infinitely better than they had been before. She seasoned our humble volume with a deep measure of faith and patience, brushing the pages with a dignity they did not otherwise possess. I taught her something of the sweet sound of a Rolls Royce Merlin inline V12 engine...she taught me how to write a book. Hey Sheila....HUGS!

To Patty Richards, my gadfly cousin, who really started everything by saying, "I beg you to write it." I have learned to do as she says. A professional photographer, Patty's work graces many of the pages here and her pursuit of excellence in classical photography has made her a sought-after teacher and mentor. The artistry of her work is totally evident in the photographs of our family members past and present. In many cases, Patty transformed cracked and faded photos I had taken during the war and transformed them into the vignettes that make it possible for the reader to "see" our story. Like Sheila, Patty Richards is a part of this story. She is also that creature of extreme rarity...a truly revered cousin.

To Tina Larson, my daughter. Tina devoted countless hours to this book. She willingly undertook the task of reading aloud hundreds of my wartime letters, the information from which formed the guts of our story. As my sight became increasingly impaired, she literally became my eyes, allowing me to reach the finish line and break the tape. Without her companionship, devotion, and diligence, I would have stopped long ago and wallowed in that parcel of pity reserved for the also-rans. Through our working partnership, we have developed a new and stronger relationship and interdependence, a bond that transcends absolutely the value of the words and visions we shared as partners. This renewed relationship is the bright star of our collaboration. It is an unforgettable gift to both of us.

There are countless others whose interest and enthusiasm made the task more pleasant and more productive: Asa Reed, Bill Murchison, Bill Rehm, Marsha Nemitz....I could go on and on. To them all, I extend my deepest thanks and appreciation.

Ed Larson —

November 2014

Ed Larson 2014

NOTES

NOTES

PART ONE

CHAPTER TWO

1. This series is still copyrighted, but see *Terry and the Pirates* dated 2/29/1936. http://en.wikipedia.org/wiki/File:Terry_and_Pirates_2-29-36_Strip.png

2. Dick Halvorsen, *Steeds in the Sky: The Fabulous Fighting Planes of WWII* (New York: Lancer Books, 1971).

CHAPTER FOUR

3. http://en.wikiquote.org/wiki/Wikiquote:Transwiki/American_History_quotes_Stock_Market_Crash

CHAPTER FIVE

4. tdhp.fr.yuku.com/topic/9755#.UpjMwMQwSjQ

5. www.donhollway.com/doolittle-geebee/

CHAPTER SIX

6. *New York Times*. "Hughes, Riding Gale, Sets Record of 7 1/2 Hours in Flight From Coast," January 24, 1937. http://www.nytimes.com/learning/general/onthisday/big/0119.html

CHAPTER SEVEN

7. www.ameliaearhart.com/about/bio2.html

8. Ibid.

9. waittinstitute.org See also:
http://tighar.org/Projects/Earhart/Archives/Research/
Bulletins/37_ItascaLogs/analysis.html

10. Amelia Earhart, Telegram to George Putnam (Purdue Collection,
June 16, 1937). searchforamelia.org/fuel-analysis

11. tenwatts.blogspot.com/2007/06/amelia-earhart-on-khaqq.html

12. "Feathering an engine (also called 'feathering a prop') is typically
done if there is some kind of serious engine problem or an engine
fire and the engine must be shut down. *Feathering* means to adjust
each blade of the propeller so that it's parallel to the direction of
flight, thus reducing drag and preventing the prop from 'windmilling'
(just spinning in the wind)."
http://forum.armyairforces.com/Feathering-engine-m90903.aspx

CHAPTER EIGHT

13. "Beyond several photo opportunities across the country to drum up
support, the Airacuda never fulfilled its purpose of bomber-
interceptor and destroyer and never would see combat action in the
Second World War. All systems were eventually scrapped with only
one prototype and twelve production models ever existing."
www.militaryfactory.com/aircraft/detail.asp?aircraft_id=662

14. www.freerepublic.com/focus/f-chat/2047977/posts

15. www.santaanahistory.com/articles/corrigan.html

16. "He wasn't mad. He was pleasant about it. The last thing he said to
me was 'get lost.' Well, two years later, I got lost! So I just did what
the government told me to do!" Corrigan's plane was reconstructed
and shown for the first time in decades at the 1988 Hawthorne Air
Faire. Volunteers at the Western Museum of Flight reassembled the
fragile aircraft and actually got the engine running, but when
Corrigan began talking with reporters about possibly taking his
"crate" up for one last flight, the FAA quickly squelched that idea.
Douglas Corrigan, Interview with Stan Miller, 1988.
www.youtube.com/watch?v=y98tz1GiJVY

17. "He bought the Robin, used, in 1933 and spent a couple of years
modifying the plane, trying to get it rated airworthy enough for
certification. He never did, and at one point officials in California
grounded the rattling bucket of bolts—which Corrigan had named
Sunshine—for six months." www.wired.com/2008/07/july-17-1938-
wrong-way-corrigan-gets-it-right

18. Ibid.

19. New York Post headline, August 1939.
    http://en.wikipedia.org/wiki/File:Wrong_Way_Corrigan.jpg

20. http://rbogash.com/B314.html

CHAPTER NINE

21. Archie Satterfield, *Alaska Bush Pilots in Float Country* (Seattle, WA: Superior Publishing Co., 1969). *Note*: "The aviator's tradition of growing a mustache started before WWII but gained more momentum during Vietnam when pilots were being shot down every day. The bulletproof 'stache was mostly a superstition but it has been documented over and over again that those who grew a mustache and then shaved it off were quickly shot down afterwards, and those pilots without 'staches in squadrons where most pilots sported the 'stache were the first ones shot down. The other reason was in rebellion of all the queep the pilots had to do while flying combat missions and losing friends every day. It was their way of scoffing the regulations while dealing with death...." Crusty Capt, USA. Source: www.mountainhome.af.mil/news/story.asp?id=123294918

CHAPTER TEN

22. This report was originally based on German propaganda. Following the war, it was determined that German bombers destroyed mostly Polish trainer planes; fighter planes, which had been dispersed to secondary fields throughout Poland, were captured and deployed to Romania, Hungary, Lithuania, Latvia, Slovenia, and Sweden for the Nazi's own use. Polish pilots and aircrews that managed to escape to France and later to Britain contributed significantly to the defense of the United Kingdom against Nazi invasion during the Battle of Britain.

23. http://military.wikia.com/wiki/Ernst_Udet

CHAPTER ELEVEN

24. www.selectiveservice.us/military-draft/7-use.shtml

CHAPTER TWELVE

25. Winston Churchill, "Speech to the House of Commons of the Parliament of the United Kingdom" (18 June 1940).

26. Winston Churchill, wartime speech (20 August 1940).

27. www.airforcemag.com/MagazineArchive/Pages/2008/August%202008/0808battle.aspx

28. Ernie Pyle, "A Dreadful Masterpiece," *The Best of Ernie Pyle's World War II Dispatches*, edited by David Nichols (Random House, 1986): Indiana University School of Journalism; http://newsinfo.iu.edu/news/page/normal/910.html

29. "In 1938, Bayerische Flugzeugwerks (BFw) incorporated the company as Messerschmitt AG and named Dr. Ing. Willy Messerschmitt Chairman and Managing Director. Heretofore, all aircraft designed by the company had carried the *Bf* prefix before the type number to signify the origin of the craft. Following the incorporation of Messerschmitt AG, all aircraft designed by the firm carried the prefix *Me* to identify the Messerschmitt factory. The Bf 109 and Me 109 identifiers are interchangeable by many history buffs, and in fact, production reports from the Messerschmitt AG factory show that labels were used interchangeably within the same report." http://109lair.hobbyvista.com/articles/bf-me/bf-me.htm

30. "Total British civilian losses from July to December 1940 were 23,002 dead and 32,138 wounded, with one of the largest single raids occurring on 19 December 1940, in which almost 3,000 civilians died. British Fighter Command lost a total of 544 military personnel of which 507 were pilots. An additional 500 were wounded. The Germans lost 1887 aircraft and roughly 2,800 military personnel, although this is an estimate because the number lost was never verified. By the end of May 1941, over 43,000 civilians, half of them in London, had been killed by bombing and more than a million houses destroyed or damaged in London alone." Sources: www.battleofbritain.eu, www.geocities.com/mchirnside/fcac.htm, http://uktv.co.uk/yesterday/item/aid/533487, and www.answers.com/topic/dunkirk-spirit

31. www.airforcemag.com/MagazineArchive/Pages/2008/August%202008/0808battle.aspx

32. http://en.wikipedia.org/wiki/Rolls-Royce_Merlin

CHAPTER THIRTEEN

33. www.rjmitchell-spitfire.co.uk/schneidertrophy/1931.asp?%20sectionID=2, also http://en.wikipedia.org/wiki/Supermarine_S.6B

34. Jeffrey L. Ethell and Steve Pace, *Spitfire* (St. Paul, Minnesota: Motorbooks International, 1997).

35. "Mitchell is reported to have said, 'Spitfire was just the sort of bloody silly name they would choose.'" Len Deighton, *Fighter: The True Story of the Battle of Britain* (London: Grafton, 1977): http://en.wikipedia.org/wiki/R._J._Mitchell

36. http://en.wikipedia.org/wiki/Little_ships_of_Dunkirk

CHAPTER FOURTEEN

37. At least ten percent of all Bf 109s were lost in takeoff and landing accidents, 1,500 of which occurred between 1939 and 1941. Walter J. Boyne, *Clash of Wings* (New York: Simon & Schuster, 1994): http://en.wikipedia.org/wiki/Messerschmitt_Bf_109#cite_note-Boyne_1994.2C_p._30-22.

38. "The Messerschmitt 109 could be summed up as a very large engine on the front of the smallest possible airframe; armament had been added almost as an afterthought. Its design could be likened to a racehorse: given the right amount of pampering and easy course, it could outrun anything. But I felt sure that a quite different breed of fighter would also have a place in any future conflict: one that could operate from ill-prepared front-line airfields; one that could be flown and maintained by men who had received only short training; and one that could absorb a reasonable amount of battle damage and still get back. This was the background thinking behind the Focke-Wulf 190; it was not to be a racehorse but a cavalry horse." http://forum.warthunder.com/index.php?/topic/109962-kurt-tank-anniversary/

39. "Account of 805 squadron and the Brewster Buffalo, 1941." www.fleetairarmarchive.net/Squadrons/805.html

CHAPTER SIXTEEN

40. http://the-american-catholic.com/2012/12/07/the-lessons-of-pearl-harbor and http://skeptoid.com/blog/2013/01/14/historical-misquotes-war

41. www.nps.gov/nr/twhp/wwwlps/lessons/18arizona/18charts1.htm

42. Franklin D. Roosevelt, Annotated typewritten copy of "Day of Infamy" speech. www.archives.gov/education/lessons/day-of-infamy/images/infamy-address-1.gif

CHAPTER SEVENTEEN

43. Licenses were issued alphabetically by the Aero Club of America.

44. www.history.navy.mil/photos/ac-usn22/f-types/f9c.htm

45. Kristin Alexander, *Clive Caldwell: Air Ace* (Crows Nest, NSW: Allen & Unwin, 2006).

46. National Museum of the US Air Force, "CURTISS P-40 Factsheet." www.nationalmuseum.af.mil/factsheets/factsheet.asp?id=2208

CHAPTER EIGHTEEN

47. ARCADIA Conference. www.britannica.com/EBchecked/topic/ 32461/Arcadia-Conference

48. James H. Doolittle, "Jimmy Doolittle Quotes," United States Air Force, Pacific Air Forces: www.pacaf.af.mil/library/pacafheritage/ jimmydoolittle/doolittle/index.asp

49. "The USS *Hornet*'s flight deck length overall was 809 feet 6 inches; however, line drawings of the ship indicate the flight deck was recessed from the bow but extended slightly further than the recessed distance past the stern with a flight deck length somewhere between 810 feet and 828 feet. Of interest, is the fact that by the end of their training, Doolittle's fully loaded B-25Bs could take off in 450 feet on land-based runways." Samuel Eliot Morison, *History of United States Naval Operations in World War II* (Boston: Little, Brown, and Company, 1947–1962).

CHAPTER NINETEEN

50. "After the start of World War II, burlap houses and chicken-wire lawns camouflaged the rooftops of Boeing Plant 2 in Seattle so that, from the air, the bomber manufacturing center looked like a quiet suburb." Boeing, "Boeing Plant 2 Rooftop Camouflage," accessed November 5, 2014, www.boeing.com/boeing/companyoffices/ gallery/roof.page

PART TWO

CHAPTER TWENTY

51. The title is equivalent to US Navy Admiral.

52. Admiral Chester W. Nimitz, Commander in Chief, US Pacific Fleet, in a communication to Admiral Ernest J. King, Commander in Chief, US Fleet and Chief of Naval Operations (29 May 1942): www.history.navy.mil/research/library/online-reading-room/title-list-alphabetically/m/midways-strategic-lessons.html

53. The United States Army Air Corps was officially renamed the United States Army Air Forces on June 21, 1941.

54. "Divine Wind" is an adapted translation of *kamikaze* (神風 or *spirit wind*), which was a term used by Japanese aviators to describe special (suicide) attacks against Allied forces.

55. Dallas Woodbury Isom, *Midway Inquest: Why the Japanese Lost the Battle of Midway* (Bloomington, IN: Indiana University Press, 2007): http://en.m.wikipedia.org/wiki/Battle_of_Midway

56. "During the attack, the USS *Enterprise*'s Torpedo Squadron Six (VT-6), led by Lieutenant Commander Eugene E. Lindsey, unsuccessfully pursued *Kaga*, losing all but five of fourteen TBDs to the Japanese defenses. Only two planes escaped from Lieutenant Commander Lance E. Massey's Torpedo Squadron Three (VT-3), from USS *Yorktown*. Six Fighting Squadron Three (VF-3) F4F-4 'Wildcats', led by Lieutenant Commander John S. Thach, tried to assist VT-3, but were so badly outnumbered by Zeros, they were unable to provide cover support." Naval History and Heritage Command, "U.S. Carrier Planes Disable *Akagi*, *Kaga* and *Sōryū* 4 June 1942," accessed November 5, 2014, www.history.navy.mil/photos/events/wwii-pac/midway/mid-4k.htm

57. The title is equivalent to US Navy Rear Admiral.

CHAPTER TWENTY-FIVE

58. Battle of Kula Gulf, 5–6 July 1943, accessed November 5, 2014, http://en.wikipedia.org/wiki/Battle_of_Kula_Gulf

CHAPTER TWENTY-SIX

59. "Kinner R-5," accessed November 5, 2014, http://all-aero.com/index.php/contactus/64-engines-power/13091-kinner-r-5-r-53-r-55-r-56-r-540

CHAPTER THIRTY-ONE

60. Harry Warren & Leo Robin, "A Journey to a Star," sung by Judy Garland (1944): www.youtube.com/watch?v=cnn9cfZdthA

CHAPTER THIRTY-TWO

61. Dwight D. Eisenhower, "Supreme Headquarters Allied Expeditionary Force Order of the Day," Dwight D. Eisenhower Archives, accessed November 5, 2014, http://eisenhower.archives.gov/research/online_documents/d_day/Order_of_the_Day.pdf

PART THREE

CHAPTER THIRTY-NINE

62. In 1939, the United States was not yet involved in the war, but military command had already concluded that Natal was the most strategic point, both for a German invasion and for the Allies to use as a supporting site to the operations in Africa. The US government created a program for development of airfields, and to avoid diplomatic involvement, Pan Am cosigned the agreement with Brazil

to establish an airfield at Natal. Source: http://www.natal-brazil.com/basics/natal-world-war.html

63. "South Atlantic air ferry routes for deployed service personnel in World War II," accessed November 5, 2014, http://en.wikipedia.org/wiki/South_Atlantic_air_ferry_route_in_World_War_II and www.ibiblio.org/hyperwar/AAF/VII/AAF-VII-3.html#page75

64. "They were an evil bastard contraption, nothing like the relatively efficient B-24 except in appearance." Ernest K. Gann, *Fate Is the Hunter* (New York: Simon & Shuster, 1961).

65. Ibid.

CHAPTER FORTY-TWO

66. Fixing up broken-down aircraft wasn't Ed's only pastime. He and his buddies made Plexiglas picture frames, canopies, and other amenities with spare parts scrounged from plane wreckage. One of their more ingenious creations was a foxhole radio built with a rusty single-edge razor blade, a cardboard toilet paper tube, a wire coat hanger, a scrap of wood, some pencil lead, and a safety pin, all fastened together with glue and screws. See: www.bizarrelabs.com/foxhole.htm

CHAPTER FORTY-THREE

67. "CHINA AIRFIELDS—From the pages of the 22nd Bomb Squadron Association Newsletter," accessed November 5, 2014, www.usaaf-in-cbi.com/341st_web/intel/china_fields.htm

CHAPTER FORTY-FIVE

68. Taiwan Documents Project, "The Surrender of Japanese Forces in the China Theatre," accessed November 5, 2014, http://taiwandocuments.org/japansurrender.htm

CHAPTER FORTY-EIGHT

69. From draft of the April 13, 1945 "Jackson Day" address. President Roosevelt died unexpectedly on April 12, the day before this speech was to be delivered. Collection FDR-FDRMSF: Franklin D. Roosevelt Master Speech Files, 01/19/1898–04/13/1945, National Archives Identifier: 577534.

EPILOGUE

70. Report provided by Aviation Archaeological Investigation & Research.

Ed Larson 2014

CREDITS

CREDITS

Ahunt

Arnold, H. H. *Target Germany: The U.S. Army Air Forces Story of the VIII Bomber Command's First Year over Europe*. London: His Majesty's Stationery Office, 1944.

Aviation Archaeological Investigation & Research

Burns, Robert. "To a mouse," *Poems, Chiefly in the Scottish Dialect*. Kilmarnock: John Wilson, 1786.

Burtt, Bob, and Bill Moore. *The Air Adventures of Jimmie Allen*. 1933–37.

Caniff, Milton. *Terry and the Pirates*. 1934–46.

Capra, Frank, and Anatole Litvak. *Divide and Conquer ("Why We Fight #3")*. United States Department of Defense: Office of War Information, 1943.

Churchill, Winston. "A Tribute to the Royal Air Force." Speech presented to the House of Commons, London, England, August 20, 1940. www.britpolitics.co.uk/quotefinder/churchill-winston-the-gratitude-of-every-home-in-our-island

Doolittle, James H. "Jimmy Doolittle Quotes." United States Air Force, Pacific Air Forces, www.pacaf.af.mil/library/pacafheritage/jimmydoolittle/doolittle/index.asp

Eisenhower, Dwight D. "Supreme Headquarters Allied Expeditionary Force, Order of the Day." Transmitted June 6, 1944. www.kansasheritage.org/abilene/graphics/ikesmessage.jpg

Gann, Ernest K. *Fate Is the Hunter*. New York: Simon & Shuster, 1961.

Google map data.

Grueskin, Tom. "Search for Amelia Earhart." January 1, 2009. http://waittinstitute.org/?s=Earhart

Halvorsen, Dick. *Steeds in the Sky: The Fabulous Fighting Planes of WWII*. New York: Lancer Books, 1971.

Hirohito. "Imperial Rescript Ending War—What Hirohito really said in his acceptance speech." Translated by William Wetherall, Yosha Research. Retrieved September 15, 2013. https://uk.news.yahoo.com/on-this-day--japan-agrees-to-surrender-24-hours-after-nagasaki-bomb-161133711.html#XxaCcqK

Hogan, Robert J. *G-8 and His Battle Aces*. New York: Popular Publications, 1933–44.

ICD-ATC. *Hump Express*. 1945.

Lakeside School, Seattle, WA

Larson, Edward C. *Spring Tides: Memories of Alaskan Towboats*. Santa Cruz, CA: Fly By Night Graphics, 1996.

Library of Congress Prints & Photographs Division

———. The Carpenter Collection, ca 1890–1923, Frank G. Carpenter, photographer.

———. Online Catalog

Lin, Ma. "Listening to Wind in Pines." National Palace Museum, Taibei, Taiwan. http://commons.wikimedia.org/wiki/File:Ma_Lin_010.jpg wikidata: Q63740.

Morison, Samuel Eliot. *History of United States Naval Operations in World War II*. 15 vols. Boston: Little, Brown and Company, 1947–62.

National Archives, Franklin D. Roosevelt Library, Public Domain Photographs, 1882–1962

———. Still Picture Branch, United States Army Signal Corps Photographs, Lieutenant Ewing, photographer.

National Museum of Naval Aviation, Robert L. Lawson Photographic Collection

National Museum of the United States Air Force

National Naval Aviation Museum

Naval Historical Center

———. Collection of Vice Admiral Walden L. Ainsworth

Naval History and Heritage Command

Nimitz, Chester W. Communication to Admiral Ernest J. King, May 29, 1942. www.history.navy.mil

Nygren, Harley D. "Unloading a float plane...Point Lay, Alaska North Slope." 1950. NOAA Photo Library. www.photolib.noaa.gov/htmls/corp1139.htm

Office of the Chief Signal Officer, United States Army. *Report from Nebraska, North Platte Canteen, August 1945*. Online Public Access of the National Archives. Identifier: 20069. Local Identifier: 111-ADC-6284.

Online Public Access of the United States National Archives & Records Administration

Pingstone, Adrian. "PT-13D Stearman."

Porter, William S. "Gee Bee."

Pyle, Ernie. "A Dreadful Masterpiece," *The Best of Ernie Pyle's World War II Dispatches*. Edited by David Nichols. New York: Random House, 1986.

Richards, Patricia D. "Blood Chit." 2013.

——. "Ed and Fiona." 2014.

——. Photo Gallery One, Photo Gallery Two, Photo Gallery Three.

Romanus, Charles F., and Riley Sunderland. *United States Army in World War II, China-Burma-India Theater: Time Runs out in CBI*. Washington, DC: Center of Military History United States Army, 1959.

Roosevelt, Franklin D. "Address at Chautauqua, NY." August 14, 1936. Online by Gerhard Peters and John T. Woolley, The American Presidency Project. www.presidency.ucsb.edu/ws/?pid=15097

——. "A Date Which Will Live in Infamy." War Address delivered to the United States Congress and the Nation, Washington, DC, December 8, 1941. www.archives.gov/education/lessons/day-of-infamy/

——. "Address to White House Correspondents' Association." Washington, DC, February 12, 1943, Online by Gerhard Peters and John T. Woolley, The American Presidency Project. www.presidency.ucsb.edu/ws/?pid=16360

——. "Address to the Nation, D-Day." Washington, DC, June 6, 1944, A Project of the Pare Lorentz Center at the FDR Presidential Library. www.fdrlibrary.marist.edu/daybyday/resource/june-1944-4/

——. "Draft of the April 13, 1945 Jackson Day Address." Collection FDR-FDRMSF: Franklin D. Roosevelt Master Speech Files, 01/19/1898–04/13/1945, National Archives Identifier: 577534.

San Diego Air & Space Museum SDASM Archives

Satterfield, Archie. *Alaska Bush Pilots in Float Country*. Seattle, WA: Superior Publishing Co., 1969.

Seattle Post-Intelligencer, August 15, 1945.

Shakespeare, William. *The Tragedy of Julius Caesar*. Reference to Scene II, lines 146–47.

Smith, Hugh. "Corrigan Flies to Dublin; U.S. Officials May Wink at Forbidden Hop in 'Crate' Lost His Way, He Says," *New York Times*, July 18, 1938, www.freerepublic.com/focus/f-chat/2047977/posts

Stars and Stripes, Issue No 285, May 8, 1945, Paris Edition, V-E Day.

State Historical Society of North Dakota, William E. (Bill) Shemorry Photography Collection

Sweeney, Charles, James A. Antonucci, and Marion K. Antonucci. *War's End: An Eyewitness Account of America's Last Atomic Mission*. New York: Quill Publishing, 1997.

Taiwan Documents Project

Terry, John. *Scorchy Smith*. 1930–61.

The International Group for Historic Aircraft Recovery (TIGHAR). "The Earhart Project: The Radio Logs of the USCG Itasca." http://tighar.org/Projects/Earhart/Archives/Research/Bulletins/37_ItascaLogs/analysis.html

Troup, Robert W. "Bobby." "(Get Your Kicks On) Route 66." 1944.

Truman, Harry S. "Radio Report to American People on the Potsdam Conference" Delivered from the White House at 10:00 p.m., August 9, 1945. www.trumanlibrary.org/publicpapers/index.php?pid=104

United States Air Force

United States Air Forces Pacific Air Forces (PACAF)

United States Army

United States Army Air Forces. "Keep 'Em Flying! Aviation Cadets Train for Air or Ground Crews." Recruiting Publicity Bureau: United States Army, 1942.

——. *Instrument Flying: Basic and Advanced*. 1943.

——. *Primary Flying Students' Manual*. Randolph Field, TX: Army Air Forces Training Command, 1944.

——. *Preparation for Surrender of Japanese Forces in China at Chihkiang*. US Army Air Forces Combat film #5142. 1945. National Archives identifier: 18941.

United States Army Military History Institute

United States Army Signal Corps

United States Department of Defense

United States Department of Transportation. *Manual on Uniform Traffic Control Devices*. 1926.

——. *Advisory Circular*. Federal Aviation Administration, 1991.

United States Military Academy, Department of History

United States Naval History and Heritage Command, Rear Admiral Samuel Eliot Morison files

United States Navy

US Navy and Marine Corps Museum, CDR Francis N. Gilreath Collection

United States War Department. *FM21-100: Basic Field Manual, Soldier's Handbook*, page 41, figure 13. Washington, DC: US Government Printing office, 1941.

Warren, Harry, and Leo Robin. "A Journey to a Star." 1944.

Wikimedia Commons/German Federal Archive (Deutsches Bundesarchiv) cooperation project

Wikiquote:Transwiki/American History quotes Stock Market Crash. "Letter from a New Jersey Resident to President Hoover, 1930." http://en.wikiquote.org/wiki/Wikiquote:Transwiki/American_History_quotes_Stock_Market_Crash

www.ibiblio.org

www.usaaf-in-cbi.com

❧✪❧

With special thanks to Suzy Moore and Jennifer Nolin.